W9-DGS-581

ADVANCE PRAISE FOR

Feminist Theologies
for a Postmodern Church

"In a remarkably lucid manner, this book examines the prospects of postmodern feminist theology by describing four divergent theologians. Attending to specific efforts and methods, Loraine MacKenzie Shepherd explores a rich tapestry of both classic Christian features—the rule of faith and the literal sense of Scripture—as well as novel reformulating that pushes through and beyond older modern criticisms. ...Shepherd avoids simplistic generalizations and challenges us to consider carefully what, at its best, a postliberal, postmodern theological position might be. By not dismissing uncritically the classical Christian tradition and by engaging some of the most promising recent efforts, she wonderfully provokes us to think about methods as well as what might be theologically a liberating word to the contemporary church at large."

Gerald Sheppard, Professor of Biblical Studies,
Emmanuel College, University of Toronto

"Loraine MacKenzie Shepherd's concern is the challenge that contemporary issues of diversity, marginalization, authority, and the interpretation of revelation present to theological reflection today. Convinced that previous theological methods, and in particular the approach of liberal theology, are inadequate, she combs the works of four current feminist theologians for insights on theological method. She finds them and then presents her own lines of reflection for a more adequate and just theological method. This is a careful, critical, and creative work, a valuable contribution to the ongoing conversation in theology today on unity in diversity."

Mary Ellen Sheehan, Professor of Feminist Theology and Pastoral
Theology, St. Michael's College, Toronto School of Theology

"In a work of exacting scholarship and exciting original thinking, Loraine MacKenzie Shepherd applies insights from four methodologically distinct contemporary feminist theologians to illumine her critique of the largely liberal, modern, dominant-centralist approach of biblical interpretation in a series of late-twentieth-century documents ón sexuality and sexual orientation of one major Canadian Protestant denomination. Her concluding suggestions of new criteria in formulating an alternative approach have the potential of inviting/challenging other faith communities in and beyond North America to attend to the various marginalized 'Other' to a radical re-ordering of 'life together'."

Wenh-In Ng, Associate Professor of Christian Education,
Emmanuel College, University of Toronto

Feminist Theologies
for a Postmodern Church

American University Studies

Series VII
Theology and Religion

Vol. 219

PETER LANG
New York • Washington, D.C./Baltimore • Bern
Frankfurt am Main • Berlin • Brussels • Vienna • Oxford

Loraine MacKenzie Shepherd

Feminist Theologies
for a Postmodern Church

Diversity, Community,
and Scripture

CABRINI COLLEGE LIBRARY
610 KING OF PRUSSIA RD.
RADNOR, PA 19087-3699

PETER LANG
New York • Washington, D.C./Baltimore • Bern
Frankfurt am Main • Berlin • Brussels • Vienna • Oxford

#47081337

Library of Congress Cataloging-in-Publication Data

Shepherd, Loraine MacKenzie.
Feminist theologies for a postmodern church: diversity, community,
and scripture/ Loraine MacKenzie Shepherd.
p. cm. — (American university studies. Series VII,
Theology and religion; vol. 219)
Includes bibliographical references (p.) and indexes.
1. Theology—Methodology. 2. Feminist theology. 3. Postmodernism—
Religious aspects—Christianity. I. Title. II. Series.
BR118 .S519   230'.082—dc21   2001037120
2002   ISBN 0-8204-5572-5
ISSN 0740-0446

Die Deutsche Bibliothek-CIP-Einheitsaufnahme

Shepherd, Loraine MacKenzie:
Feminist theologies for a postmodern church: diversity, community,
and scripture/ Loraine MacKenzie Shepherd.
–New York; Washington, D.C./Baltimore; Bern;
Frankfurt am Main; Berlin; Brussels; Vienna; Oxford: Lang.
(American university studies: Ser. 7, Theology and religion; Vol. 219)
ISBN 0-8204-5572-5

The paper in this book meets the guidelines for permanence and durability
of the Committee on Production Guidelines for Book Longevity
of the Council of Library Resources.

© 2002 Peter Lang Publishing, Inc., New York

All rights reserved.
Reprint or reproduction, even partially, in all forms such as microfilm,
xerography, microfiche, microcard, and offset strictly prohibited.

Printed in the United States of America

Dedicated to Nancy Pinnell,
my beloved life-partner,
who has gifted me with
patience, love, and wisdom.

&

In Memory of George Schner,
my wise mentor and critic,
who offered boundless
time, energy, and support.

Contents

Acknowledgements

I am deeply appreciative of the careful editing and suggestions given by Cathie Clement, Karen Ridd, and Linda Watson. I am also grateful for the critique which Cora Krommenhoek, Sue Jackson, Barbara Paleczny, Marion Pope, Catherine Rose, George Schner, and Mary Ellen Sheehan gave on an earlier form of this manuscript. My thanks to Gerald Sheppard and Wenh-In Ng for their careful reading and support.

A grant given by the University of Winnipeg facilitated the helpful assistance of Lowell Siemens with the indexes and glossary. Gratitude is also extended to the Centre for Christian Studies, who generously offered the use of their printer.

For family and friends who provide a constant circle of support and love, I am deeply grateful. From social justice companions who persevere with courageous and absurd audacity, I receive inspiration. May we continue to work towards the kin-dom of God!

Part One

Feminist Theological Methods

Chapter 1

Marginalized by the Liberal, Modern Church & Academy

In my work as a minister in The United Church of Canada, and as a theological educator, I have often felt daunted by the use of scripture. I have also found that I am not alone in this intimidation. Many of us who are not well versed in the latest historical-critical conclusions feel inadequate in our use of scripture. As Christian theologians and pastors, however, scripture is integral to our theologies and ministries. This dilemma prompted me to explore the use of scripture within theological methods. I have also become increasingly concerned about the use of scripture and traditional doctrine for oppressive ends, and the inadequacy of modern, liberal theological approaches to address this. For instance, those who are marginalized by sexual orientation have become further marginalized by the church's attempt to become more inclusive. Because of these concerns, I have focused my research on the development of a feminist theological method that seriously considers the use of scripture and attends to issues of marginalization and diversity within a Protestant context.

I will be using the term "feminist" to describe an approach that is attentive to multiplicative[1] sources of domination within church and society, only one of which concerns gender. In this book I have concentrated upon issues of gender and sexual orientation, while making some connections with colonialism. This use of the term "feminist" implies a liberative approach that sets as two of its criteria the liberation of the oppressed and the respect of diversity.

The following incidents illustrate my concerns and raise further questions which will be addressed in this book. From 1986 to 2000 I served in a number of rural and urban United Church pastoral charges as their minister. For some of them, I was their first or second "woman minister." During my first sermon in one congregation a woman elbowed her husband

and warned him not to cause trouble for *this* woman minister. Their first woman minister only lasted one year. My experience was more gracious, in spite of two separate incidents of sexual abuse at the hands of two male parishioners, and physical assault by a Roman Catholic priest as we were vesting for an ecumenical service. For most congregations, if not all of them, I was also their first lesbian, albeit closeted, minister. In retrospect, I was not as closeted as I had thought!

During this time the United Church underwent its most divisive experience when it supported the ordination and commissioning of lesbian and gay candidates. Anger erupted across the country and in virtually every United Church congregation. I found myself living daily contradictions as I ministered to people livid about the United Church's decision. I provided pastoral care for individuals feeling alienated from the United Church and incensed about the moral depravity of a church that would allow perverts into the church at all, let alone into ministry. As I visited a dying man in the hospital, he told me that he wished he could round up every homosexual in the world, put them on a raft and sink it. "Now that's a charitable, Christian attitude," I replied with a nervous laugh. I supported families whose children became homophobic targets at school as non-United Church children parroted their parents' hate and fear. One congregation I served passed a motion forbidding homosexuals from ministering in their church. Because I was committed to empowering the voices of marginalized rural congregations, I helped them write a letter to the national church expressing their dismay over the national church's decision, while I preached about God's inclusive love and grace for all people. In contrast, the other two congregations of the multi-point pastoral charge I served refused to endorse the motion of the first congregation, because they were committed to an open, inclusive church. And in the meantime my partner and I made emergency get-away plans should we come home to a manse sprayed with homophobic graffiti. In its attempt to become inclusive, the church had become a dangerous place for me.

At another pastoral charge a few years later, a meeting was held to discuss a United Church document on sexual orientation. Some people quoted verses out of scripture (and out of context) to support their abhorrence of homosexuality and insistence that the United Church was abandoning its faith traditions. Others replied with different quotes, also taken out of context, to emphasize the inclusive, nonjudgmental nature of Jesus' message, and the importance of heeding modern scientific findings instead of antiquated church traditions. Those of us present who were lesbian and gay were silenced. Later one man confided to me that the underlying problem with homosexuality was its hindrance to the propagation of the white race, as if only white people were homosexual. Even worse were the white supremacist overtones to his concern about the purity of the white race.

These experiences led me to reflect upon the following questions. At whose expense are inclusive decisions about women, and lesbian and gay people made? Without an analysis of power, accompanied by protective policies, how effective and safe are inclusive decisions? Did one have to abandon church tradition in order to support lesbian and gay people? How could scripture be helpful when its diversity allowed people to choose passages that supported their pre-formed opinions? Everyone was welcomed into this discussion, but a simple inclusion of all voices did not provide lesbian and gay people, or people of colour, the safety necessary to risk speaking. Did we need to move beyond a liberal model of inclusion in order to allow all voices to be heard? The racist comment indicated that connections needed to be made with other sources of oppression. How could multiplicative oppressions be addressed?

Another incident occurred in the late 1980's. A woman approached me with a concern that was weighing heavily upon her. How could she continue reading the Bible when she felt violated by it? I was her minister in a rural pastoral charge and she was hoping that I, as another woman, had found a way to read the Bible without being upset. She had just read one of the biblical passages which Phyllis Trible has named a "text of terror." The violence portrayed against women, which appeared to her to be condoned in this passage, distressed her. She was in the habit of reading scripture every day, but was finding that the Word of Life was becoming the Word of Death. She had come from another denomination which equated scripture with the literal Word of God, and had used passages such as these to justify the subordination of women. She questioned if there was any other way to read these passages. How could United Church feminists, such as myself, still read the Bible? I understood her dilemma, as I had been a Southern Baptist for ten years before joining the United Church, and had been wounded by devout Christians who used scripture to cut down and maim those who challenged the patriarchal status quo. Sword drills (races to find biblical verses) took on a whole new meaning!

The last incident happened more recently. A colleague within the doctoral program of the Toronto School of Theology began to tell me of her pain, exhaustion and loneliness trying to think in the western style of Canadian academics. She was a foreign-exchange student from Korea, and was finding it difficult to work in a Western mindset. She asked why theology must be done from a linear perspective that isolates the mind from the body, the individual from community, and Christian beliefs from other religious traditions. Why has Christian theology so readily adopted western, abstract, philosophical traditions while remaining uneasy with the use of eastern, holistic, philosophical traditions?

These incidents have contributed to my growing passion for justice, and my social activist work on issues of human rights, gender, sexual orientation, anti-racism, ecology, and the global economy. They have also helped me to recognize my own areas of privilege as a white, middle-class, formally-educated, able-bodied Canadian, and the ways in which these areas of privilege are complicit in the oppression of others. Oppressions are not isolated, but inextricably linked, as demonstrated by hate crimes which jointly target Jews, lesbians and gays, and people of colour.

These incidents also raise questions that illuminate the growing diversity of our Canadian society, and the need for churches to address questions of marginalization and diversity within their own faith communities and traditions. In addition, these incidents indicate the need for systematic theologians to take biblical interpretation seriously.

Theologians who are not familiar with the latest findings of biblical studies often ignore the scriptures, for fear of displaying their ignorance. The increasing specialization within academic disciplines encourages this separation of theology from biblical studies, as well as other disciplines. Interdisciplinary studies are becoming more difficult to do, and are accused of superficiality. Without such an interdisciplinary approach, however, theology will become increasingly irrelevant. It is for this reason that I am risking a multi-disciplinary interconnection of systematic theology, feminist theory, ethics, literary theory, history, and biblical interpretation. I am particularly hopeful that this work will contribute to a dialogue with biblical scholars in the search for an adequate theological method.

The intended audience for this book is those working in academics as professors, researchers, and graduate students, as well as those responsible for policy statements and theological guidance in Protestant denominations. I have included a glossary at the back of the book in order to make some of the terms and philosophies found in this book more accessible to readers without a background in postmodern theory.

Contemporary theology has arrived at a critical moment. Postmodern thought has challenged sources of authority that have been taken for granted in the modern era. The liberal, modern paradigm which has largely governed theological method in this century has tended to support the status quo at the expense of the marginalized. As a corrective, marginalized voices are being heeded now, more than ever before, and are calling for a radical shift in theological method.

This is particularly the case for lesbian, gay, bisexual, and transgendered people within the church. As mainline, Protestant denominations begin to become more inclusive of different sexual orientations within their membership and leadership, questions emerge concerning biblical interpretation, revelation, authoritative criteria, and the credibility of the experiences and biblical interpretations of anyone who is not heterosexual. In turn, those of us who have a minority sexual orientation find ourselves further marginalized by these liberal attempts to become more inclusive, as will be explained further in the second part of this book. In addition, backlash creates a hostile environment in which homophobic policies or practices become entrenched.

Modern suspicion of subjective experience, and assumptions that experts can more accurately (and safely?) describe the identities and needs of those marginalized by sexual orientation, leads to an elevation of objective analysis. It also leads to an assumption that accurate and complete representations of our own reality or that of others can be made. Modern emphasis upon the empirical scientific method has also granted authority to the biblical interpretations of impartial scholars, rather than faith communities or church support groups for lesbian, gay, bisexual and transgendered people. In contrast to the Protestant emphasis on the priesthood of all believers, the Bible has been taken out of the hands of the church and its people in order to preserve the "correct" interpretation of the

Bible.

These modern and liberal assumptions have proven to preserve the status quo at the expense of the marginalized. Alternative theological methods are needed that more adequately address issues of marginalization, diversity, accountability and authority within churches. I am particularly interested in theological methods that are appropriate within Protestant churches. Among the many alternative theological methods which address this crisis of authority, I will consider four: critical modern, poststructural, postcolonial and postliberal. Each of these methods offers promising alternatives as well as problems. However, when their strengths are braided together, they offer an alternative theological method that honours diversity, addresses marginalization, and respects the church community.

Various feminist theologians are beginning to adopt one or another of these four perspectives in their search for a theological method that more adequately addresses issues of diversity and marginalization. They are realizing that their earlier attempts to deal with the marginalization of women within male theological discourse[2] have themselves marginalized Aboriginal women, third world women[3] and women of colour. As feminists hope to better "attend to the other"[4] from each of these four perspectives, they also provide a corrective to other theorists from the same perspectives who tend to ignore gender analysis and its impact upon diversity and marginalization. Because of this feminist potential for deeper analysis, I will focus upon the following four feminist theologians who each represent one of these four perspectives: Elisabeth Schüssler Fiorenza as critical modern; Mary McClintock Fulkerson as poststructural; Kwok Pui-lan as postcolonial; and Kathryn Tanner as postliberal.

It must be noted at this point that categorization always risks oversimplification because there will be overlap amongst categories, certain works defy classification, and other works are in transition between categories. Such is the case for each of these four feminists. However, categorization does aid in the clarification, comparison, and critique of these different methods.

My critical examination of each of these positions will uncover similarities and differences amongst them. I will then determine aspects of each theological method which might contribute to the development of a feminist theological method that more adequately addresses issues of diversity and marginalization within Protestant churches. In order to determine these elements, I will contrast these theological methods with the liberal, modern approach which The United Church of Canada has taken in documents addressing issues of sexuality. Many of the concerns about these documents pertain to the types of theological method and biblical interpretation that were employed. Some believe that the documents' liberal and modern approach hindered the full inclusion of gay and lesbian people. Others believe that this approach erred in its departure from United Church traditions. I will demonstrate that both concerns are valid for particular sexuality documents, and suggest elements of a feminist theological method that can more adequately address issues of marginalization and diversity for Protestant churches in a postmodern era.

To begin, I will give a brief background of the four different feminist approaches. I am naming the first alternative "critical modern" to describe those who continue to use a modern approach while critically examining the impact of these modern assumptions and methods. Friedrich Nietzsche, Sigmund Freud and Karl Marx, commonly referred to as the masters of suspicion, began to question critically the basic principles of the modern era. These critiques were more fully developed by the Frankfurt School of Social Critical Theory, whose members were particularly concerned about ideological control and reification of the masses. They argued that the identities of those who were marginalized from positions of power within society were subsumed into the identity of the dominant culture.

I will consider Elisabeth Schüssler Fiorenza as a representative of this critical modern approach. She is primarily concerned about the marginalized voices which have been erased from history and from the Bible. In order to honour these voices, as well as those who are marginalized today, Schüssler Fiorenza chooses to use a rhetorical method of biblical interpretation. She uses modern tools and methods critically, questioning many of the above-mentioned difficulties with liberal modernism, but also rejecting some of the more problematic aspects of postmodernism. Although she is drawing much more upon poststructuralism in her later work, a critical modern approach remains for her the most politically viable way in which to respect diversity and struggle against multiple oppressions.

Poststructuralism, as the second alternative, emanated from France primarily through the works of Michel Foucault, Jacques Derrida, Jean-François Lyotard, Jacques Lacan, and the French feminists, Hélène Cixous, Luce Irigaray and Julia Kristeva. Although poststructuralism by its very nature resists definition, there are certain elements held in common by most poststructuralists. They resist the foundationalism of modernism, suggesting that foundations are social constructions and context dependent. They also resist modernity's totalizing attempts to explain and contain every aspect of an issue from one perspective.[5] A "God's eye view" that can capture all of reality is humanly impossible.[6]

Postmodernism is another, perhaps even more, elusive term that is often used interchangeably with poststructuralism. Because the term "postmodernism" has been used to describe both poststructuralism and postliberalism, which I am attempting to contrast, I prefer the term poststructuralism. This is also the term of preference for Mary McClintock Fulkerson to describe her own work.

Mary McClintock Fulkerson is concerned about the feminist dismissal of women whose biblical interpretations or political goals are not overtly feminist. In this respect she argues that modern feminism obliterates difference. Fulkerson suggests that poststructural views can best attend to "the other" within particular faith communities.

Postcolonialism, the third alternative, asks similar questions in reference to the effects of colonization by addressing issues of representation, multiculturalism and Western imperialism. Postcolonialists suggest that Western representations of colonized people may say more about the West than about the colony. The works of Gayatri Chakravorty Spivak, Trinh T. Minh-Ha, Edward Said, and Rasiah S. Sugirtharajah have been formative for this approach, in addition to that of poststructuralists.

Kwok Pui-lan identifies her work as postcolonial and draws upon postmodern thought to question the authority and universality of truth claims within colonialist discourse. She proposes a multifaith hermeneutics that she believes best honours the cultural and religious complexity of the scriptures themselves, as well as the multiple identities of Christian communities.

Postliberalism is a more recent development, particular to Christian theology. It is based primarily upon the work of George Lindbeck and Hans Frei, who in turn give significant reference to the work of Ludwig

Wittgenstein, Karl Barth, and Reinhold Niebuhr. Postliberals seek to move beyond the historical-critical methods of modernity and reclaim traditional theological methods and types of biblical interpretation.[7] Emphasis is given to the literal sense of scripture and traditional Christian doctrine while honouring the diversity of voices within the biblical text and the interpreting communities.

Kathryn Tanner is one of the few feminists who has taken a postliberal approach. She draws upon the work of George Lindbeck and Hans Frei to recommend an internal, self-critical approach to Christian faith. This allows traditional Christian beliefs to critique the dominant, oppressive practices of Christian faith communities, and to challenge the church to attend to the marginalized. Although she is moving away from postliberalism in her later work, and is relying more upon poststructuralism, she remains committed to the internal critique of traditional Christian beliefs within their diverse uses and meanings.

Each of these four feminists are committed to theological methods that fully honour the diversity of experiences and cultural communities, while retaining clear, authoritative criteria that enable a liberative stance on behalf of society's marginalized. At the same time, each one of their approaches has limitations. After examining each of their methods in depth, I will suggest a braided approach that might more adequately attend to issues of diversity and marginalization within Protestant churches.

Notes to Chapter 1

1. I follow Elisabeth Schüssler Fiorenza's understanding that the effects of multiple oppressions are not only added to each other, but multiplied by each other. Thus, a First Nations lesbian has not only three different sources of oppression, but the multiplicative effects of each source of oppression impacting the other. See Glossary.

2. For a discussion on the term "discourse" see A. K. M. Adam, *What is Postmodern Biblical Criticism?* New Testament Series (Minneapolis: Fortress Press, 1995), p. xiii. See Glossary.

3. For reasons given in the definition of "third world" in the Glossary, I prefer the term "third world" for this book.

4. The term "attending" suggests that those of us in positions of privilege are in as much need of liberation as is the oppressed other. See Glossary, and Mary McClintock Fulkerson, *Changing the Subject: Women's Discourses and Feminist Theology* (Minneapolis: Fortress Press, 1994), p. 4–5. I also recognize that the multiple forms of oppression, in some situations, place us outside of the circles of privilege as the oppressed, and in other situations place us inside. Thus, the lines of demarcation between privileged and oppressed, the other and the dominant, are blurred.

5. For a helpful introduction to poststructuralism within biblical studies (named postmodernism in this reference), see Adam, *What is Postmodern Biblical Criticism?*

6. Morny Joy uses the phrase "God's eye view" in reference to postcolonial critique. See "Beyond a God's Eyeview: Alternative Perspectives in the Study of Religion," presentation, Canadian Society for the Study of Religion, Brock University, St. Catharines, Ontario, May 1996.

7. For this reason some postliberals refer to themselves as postcritical. See Peter Ochs, "Scriptural Logic: Diagrams for a Postcritical Metaphysics," *Modern Theology*, 11, 1 (January 1995): 65–92.

Chapter 2

Critical Modern Response: Elisabeth Schüssler Fiorenza

"A feminist critical hermeneutics of suspicion
places a warning label on all biblical texts:
Caution! Could be dangerous to your health and survival."
—Elisabeth Schüssler Fiorenza, "The Will to Choose or to Reject"

Elisabeth Schüssler Fiorenza was born in Germany in 1938, on the same day as the Kristallnacht. The coincidence of her birthdate with Kristallnacht has increased her awareness of the violence instigated in the name of Christianity, of the need to include the voices of others in biblical scholarship, and of the responsibility for religious studies to contribute to a more humane world.[1] Her family became fugitives in Austria during the war, and later resettled in West Germany.[2] These experiences contributed to her commitment to the liberation of the oppressed, as shaped by her Christian faith. Schüssler Fiorenza felt drawn to ministry within the Roman Catholic Church, but was frustrated by gender restrictions. In her doctoral studies at the University of Münster she also encountered closed doors because of her gender. In spite of completing two theological degrees *summa cum laude* and publishing a book, Schüssler Fiorenza was refused a scholarship because, as a woman, she "had no future in the academy."[3] After she moved to the United States in 1970 to accept a teaching position at the University of Notre Dame, these previous experiences, together with the burgeoning women's liberation movement, sparked her interest in feminist biblical studies.[4]

In a 1990 article Schüssler Fiorenza recognized three distinct periods of her own writing, corresponding to the decades of the 1960s, 1970s and 1980s.[5] However, I have discerned a shift in her writing in the late 1980s. Beginning with articles published in 1989, I have found an increasing sophistication in Schüssler Fiorenza's analysis. With the help of womanist, mujerista, and global feminist theories, she refines her methodologies so as to better honour women's diversity, she further develops her rhetorical method, and she begins to incorporate aspects of poststructural theory. For the purposes of this book, I will refer primarily to two periods of her writing: the late 1970s until the late 1980s, which I call her earlier work, and the late 1980s through the 1990s, which I call her later work.

From the outset Schüssler Fiorenza has been concerned not only with the liberation of those who are oppressed, but also with the complicity of Christian theology in this oppression. In order to address these concerns, she has drawn upon liberation theology, as well as feminist and political critical theories, to develop a theological method and approach to biblical interpretation. For most of her work she has used the descriptor "critical" to indicate her indebtedness to Jürgen Habermas, a social critical theorist with whom she connects the Frankfurt School. The term "critical" also distances her work from liberal hermeneutics.[6] As outlined below, she has found that certain elements indicative of liberal and modern approaches to theology and biblical studies contribute to the oppression of the marginalized. At the same time, she still finds aspects of modernity and liberalism helpful. She utilizes some modern, historical-critical methods which are resisted or ignored in most postmodern, postliberal, and postcolonial writings. Even though she also draws explicitly upon some poststructural theories in her later writings, her critical use of modern theories remains her primary methodology and she clearly distinguishes her work from poststructuralist.[7] It is for these reasons that I refer to her approach as critical modern.[8]

Critique of Modernity and Liberalism

Modernity, arising from the eighteenth century Enlightenment, introduced a sorely needed critique of doctrinal and ecclesial authority through its emphasis upon reason and scientific method. Liberalism, evolving from a nineteenth century rise in historical consciousness, heralded human rights, equality, individual freedom and democracy.[9] While Schüssler Fiorenza acknowledges the importance of these contributions,[10] she addresses certain problems which have emerged from modern and liberal approaches: claims to impartiality, positivism, individualism, and the logic of identity. Each of these problems will be elaborated below.

Impartiality

Early modern thinkers believed that rational critiques were best accomplished by researchers who were detached emotionally and politically from their object of study. Schüssler Fiorenza describes such a researcher as "the transcendent abstract subject of Enlightenment reason positioned outside time and space who has privileged access to truth and knowledge."[11] The intent of this goal of impartiality was to prevent biases, values and interests from interfering with the collection of data and interpretation of results. However, Schüssler Fiorenza points out that a declaration of impartiality, objectivity, and disinterest is problematic for three reasons. The first is that it serves merely to mask hidden ideologies, political commitments, relationships of power, and interests of the biblical interpreter.[12] She refers to Albert Schweitzer's observation that historical-critical scholars seeking the historical Jesus will inevitably find him to be "fashioned in their own image and likeness."[13] She also draws upon the work of womanist, mujerista and Asian women theologians who have revealed the economic, institutional, cultural, racial, and colonial interests embedded within dominant biblical interpretations.[14]

This pretense to impartiality prevents biblical scholars and theologians from realizing that their own methods and interpretations are socially constructed.[15] It ignores the political pressures of audiences, publishers or places of employment. It also ignores the political implications of the work.[16] The Holocaust, slavery, the denigration of women, colonization, and global economic disparity have all been justified by particular Christian theologies and biblical interpretations. To ignore the political implications of one's own scholarly work may well be to implicitly support dominant structures of oppression.

The second problem with a declaration of impartiality is that it procures a false confidence in universally valid conclusions. Without realizing the effect of their own social location, presuppositions, and privileges on their work, theologians and biblical scholars will assume that their objective results will be valid and applicable globally. When a particular biblical interpretation is understood as a discovery of historical reality from which revelatory truth claims can be derived, historically limited experiences and values in scripture are posited as universal.[17]

The third problem with claims to impartiality concerns unitary thought. When historical-critical tools are used to unearth hidden facts and discern the one, true meaning of the text, any alternative meanings are either collapsed into this one, or are shown to be false. Schüssler Fiorenza insists that a supposedly objective and empirical study only produces one amongst many socially determined interpretations. If one acknowledges that conclusions are informed by the socio-political location of the interpreter, the diversity of interpreters will necessitate a diversity of interpretations.[18] While Schüssler Fiorenza wants to affirm this diversity of interpretations, she also resists absolute relativism, as shall be discussed later. This last problem of unitary thought is connected with the modern tendencies towards historical and textual positivism.

Positivism

Schüssler Fiorenza notes that modern approaches to biblical interpretation have relied upon historical-critical methods to uncover the historical reality behind the texts. These texts are understood as reflections of "how it really was."[19] Such an approach ignores the rhetorical nature of the text in its social context and construction. It also ignores the fact that history was written by the "winners," thereby reflecting their perspective.[20] This leads to a false assumption that those marginalized or absent in the texts were also marginalized or absent in historical reality. Schüssler Fiorenza demonstrates that this methodology has caused women to have been mistakenly erased from biblical history. Although she recognizes that most contemporary biblical scholars have acknowledged the "referential fallacy" of historical positivism, they still abide by a "modified positivist value-neutral stance" and overlook the ethical implications of their work.[21]

Historical positivism also removes the text from the contemporary world, making it an "artifact of antiquity," accessible only through historical-scientific research.[22] Such an understanding contributes to the separation and consequential isolation of biblical and theological disciplines.[23] Schüssler Fiorenza notes that this approach restricts anyone who does not have use of historical-critical tools from accessing the biblical texts. Biblical scholars defend this restricted access through their supposition that the original meaning, assumed to be accessible only through historical-critical methods, is definitive.

As a correction to historical positivism, Schüssler Fiorenza points to hermeneutics and the sociology of knowledge which question the objective, factual assumptions of historical criticism.[24] In her later writing she adds critical theory to this list of correctives.[25] Hermeneutical theory, such as that of Paul Ricoeur, proposed that meaning is found not behind the text, but in front of the text. What is of primary importance is not the historical reality revealed by the text, but the meaning inherent within the text itself, distanced from the author and the original context. Schüssler Fiorenza refers to this as textual positivism, still enmeshed in the modern elevation of rational, objective, apolitical, and neutral methods.[26] No critical or rhetorical questions are asked of the text itself. The text is absolute.

Another concern Schüssler Fiorenza has with hermeneutical theory, and later developments in literary theory, is its disregard of history. As the primary focus is with the text itself, and reality is constructed by the language of the text, actual historical reality is deemed both inaccessible and irrelevant. Schüssler Fiorenza is troubled by both the radical difference between text and reality posited by textual positivism, and the radical identity between text and reality posited by historical positivism.[27]

In some of her more recent writings, Schüssler Fiorenza names theological positivism as a concern. She uses this term to describe fundamentalist or neo-orthodox attempts to reduce multiple theological expression to those which neatly line up with the central theological doctrines and canons of the church.[28]

Individualism and the Logic of Identity

The modern problems of impartial claims and positivism are accentuated by the liberal emphasis upon the emancipation of the individual. Schüssler Fiorenza suggests that this has encouraged the privatizing of particular interpretations. This relativizes them even as they are still dependent upon the objectivity of historical-critical studies in order to be universally credible.[29] In contrast to the universal absolutism of the empirical scientific method, liberalism tends towards absolute relativism.[30] However, its particular relativism is confused with its dependence upon the universal validity of its objective findings.[31] It claims both particularity and universality.

The liberal emphasis upon the individual also informs the liberal commitment to equal rights. However, in her discussion of democracy, Schüssler Fiorenza suggests that the liberal movement for equal rights merely reinforces the patriarchal or "kyriarchal" Greco-Roman origins of democracy because the structures of domination are not addressed.[32] By not challenging the interlocking systems of racism, sexism, classism, colonialism, and heterosexism, equality cannot be achieved. The "patriarchal politics of otherness" remains entrenched.

In order to avoid the liberal, gender-specific interpretation of patriarchy, Schüssler Fiorenza has described patriarchy early in her work as "a complex political-economic-legal system that found its classical expression in Athenian democracy and its systemic articulation in Aristotelian philosophy."[33] She does not want to limit patriarchy to the dualistic gender framework of sexism and androcentrism, but defines it as "a shifting pyramidal political structure of dominance and subordination, stratified by gender, race, class, sexuality, religion, nation, culture, and other historical formations of domination."[34] In order to further distinguish her work from liberal, gender-specific interpretations of patriarchy, she coined the term "kyriarchy" in her later work, which she now prefers to the term patriarchy.[35] Kyriarchy means master-centred and refers to the classic Greek interlocking systems of domination. It indicates that not all men dominate all women. Rather, "elite, Western-educated, propertied, Euro-American men" have benefited from the exploitation of women, children, and other men.[36]

Another difficulty with the liberal movement for equal rights is that its standard measure for equality is "elite white men." It has coopted the dualistic Western gender system which has positioned woman as "the other" of man.[37] In her later work, Schüssler Fiorenza analyzes this through the "logic of identity," in which all difference is subsumed into the identity of those in power.[38] The creation of universal interpretations and norms is based upon a common essence, particular to the dominant group (usually white, European men) and assumed to be descriptive and relevant for all. This essentialism corresponds with the drive for unitary thought and eliminates as many variables (and hence human difference and diversity of biblical interpretation) as possible in its attempts to contain reality within a total system.[39] Schüssler Fiorenza refers to Simone de Beauvoir's analysis of women within this system as the "other" of men. She then refers to global feminist discourse which describes women of subordinated races, classes, cultures, and religions as the "others" of the "others."[40] Global feminism has critiqued white, middle-class feminists for continuing the same essentializing discourse about women which subsumes the diversity of women into a unitary logic of identity.[41]

Although Schüssler Fiorenza takes issue with a number of elements associated with modernity and liberalism, she does note her appreciation for the modern methods of empirical research, analytical scholarship and critical abstraction.[42] She herself employs such methods in her historical-critical studies. She also notes her appreciation for the liberal emphasis upon freedom, equality, justice, and democracy, all of which are central in her own work. It is not with modernity or liberalism per se with which she has difficulty. Rather, it is an uncritical adoption of these approaches and principles that have led to the above problems. By not submitting its own work to ideological critique, the modern approach fails to abide by its own critical principle of the Enlightenment.[43]

Theological Method

Elisabeth Schüssler Fiorenza describes her method as "a feminist critical theology of liberation"[44] or "a critical feminist rhetorical interpretation for liberation."[45] She is aware of womanist and mujerista critiques that the term "feminist" has been largely descriptive of white, middle-class women. However, because of the political impact of the term "feminist" throughout the world and its continued use by some Third World women, she continues to use this term for her own work.[46] At the same time, she wants to problematize this term, so as to leave it open to critiques and corresponding shifts in meaning.[47]

As indicative of liberation theology, Schüssler Fiorenza intentionally takes an advocacy position on behalf of the oppressed, rather than assuming neutrality. "Intellectual neutrality is not possible in a historical world of exploitation and oppression."[48] She calls for a paradigm shift from "value-detached scientism" to "public rhetoric," from a "hermeneutical model of conversation" to a "practical model of collaboration."[49] Schüssler Fiorenza bases her call for this paradigm shift upon Thomas Kuhn's work in which "a paradigm represents a coherent research tradition created and sustained by a scientific community."[50] She believes that the feminist paradigm has created and is sustained by its own academic institutions and communities which need to be both strengthened and taken seriously by the patriarchal institutions. However, it is to the women's movement, not the academy, that Schüssler Fiorenza wants to be accountable. Her goal is to establish a new paradigm for biblical interpretation that will more adequately address the experiences and concerns of women. In her later work she also includes concern for men who are outside of the dominant white, elite, Western-educated, male purview, although her emphasis still remains with women.

Community and Diversity

Schüssler Fiorenza maintains a "critical commitment to the Christian community and its traditions."[51] In contrast to postbiblical feminists, she insists on working within the Christian tradition because it continues to be influential in the lives of women throughout the world. She is able to find signs of hope within the Bible and Christian tradition that resist the patriarchal overlay of the texts. However, she does not view the Bible as an authoritative source in itself. It is only a resource in which evidence of women's struggles for liberation can be found.[52] In order to reconstruct these marginalized stories of women, she draws on the biblical texts as well as extra-canonical material. Questions and commitments that arise out of contemporary women's liberation movements around the world inform this reconstruction and provide both guidance and the means for the celebration of these re-membered stories. Thus, her critical feminist hermeneutics begins with the experiences of both contemporary and historical women struggling against patriarchal oppression.[53] Central to this process of biblical interpretation is what Schüssler Fiorenza calls the "ekklēsia of wo/men."[54]

Schüssler Fiorenza has an evolving definition of ekklēsia of wo/men, which may yet take on new dimensions. Her original 1982 term, "ekklēsia of women," was based upon the Greek word for church, which was the common word for the assembly of free citizens gathering to decide their own spiritual and political affairs. Schüssler Fiorenza qualified ekklēsia with the phrase "of women" to indicate that the church will never be the complete democratic assembly of the saints until women are fully included.[55] At first Schüssler Fiorenza alternated between the terms "ekklēsia" and "synagogē." However, after realizing that this obscured the differing relationships of power between Christians and Jews, as well as the history of genocide of the Jewish people, she used only ekklēsia.[56]

In her earlier writing the ekklēsia of women is inclusive of all women of the past and present who have acted and continue to act in the "life-giving Sophia-Spirit." It overcomes patriarchal dualisms between Jewish and Christian women, lay and "nun-women," homemakers and career women, active and contemplative, Protestant and Roman Catholic, married and single, physical and spiritual mothers, heterosexual and lesbian, the church and the world, the sacred and the secular.[57] The ekklēsia of women is not an end in itself, but seeks to reconstruct "women's heritage as church" and to transform the patriarchal church into a discipleship of equals as part of the *basileia* of God.[58] Patterned after the Jesus movement, the ekklēsia of women is committed to the liberation of all who are marginalized from society.[59]

Schüssler Fiorenza's definition of the ekklēsia of women was originally exclusive of men. She believed that women first had to meet alone, without men, in order to "reclaim their spiritual powers and to exorcise their possession by male idolatry" before mutuality with men would be possible.[60] Within a year, however, she used the terms "ekklesia gynaikon," "women-church," and "ekklesia of women" interchangeably to mean "the movement of self-identified women and women-identified men … as the dialogical community of equals in which critical judgement takes place and public freedom becomes tangible."[61] Men were now included if they were "women-identified."[62] This expanded definition of ekklēsia of women invites men to identify with women's struggle for equality, authority and citizenship in the church.[63] She wants to keep the focus on women in order to raise consciousness about their absence from particular ecclesial circles and to allow women a space where a different theology can be envisioned and enacted.[64]

In one of her most recent writings she uses the term "woma[e]n" to intentionally jar the reader into realizing that the terms "women" and "woman" are culturally constructed and need to be destabilized.[65] However, Schüssler Fiorenza is inconsistent with her use of "woma[e]n," at times within the same sentence, creating more confusing instability of the text than I think she intends. Most confusing is her use of the term "everywoman" in the same article. I cannot think of a more essentializing term for women!

In her struggle to find a term that best honours the multiple identities of women and oppressed men, she has settled on "wo/men."[66] Some of her latest writing uses this term to denote the multiple identities of women, foreclosing a unitary essence, while still enabling Schüssler Fiorenza to use "women" as a political category. It also indicates a concern for men of subordinated races, classes, countries and religions. Thus, the ekklēsia of wo/men now fully includes all people, women and men, who are oppressed.[67]

Although this is her stated intent, it is also clear that in certain instances she is only referring to women by this term. She hopes that the term "wo/men" will invite men to "think twice and to experience what it means not to be addressed explicitly."[68] However, it also causes women to think twice as to whether Schüssler Fiorenza is referring to women or to all oppressed peoples. Lack of an explicitly gendered reference makes political analysis more difficult. By broadening the term "wo/men" to now include all of the oppressed men and women, one could question whether or not she has retained women as subjects. By changing the definition of women to include all of the globally oppressed, she is subsuming women into a larger, generic category of the oppressed. Just as Donna Haraway has been criticized for subsuming women into her cyborg and obliterating their subjecthood, Elisabeth Schüssler Fiorenza could be accused of obliterating the subjecthood of women.[69] Susan Wood makes an interesting observation that Schüssler Fiorenza's theological method, "begun in an experience of gender oppression, ultimately transcends gender."[70]

One of the difficulties Schüssler Fiorenza encountered with her evolving construct of the ekklēsia of wo/men was the concept of women's common experience. In her earlier writing, she speaks of "a common experience" which "women as a group share," while acknowledging the diversity of individual perceptions and interpretations of this experience.[71] Elsewhere, Schüssler Fiorenza wrote at the same time that raw, common experience does not exist. It is only the particular and individual experience, shaped by historical and cultural conditions, that exists.[72] The following year Schüssler Fiorenza tries again to reclaim the notion of common experience, suggesting that it is not derived from biological sex nor essential gender differences, but from the struggle against patriarchy.[73]

In her later work she eventually abandons altogether this essentialist notion of women's common experience. Speaking "as a woman," she explains, introduces a problematic notion that all women share a common, essential nature. She draws upon womanist, mujerista and global feminist theories to warn against the construction of a unitary identity of women. This essentialism only perpetuates the kyriarchal politics of otherness.[74]

These continuous revisions to her work give evidence of her commitment to hearing and incorporating the critiques of womanist, mujerista, and Asian feminist theologians. She has always been sensitive to the diversity of women and the problem of speaking for all women. For instance, in her earlier work she refers to the double and triple oppression of poor women and women of colour.[75] In her later work she notes that oppression is not merely multiplied (doubled or tripled), but is multiplicative (one oppression multiplied by another, multiplied by another).[76]

As the diversity of women is becoming more fully acknowledged by feminists in general, Schüssler Fiorenza cautions against reinforcing the patriarchal status divisions that are established on the basis of the inequality of class, gender, race, ethnicity, and age. A celebration of difference, she warns, can inadvertently reinforce these divisions. Biological, social and cultural diversities should be recognized within their historical and geographical limitations. Differences should be "denaturalized" in order to avoid essentializing them in a male-female dualism or ontologizing them with inherent qualities. This deconstruction will prevent a reification of differences by emphasizing their historical and cultural construction.[77] It will also reveal the historical multiplicity of every person, even within their own groups of identity. Lesbian women, for instance, do not form a monolithic, undifferentiated group.[78]

Because of this, she suggests it is problematic for women to form groups on the basis of a shared victimization or a homogeneous identity of "woman." It is also problematic for women to form noncompetitive, structureless collectives which discourage self-critique or responsibility for their own roles as oppressors.[79] When such groups are formed around these common experiences, identities, or protectionist attitudes, they follow the logic of identity and exclude or obliterate differences amongst women.

This, she admits, has been the case for women-church, which has remained a "homogeneous white women's movement."[80] Although she acknowledges that women-church gatherings have been primarily white and middle-class, she doesn't acknowledge that her original essentialist definitions of women-church may have contributed to its homogeneity.

In light of these difficulties with the definition and reality of the ekklēsia of wo/men, Schüssler Fiorenza could dispense with the notion of women-church and simply refer to diverse, emancipatory faith communities. Her explicitly feminist criteria would still allow critical analysis of multiplicative oppressions, including those based on gender. I suspect that one of the reasons she retains the ekklēsia of wo/men is that she is unwilling to relinquish her earlier statements that women's perspectives give a more accurate account of reality. This assumption becomes evident when she supports the use of standpoint theory, as will be discussed later. Thus, women's communities are given normative status, not only because of their political commitments, but also because of their epistemological privilege *as women*.[81] At the same time, Schüssler Fiorenza clearly situates the ekklēsia of wo/men within a politics of struggle rather than a politics of identity.[82]

To counteract the white, middle-class nature of women-church gatherings, she joins with Chandra Talpade Mohanty to call for a *political* common ground upon which communities, including the ekklēsia of wo/men, be formed and alliances be made.[83] This political common ground should make international, intergenerational, and inter-religious connections simultaneously in order to better understand the interconnection of systemic systems of domination.[84] She believes that the ekklēsia of wo/men can be a coalition of diverse women's groups which form an alliance of solidarity around the common commitment to the vision of G*d's[85] *basileia* and to the struggle against the multiplicative structures of patriarchal oppression.[86]

It is from within the ekklēsia of wo/men that biblical interpretation should take place. Schüssler Fiorenza faults biblical scholars for being accountable to the academy, but not to the community of faith.[87] She lifts up the example of liberation theology, which forms its biblical interpretation primarily from the experiences of its members instead of European academic scholarship. Base communities study the Bible in order to gain strength and vision for their struggle to achieve liberation. Schüssler Fiorenza stresses the importance of this purpose for biblical hermeneutics.[88]

Authoritative Criteria

The authority of the ekklēsia of wo/men rests upon G*d's presence revealed in the struggles against dehumanization and injustice, with particular emphasis upon women's liberation.[89] Authority is not located in the experiences of *all* women, but is limited to those who were part of the historical Jesus movement (companions of Jesus and members of the early church), as well as all others throughout history who have worked for justice.[90] The goal of Schüssler Fiorenza's critical feminist hermeneutics is to make present as historical actors those whom the biblical texts have marginalized or excluded.[91] On this basis, "the personally and politically reflected experience of oppression and liberation must become the criterion of appropriateness for biblical interpretations and evaluation of biblical authority claims."[92]

These reflections are not meant to be individualistic, but to be situated within a community patterned after the Jesus movement. Even though Schüssler Fiorenza resists positing Jesus of Nazareth as the authoritative norm, as shall be discussed later, the Jesus movement is central for her. The Jesus traditions do not attribute misogynist statements to Jesus, which is remarkable, she notes, since the gospels were written after the patriarchalization of Christianity was well under way. Instead, these Jesus traditions reflect the emancipatory attitude of Jesus towards women, as well as his recognition of female disciples and leaders.[93] They also reflect the emancipatory commitment of the Jesus movement, which Schüssler Fiorenza is careful to describe as one amongst other Jewish renewal movements, so as not to place it in opposition to Judaism. The early church therefore provides glimpses of the discipleship of equals. It is this communal experience of G*d's *basileia* to which Schüssler Fiorenza gives authority. She therefore reverses the second century shift from charismatic and communal authority to institutional patriarchal leadership.[94]

Although Schüssler Fiorenza wants to honour the authority and diversity of religious communities in their interpretations of scripture, she is careful not to lapse into absolute relativism. Authority is given to those interpretations which meet certain criteria which she believes are universally applicable for all communities. She expands upon David Tracy's criteria to call for an adequacy to the historical-literary methods of interpretation and appropriateness to the struggle of the oppressed for liberation.[95] To be adequate, historical research must submit to public testing in three areas: it must use relevant sources and current research; it must reach plausible conclusions that are "fitting" to its rhetorical context; and it must be logically rigorous, consistent and coherent.[96] To be appropriate, it must evaluate critically the patriarchal formation of the biblical texts, and the ideological distortions of biblical interpretation which have contributed to the oppression of the marginalized.[97]

These two criteria of adequacy and appropriateness coincide with her double ethics of historical reading and of accountability. An ethics of historical reading uses historical-critical tools to discern and prioritize the "original meanings" of a text over later editions. This allows the text to retain its critical distance from the reader and not be subsumed into the reader's world. The text and the reader enter into a relationship of mutual critique.[98] An ethics of accountability stresses the responsibility of the reader for the particular interpretive model chosen, and for the ethical consequences of the biblical texts and their interpretation.[99]

Schüssler Fiorenza later added to these criteria an ethics of solidarity. The diverse social locations of feminist theology will produce diverse, sometimes opposing, interpretations that will require adjudication. The authoritative basis for this judgement would depend upon the above criteria within "responsible debate and practical deliberation."[100] The ekklēsia of wo/men must therefore be open to continual self-critique and transformation as an act of solidarity. Methodologies must always be open to more adequate ways to address multiplicative oppressions and visions of G*d's *basileia*.

In order to avoid a "paralyzing pluralism," an ethics of solidarity operates with "radical democracy." Attention is given to the silencing and welcoming of different voices and to strategies for analyzing and critiquing structures of domination.[101] So as not to perpetuate the modern drive towards unity, Schüssler Fiorenza stresses that the truth claims emerging from these debates be relative, not absolute, because they are historically and culturally conditioned. However, in order to avoid relativistic nihilism, emancipatory discourses are privileged over patriarchal ones.[102] The strategies and theories of feminists who speak from the experience of multiplicative oppressions must also be privileged in this debate.[103] In this respect, she supports the hermeneutical privilege of the oppressed.[104]

In order to help assess the degree to which a social group is oppressed, Schüssler Fiorenza has recently revised a list of criteria originally created by Iris Marion Young. She asks the degree to which wo/men are:

- exploited economically, culturally, and politically;
- marginalized in cultural, religious, and scientific institutions;
- powerless in political, cultural, and religious decision-making;
- made invisible by cultural imperialism;
- the victims of physical and mental systemic violence;
- silenced from public speaking, preaching, or teaching;
- vilified or trivialized.[105]

Revelation

Because the Bible and Christian tradition have contributed to the abuse and silencing of women, Schüssler Fiorenza cannot trust or accept either simply as divine revelation.[106] She understands both to be deeply imbued with the patriarchal attitudes of the authors and editors. With the support of historical criticism, she insists that biblical texts are not verbally inspired revelation but are historical constructions within religious communities.[107] However, she believes that the Bible and extra-canonical writings can be used as resources which can provide clues to the erased experiences of women. Revelation and truth can be found in biblical texts which transcend their patriarchal frameworks and reveal the historical agency of women. This does not mean that a revelatory essence be abstracted from its accidental, socio-political formations. Rather, women's struggles against oppression can only be understood within their patriarchal context.[108] "*The* litmus test for invoking Scripture as the Word of God must be whether or not biblical texts and traditions seek to end relations of domination and exploitation."[109]

Schüssler Fiorenza compares the views of revelation taken by differing theological approaches throughout the last few decades. In contrast to the doctrinal, historical, or hermeneutical-contextual paradigms as outlined below, she prefers the pastoral-theological paradigm. In her later writing she names these the doctrinal-fundamentalist (this is an unfortunate addition, as many postliberals who prioritize the doctrines of the church are far from fundamentalist), the scientific-historical, the hermeneutic-(post)modern (this is also an unfortunate addition, as postmodern theorists are quite different from modern literary theorists), and the rhetorical-emancipatory paradigm.[110]

Schüssler Fiorenza suggests that the doctrinal paradigm declares texts which support particular ecclesial doctrines as revelatory. The historical paradigm declares the earliest historically verifiable traditions to be true and therefore revelatory. Schüssler Fiorenza's definition of the hermeneutical-contextual paradigm is less clear, as she attempts to group literary theory together with various liberation theologies. However, she suggests that these latter approaches all base their judgements upon the fixed biblical canon and the norm of Jesus Christ or the norm of a canonical principle, such as salvation history or prophetic justice. She rejects the christological norm because the historical Jesus is inaccessible, and she resists positing a male norm for women.[111]

It is difficult to follow her logic on these two points. First, the historical Jesus is no more inaccessible than are the women of the Jesus movement. Conversely, Jesus is just as accessible as the women through rhetorical analysis and reconstruction. Indeed she does describe aspects of Jesus' emancipatory life and ministry in order to support her claims for the emancipatory commitments of the Jesus movement. Secondly, she suggests that feminists who dismiss the importance of Jesus' masculinity ignore and therefore reify the kyriarchal sex/gender system.[112] However, her elevation of Jesus' gender as a reason for his dismissal seems itself to be a fixation and therefore a reification of the sex/gender system. Kwok Pui-lan notes that the concern with Jesus' male identity seems to be a preoccupation only of western feminists. Asian feminists understand the maleness of Jesus to be "a historical accident rather than an ontological necessity in the liberation process."[113]

Schüssler Fiorenza's alternative is the pastoral-theological paradigm which declares revelatory those texts which are deemed by emancipatory Christian communities to contribute to our salvation.[114] She understands salvation in the biblical sense as pertaining to the welfare of the whole person, and not simply to their soul. Correspondingly, sin is not limited to the personal, but includes the structural sins of domination.[115] As her primary concern is the liberation of the oppressed, she recommends that soteriological discussion of this nature take priority over christological concerns.[116] This division of soteriology from christology is problematic. If she derives her soteriology from the Jesus movement, she cannot avoid christological discussion. The very separation of christology from soteriology may have contributed to the abstract christological debates which she rejects.

Schüssler Fiorenza notes that this concept of revelation, which is dependent upon the salvific relevance of texts to an ecclesial community, is more familiar for Roman Catholics than for Protestants.[117] She refers to Vatican II's document on divine revelation in which revealed truth and inerrancy is limited "to matters pertaining to the salvation of the Christian and human community." Scripture *contains* revelation but not all of Scripture *is* revelation.[118] This position may be closer to traditional Protestant beliefs than Schüssler Fiorenza realizes, particularly regarding the distinction between the revealed Word of God and the biblical texts. Foremost Protestant theologians in the earlier part of this century, such as Paul Tillich, Emil Brunner, and Karl Barth, all agree that the Word of God is not to be equated with Scripture but with Jesus Christ. The Word of God is contained in and revealed through Scripture, but is not Scripture itself. While Schüssler Fiorenza would differ on her view of the Word of God and its normative equation with Jesus the Christ, her warning that the biblical text not be viewed revelatory in itself would be similar to the views held by these Protestant theologians.[119]

According to her concept of biblical revelation, Schüssler Fiorenza posits the Bible as a prototype or formative root model of how religious communities respond to their historical situations. Understanding the Bible as a prototype resists its reduction to universal principles or certain inspired passages. Rather, it honours the pluriformity of biblical texts and encourages their critical transformation.[120] It does not ignore or silence the more oppressive passages, nor does it read the more liberative passages in an anti-Jewish manner.[121] She contrasts this with the traditional understanding of the Bible as an archetype of unchanging pattern and ideal form.[122] A normative archetype can only be received or rejected, but not critically evaluated. It takes historically limited experiences and posits them as universals, authoritative for all cultures and times.[123]

Understanding the Bible as a formative prototype, according to

Schüssler Fiorenza, is also in accord with the early Church. The early Christian communities believed that revelation "happened decisively in Jesus of Nazareth" and continues to happen through the Holy Spirit. The New Testament writings were not intended to be universal, revelatory norms. Rather, they were intended to interpret this dialectical understanding of past and present revelation according to the needs and particularities of each community.[124] Revelation, therefore, should not be located in the androcentric text, but in the Jesus movement and the subsequent Christian communities.

In Schüssler Fiorenza's later writing, she suggests that "whitemale" biblical hermeneutics and white feminist hermeneutics are preoccupied with the normativity and authority of scripture because they operate out of the Eurocentric logic of identity. Schüssler Fiorenza refers to African-American critiques of white anxiety over biblical authority. She notes that African-American women avoided their own subsumption into the logic of identity by claiming the authority of their personal experiences of God's liberation within the context of slavery. Only as a secondary source of authority would biblical stories be invoked to illuminate their experiences.[125]

While Schüssler Fiorenza's assessment of a white preoccupation with biblical authority may be true in certain circles, I have found biblical authority to be of utmost importance for many Korean, Chinese, First Nations, and African Canadian Protestant churches. The preoccupation with biblical authority may well be more a difference between Protestant and Roman Catholic traditions, than between ethnic groups. From a Protestant perspective, it is difficult to study or preach from biblical texts without addressing their authority.[126] Interestingly enough, in Schüssler Fiorenza's latest works, she still continues not only to address issues of biblical authority, but also to recommend a revised definition of biblical and canonical authority. Obviously the authority of scripture is still of concern to her.

Schüssler Fiorenza's primary concern with people's preoccupation of biblical authority is their accompanying need to find clear, unambiguous answers. This unrelenting urge towards unitary thinking attempts to eliminate all uncertainty and unpredictability, thereby subsuming otherness into itself.[127] Schüssler Fiorenza suggests that revelation should not be derived out of a logic of identity but out of a "logic of democracy." A logic of identity understands truth to be a hidden, metaphysical given which must be uncovered. A logic of democracy, on the other hand, understands truth to be a moment in the process of global emancipatory and democratic struggles. It is constituted through communicative practices, not as a hidden essence to be discovered, but as a point of realization to be determined.[128]

Revelation is thus located within the experiences of religious communities, as they define their own canons of authority. Schüssler Fiorenza is careful not to endow the patriarchal church with revelatory status, however, by clarifying that revelation is found in the struggles of all women against patriarchal oppression.[129] Thus, it is specifically the ekklēsia of wo/men, as a religious community, that is revelatory. Revelation is found elsewhere only to the extent that the liberation of all the oppressed, including women, is sought.

This understanding of revelation resists the distorted use of scripture for oppressive means. If revelation is located in scripture, debate is focused upon the normativity and authority of the biblical texts. If revelation is located in the justice-seeking community, debate is focused upon their struggles against oppression. The latter option would prevent opposing sides both claiming scriptural authority regarding issues of women's full ecclesial participation, of slavery, of economic equity, or of the rights of lesbian and gay people.[130]

Schüssler Fiorenza's concept of revelation necessitates a critical examination not only of the biblical texts, but also of their canonical formation. The canon was chosen by the winners of the debates over orthodoxy and heresy. Central to these debates was the question of women's leadership. Those who emerged the winners disputed the validity of women's leadership and equated it with heresy. These beliefs were reflected in the choice of books both rejected, such as *The Acts of Paul and Thecla*, and included in the canon.[131] "By claiming to be the only 'orthodox' word of God, the canon scripturalized traditions of subordination and domination."[132]

Schüssler Fiorenza addresses these problematic aspects of the canon by redefining and expanding the notion of canon. She does not want to dispense with the traditional canon, for even within these patriarchal, canonical books evidence can be found of earlier egalitarian traditions welcoming women's leadership.[133] Rather than understanding canon as a limited set of revelatory texts that cast a negative judgement on other early Christian writings, Schüssler Fiorenza suggests that canon be viewed as an inclusive collection of diverse models of Christian community and life.[134]

This would preclude the search for a revelatory canon within the canon, whether that be the historical Jesus, the earliest apostolic witness, or a liberating theological principle. Such a search operates out of a logic of identity in its attempts to find an authoritative essence underlying scripture. The establishment of a canon within the canon reduces the historical particularities and pluralities of the biblical texts and images into one unitary norm.[135]

By understanding the canon as an inclusive collection of texts, she wants to protect the diversity of these texts and break open the boundaries of the traditional canon. She expands the functional definition of canon beyond texts to include the liberation struggles of all women.[136] She also intentionally transcends the boundaries of the traditional biblical canon to include extra-canonical writings and commentaries from Jewish and post-Christian perspectives. This transgression of canonical boundaries protests the heretical branding and dismissal of women that occurred through the formation of the canon.[137]

Schüssler Fiorenza's intention is not to produce an alternate, feminist canon. She wants to deconstruct, not reconstruct, the canon in order to destabilize canonical authority and its continuing historical impact upon women. Relationships of people with their sacred scriptures is her central concern, rather than the authority and normativity of a fixed canon. Thus, she does not support the Protestant notion of a revealed canon.[138] In this deconstruction, however, she proposes an alternate and more fluid definition of canon. She suggests that the canon be perceived as the "open, cosmic house of divine Wisdom." Its authority is based upon the original meaning of the Latin word for authority, *augere/auctoritas*: to nurture creativity and foster growth. In this respect, Schüssler Fiorenza does not eschew biblical or canonical authority, but redefines it as fostering creativity, strength, and freedom.[139]

Rhetorical Reading Strategies
In order for Schüssler Fiorenza to ascertain both the liberative and

patriarchal aspects of the biblical texts, she analyzes their socio-political contexts with the help of historical-critical methods, literary criticism, liberation theologies and feminist critical theory. She is particularly interested in traces of the silenced or marginalized voices, and draws upon rhetorical criticism to reconstruct their histories. Her intent is not to search for the "true, pristine, orthodox beginnings" which were later corrupted by the established church. The Jesus movement not only struggled against patriarchal views, but was also steeped in them. Nor is she attempting to construct a more accurate account of historical reality. Rather, she seeks to reconstruct a different account of history from the perspective of the marginalized.

Schüssler Fiorenza has often been criticized for seeking a truer account of a purely egalitarian Jesus movement. Indeed, her earlier work could be interpreted as such, even though she states otherwise, dismissing most of her critics with the accusation that they have misread her work. I suggest that if such a large number of intelligent readers are indeed guilty of misreading, then her work must surely lend itself to this confusion. In fact, she acknowledges in one of her later writings that her earlier work might have inadvertently fostered historically positivist misreadings.[140] I believe that this confusion results from her refinement and subtle shifts between her earlier and later work. Unfortunately, she adds to this confusion by insisting that she has not changed, but is simply elaborating upon her earlier work.[141] Her development of rhetorical method in her work is a good example. It is not until her later work, particularly with *Jesus*, that she refines her rhetorical method and clearly refutes any suspicion that she is searching for a more accurate historical account of the Jesus movement.[142] It has become clear only in her later work that she is relying upon a poststructural understanding of language not as a representation of reality, but as a sociocultural linguistic system constructed through discourse.[143]

Within such a reconstruction of history, Schüssler Fiorenza can discover glimpses in the early church of the egalitarian vision in the midst of struggles against patriarchal domination.[144] She hopes that this vision will aid not only the liberation of women, but also "the emancipation of biblical religion from patriarchal structures and ideologies."[145] Schüssler Fiorenza proposes four reading strategies for this type of emancipatory biblical interpretation. Biblical texts should be critically analyzed through a hermeneutics of suspicion, of remembrance and reconstruction, of evaluation and proclamation, and of imagination and ritualization.

A hermeneutics of suspicion entails an ideological critique of patriarchal elements in both contemporary interpretations and the texts themselves. It reads the biblical texts against their ideological grain and positions them within the historical, early Christian debate.[146] This strategy is based upon four presuppositions:

1. Texts and historical sources must be read as androcentric texts.
2. The glorification, denigration and marginalization of women must be read as patriarchal social construction or projection.
3. Formal patriarchal laws are generally more restrictive than the actual interaction of men and women.
4. Women's actual social-religious status must be determined by their economic autonomy and social roles rather than by ideological or prescriptive statements.[147]

Schüssler Fiorenza compares this strategy to the work of a detective or sleuth.[148]

A hermeneutics of remembrance and reconstruction recovers all biblical texts, including those supporting patriarchal views, in order to best reconstruct a history of women in the early Christian movement. Schüssler Fiorenza refers to Johann Metz's concept of a dangerous or subversive memory that reclaims the visions and sufferings of the dead.[149] This strategy involves imagination, but Schüssler Fiorenza is quick to distinguish this imaginative historical reconstruction, based upon historical-critical evidence, from fiction.[150] An historical reconstruction resembles a quilt-maker, piecing together historical patches into a new, and more plausible, design.[151] Schüssler Fiorenza seems most unconvincing to many readers on this point. They suggest that she needs more plausible support to distinguish certain aspects of her work from fiction.[152]

A hermeneutics of evaluation and proclamation assesses the Bible's theological and ethical significance for the contemporary community of faith. Texts deemed patriarchal by the ekklēsia of wo/men should be eliminated from worship and Christian education, while those considered to "transcend" their patriarchal contexts should be included.[153] Masculine language should be perceived as generic, unless specifically stated otherwise. This strategy is likened to a health inspector checking food and medicine for harmful ingredients.[154] The quote at the beginning of this chapter emerges from this strategy.

Lastly, a hermeneutics of imagination and ritualization, also referred to as a hermeneutics of creative actualization and liberative vision, allows women to celebrate this reconstructed history through artistic recreation and liturgy. This celebration makes present the suffering and victories of biblical foremothers, and actualizes their emancipatory visions.[155]

In her later refinement of this approach, she notes that these strategies should not be undertaken linearly or progressively from one step to the next. Rather, each movement informs the others in a "dance of biblical interpretation."[156] Each one also takes into consideration four levels of meaning: agent (reader and writer), text (including context and intertextual relationship), world (contemporary and historical sociopolitical forces and institutions), and ideology (inscribed in the language and practices of the text and the reader).[157]

In one of her writings, Schüssler Fiorenza has simplified this process into two strategies: suspicion or critical evaluation, and re-vision or reconstruction. She suggests that a hermeneutics of suspicion searches texts for evidence of patriarchal oppression while a hermeneutics of re-vision searches for liberative values and visions.

In some of her most recent writing Schüssler Fiorenza expands the four strategies to seven, in order to stress the importance of analyzing the social location of our own experience and the dominant ideologies that influence both us and the text. She also adds a final strategy of change and transformation. The seven strategies are named as a hermeneutics of experience (beginning not simply with experience, but with "systemically analyzed and reflected experience"[158]), a hermeneutics of domination, of suspicion, of assessment and evaluation, of reimagination, of reconstruction, and of change and transformation.[159]

Elsewhere in the same writing Schüssler Fiorenza also talks about a hermeneutics of desire (a yearning of the ekklēsia of wo/men for the *basileia* of G*d), a hermeneutics of indeterminancy (honouring the plurality of readings of a text), and a hermeneutics of transformation (evaluates various readings according to their political impact and supports those which resist systems of domination).[160] These three hermeneutics are meant to work together, each one challenging and balancing the other.

It is clear that Schüssler Fiorenza has never intended her hermeneutical strategies to remain static and fixed. She is always revising, adding, and massaging the strategies so as to best address the ever-shifting patterns of domination, and take seriously the continuous critique of marginalized wo/men. Within all of these strategies, though, there is a consistent emphasis upon rhetorical criticism. This is particularly evident within the hermeneutics of suspicion and of reconstruction.

As previously noted, Schüssler Fiorenza uses the rhetorical method in her earlier writing but has refined it and given greater emphasis to it in her later work. She distinguishes the popular use of rhetoric as "mere talk" from her use of the ancient practice of rhetoric as a "communicative practice that involves interests, values, and visions."[161] Rhetorical criticism asks how meaning is constructed, whose interests are served, what values, visions, duties, and roles are advocated, which communities and socio-political practices are considered authoritative, etc. In short, rhetorical criticism is concerned with issues of power.

As Schüssler Fiorenza applies rhetorical criticism to texts, she seeks to determine how the text worked in its complex historical, cultural, social, and religious contexts. This use of rhetorical criticism purports that the context is as important as the text, that our social location will determine how we view the world and interpret biblical texts, and that historical sources can only reveal perspectival discourses and not historical reality. Thus, a text will have multiple meanings, according to the interpreters' varying frameworks. With this understanding, the rhetorical method is less interested in determining a text's meaning as it is in determining how the text operates within socio-historical contexts. Rhetorical criticism is particularly helpful in determining the ideological constructs of the text which include or silence others.[162] Questions from feminists, liberation theologians, third world theologians, and others who have been marginalized in biblical hermeneutics are therefore central to this analysis.[163]

Schüssler Fiorenza delineates four stages in her use of the rhetorical method. First, she identifies the rhetorical interests and models of contemporary interpretation. Secondly, she delineates the rhetorical arrangement and interests of the author of the text. Thirdly, she establishes the rhetorical, socio-political situation of the text. Lastly, she seeks to reconstruct the historical situation of the author and audience.[164]

Throughout this rhetorical analysis Schüssler Fiorenza employs feminist standpoint epistemologies. Because women are both participants in and outsiders to the patriarchal culture, our world view differs from the dominant world view. This renders an epistemologically privileged standpoint of women, as we must understand the patriarchal culture in order to live in it, and at the same time understand our own marginalized space. Thus, we are able to give a "truer, more adequate account of a 'real' world and human history."[165]

Although Schüssler Fiorenza wants to avoid an essentializing of women, she does not accept postmodern critique of feminist standpoint theory. Women must still be political subjects and must resist complete relativization of their experiences. Thus, Schüssler Fiorenza stresses that standpoint theory is informed by global feminist theories and diverse experiences of women within a partisan commitment to socio-political emancipation. Standpoint theory will help first to deconstruct the politics of otherness within the biblical texts and then to reconstruct the texts in order to construct a different socio-historical reality and empower women.[166]

While consistently eschewing a modern assumption of universally valid conclusions, Schüssler Fiorenza is unwilling to relinquish universal norms. Her criteria of adequacy and accountability, her ethics of solidarity, and her liberative principle of textual adjudication form the basis of her critique of other biblical interpretations.[167] These are normative for her own work and provide standards of judgement for all others.

Schüssler Fiorenza does stress the importance of multiple, often competing readings arising from diverse social locations in order to best respect the diversity of the biblical texts and the diversity of the interpreters. However, she has long puzzled critics who point to both her avowed openness and her subsequent critique and dismissal of competing interpretations.[168] I suggest that it is the *method* of biblical interpretation with its accompanying criteria which she recommends as universally valid. She welcomes diverse interpretations that operate within this same method, and resists universalizing any one particular interpretation. In this manner she attempts to respect the diversity of communities with their own diverse interpretations while retaining universal criteria and avoiding postmodernism's tendency towards absolute relativity.

Conclusion

Schüssler Fiorenza has consistently worked from a liberation perspective. Through personal experiences and her involvement with Roman Catholic women's organizations, she has been painfully aware of the church's marginalization and silencing of women. Early in her work she became aware of the need for a paradigm shift in theological method that would address this problem. She came to see that the modern and liberal paradigms, which were originally developed to address the hegemony of church authority, have unwittingly perpetuated the hegemony of white, male Eurocentric thought. In her critique of modern and liberal approaches, however, she hesitates to abandon this paradigm altogether. Rather, she uses modern historical-critical methods *critically*, avoiding their claims of impartiality and universalism, while guarding against their tendencies towards unitary thought, historical and textual positivism, individualism, essentialism, and the collapse of the other into the logic of identity.

The rhetorical method has proven vital in Schüssler Fiorenza's attempts to avoid and critique the problems of modernity and liberalism. Her ongoing refinement of the ancient practice of rhetoric within her own work has allowed her to focus upon the socio-political contexts and communities of the biblical texts while reconstructing the voices that have been marginalized within these texts. As part of this rhetorical method, she has developed reading strategies that focus on a hermeneutics of suspicion, proclamation, remembrance and creative actualization.

Schüssler Fiorenza intends these reading strategies to be conducted not by individuals, but within faith communities. In order to raise up the voices of the marginalized, Schüssler Fiorenza focuses upon the ekklēsia of wo/men, rather than institutional churches. Her goal is to establish a new emancipatory paradigm for biblical interpretation that will seek the liberation of all oppressed peoples, with particular concern for women. For this reason, she privileges the interpretations of faith communities of oppressed peoples struggling for liberation and political solidarity across the world, and considers these part of the ekklēsia of wo/men. Schüssler Fiorenza notes that the diversity of these communities and their members is essential if the Bible is truly to become Scripture again for the community of faith.

Although Schüssler Fiorenza addresses her writing in part to the academy, it is to the ekklēsia of wo/men, rather than the academy, that Schüssler Fiorenza chooses to be primarily accountable, and to whom she grants authority. In the interaction of these diverse communities with the biblical texts, diverse meanings are constructed and evaluated according to a triple ethics of historical reading, accountability and solidarity. Those texts and readings which resist patriarchal or kyriarchal structures of domination are deemed revelatory according to her pragmatic, ethical criteria. However, she also insists that revelation is located not in the text itself, but in its interaction with the community in the midst of emancipatory struggles. This concept of revelation relates to her understanding of the Bible as a prototype or formative root model for communities of faith. Such an understanding resists the reduction of the biblical texts to universal principles and honours its diversity and multiple meanings for different communities. It also allows critical evaluation and reconstruction of the biblical texts and the canon, while focusing authority not on the Bible, but on the interpreting community.

In the following chapter we will see both similarities and differences between Schüssler Fiorenza and Fulkerson. They have similar critiques of modernity and liberalism, and both draw upon poststructural theory to varying extents in order to respect the diversity of the biblical texts and faith communities. They also propose pragmatic, liberative criteria that move beyond the apolitical impasse of postmodernism. Their methods differ according to their different purposes. Fulkerson is interested in the women whom Schüssler Fiorenza dismisses. To honour their voices and biblical interpretation, Fulkerson proposes a different approach.

Notes to Chapter 2

1. Elisabeth Schüssler Fiorenza, "Biblical Interpretation and Critical Commitment," *Studia Theologica* 43, no. 1 (1989): 6.

2. Elisabeth Schüssler Fiorenza, *The Inside Stories: Thirteen Valiant Women Challenging the Church*, interviewed by Annie Lally Milhaven (Mystic, Ct.: Twenty-Third Publishers, 1987), 43.

3. Elisabeth Schüssler Fiorenza, "Changing the Paradigms," "How My Mind Has Changed" Series, *The Christian Century* 107, no. 25 (September 5–12 1990): 797.

4. Elisabeth Schüssler Fiorenza, "Biblical Interpretation in the Context of Church and Ministry," *Word & World* 10, no. 4 (Fall 1990): 321.

5. Schüssler Fiorenza, "Changing the Paradigms," 796–800.

6. Elisabeth Schüssler Fiorenza, *Discipleship of Equals: A Critical Feminist Ekklesia-Logy of Liberation* (New York: Crossroad, 1993), 54.

7. Elisabeth Schüssler Fiorenza, "Struggle is a Name for Hope: A Critical Feminist Interpretation for Liberation," *Pacifica* 10 (June 1997): 235.

8. In a recent paper, Schüssler Fiorenza identifies her work as postcolonial. However, because she still utilizes modern historical-critical methods which are resisted or ignored in most postcolonial writing, I am not categorizing her work as postcolonial. See Elisabeth Schüssler Fiorenza, "The Ethos of Interpretation: Biblical Studies in a Postmodern and Postcolonial Context," presented at The Association of Korean Theologians, October 26, 1996, at Usong, Republic of Korea.

9. Elisabeth Schüssler Fiorenza and David Tracy, "The Holocaust as Interruption and the Christian Return Into History," in *The Holocaust as Interruption*, ed. Elisabeth Schüssler Fiorenza and David Tracy, Concilium Series (Edinburgh: T. & T. Clark Ltd., 1984), 83. For an excellent overview of the rise of modernity and the critiques given by critical theory and postmodernism, see Sheila Greeve Davaney, "Problems with Feminist Theory: Historicity and the Search for Sure Foundations," in *Embodied Love: Sensuality and Relationship as Feminist Values*, ed. Paula M. Cooey, Sharon A. Farmer and Mary Ellen Ross (San Francisco: Harper & Row, 1987), 79–84.

10. Elisabeth Schüssler Fiorenza, *But She Said: Feminist Practices of Biblical Interpretation* (Boston: Beacon Press, 1992), 132.

11. Elisabeth Schüssler Fiorenza, "Text and Reality—Reality as Text: The Problem of a Feminist Historical and Social Reconstruction Based on Texts," *Studia Theologica* 43 (1989): 26.

12. Schüssler Fiorenza adopts the postmodern definition of ideology, described by Teresa L. Ebert, as "the organization of material signifying practices that constitute subjectivities and produce the lived relations by which subjects are connected to the dominant relations of power in a dominant social formation." See Schüssler Fiorenza, *But She Said*, 243–44, ftnt. 2. Elsewhere she defines ideology as "distorted communication rather than false consciousness." See Elisabeth Schüssler Fiorenza, "Ecclesia Semper Reformanda: Theology as Ideology Critique," *Concilium* 1 (1999): 75.

13. Elisabeth Schüssler Fiorenza, *Jesus: Miriam's Child, Sophia's Prophet: Critical Issues in Feminist Christology* (New York: Continuum, 1994), 83.

14. Schüssler Fiorenza, *But She Said*, 37–39.

15. Schüssler Fiorenza, *Jesus*, 29–30.

16. Schüssler Fiorenza, "Text and Reality," 21.

17. Elisabeth Schüssler Fiorenza, *Bread not Stone: The Challenge of Feminist Biblical Interpretation* (Boston: Beacon Press, 1984), 11. Schüssler Fiorenza faults feminist theologians, such as Rosemary Radford Ruether and Letty Russell, for using this same universal logic in their elevation of biblical principles or normative biblical traditions. See *Bread Not Stone*, 12–15.

18. Elisabeth Schüssler Fiorenza, "The Politics of Otherness: Biblical Interpretation as a Critical Praxis for Liberation," in *The Future of Liberation Theology: Essays in Honor of Gustavo Gutiérrez*, ed. Marc Ellis and Otto Maduro (New York: Orbis Books, 1989), 322.

19. Schüssler Fiorenza translates this from the famous expression of Leopold von Ranke: *wie es eigentlich gewesen*. See Schüssler Fiorenza, *Bread Not Stone*, 168, ftnt. 9.

20. Schüssler Fiorenza, *Bread Not Stone*, 102.

21. Schüssler Fiorenza, *But She Said*, 82–83.

22. Elisabeth Schüssler Fiorenza, "The Bible, the Global Context, and the Discipleship of Equals," in *Reconstructing Christian Theology*, ed. Rebecca S. Chopp and Mark Lewis Taylor (Minneapolis: Fortress Press, 1994), 84.

23. Schüssler Fiorenza, *Discipleship of Equals*, 284.

24. Schüssler Fiorenza, *Bread Not Stone*, 25.

25. Schüssler Fiorenza, *Discipleship of Equals*, 285.

26. Schüssler Fiorenza, "The Bible, the Global Context," 83.

27. Schüssler Fiorenza, "Text and Reality," 20–22.

28. Schüssler Fiorenza, "Jesus and the Politics of Interpretation," *Harvard Theological Review* 90, no. 4 (October, 1997): 345, 351.

29. As an example, Schüssler Fiorenza notes the recent proliferation of books on the historical Jesus. See Schüssler Fiorenza, *Jesus*, 9.

30. Schüssler Fiorenza, *But She Said*, 190–91.

31. Schüssler Fiorenza, *Jesus*, 73.

32. Schüssler Fiorenza, *Jesus*, 16–17.

33. Schüssler Fiorenza, *Discipleship of Equals*, 213–14.

34. Schüssler Fiorenza, *Discipleship of Equals*, 341.

35. Schüssler Fiorenza, "G*d at Work in Our Midst: From a Politics of Identity to a Politics of Struggle." *Feminist Theology* 13 (S 1996): 63.

36. Schüssler Fiorenza, *Discipleship of Equals*, 363; Schüssler Fiorenza, *Jesus*, 14.

37. Schüssler Fiorenza, *Discipleship of Equals*, 360.

38. The term "logic of identity" was coined by Theodore Adorno, a member of the Frankfurt School, but she does not credit him accordingly.

39. Schüssler Fiorenza, *But She Said*, 139–40, 145, 147.

40. Schüssler Fiorenza, "Politics of Otherness," 311.

41. Schüssler Fiorenza, *But She Said*, 135–36.

42. Schüssler Fiorenza, *Discipleship of Equals*, 284.

43. Schüssler Fiorenza, "Biblical Interpretation and Critical Commitment," 8.

44. Schüssler Fiorenza, Introduction to *Bread Not Stone*, xvi.

45. Schüssler Fiorenza, *But She Said*, 47.

46. Elisabeth Schüssler Fiorenza, "Introduction: Transforming the Legacy of *The Woman's Bible*," in *Searching the Scriptures: Volume I: A Feminist Introduction*, ed. Elisabeth Schüssler Fiorenza (New York: Crossroad, 1993), 16–18.

47. Elisabeth Schüssler Fiorenza, *Sharing Her Word: Feminist Biblical Interpretation in Context* (Boston: Beacon Press, 1998), 39; Elisabeth Schüssler Fiorenza, "Introduction: Feminist Liberation Theology as Critical Sophialogy," *The Power of Naming*, A Concilium Reader in Feminist Liberation Theology (Maryknoll: Orbis Books, 1996), xvii–xx.

48. Schüssler Fiorenza, *Bread Not Stone*, 45.

49. Schüssler Fiorenza, *Discipleship of Equals*, 278.

50. Schüssler Fiorenza, *Bread Not Stone*, xxi-xxii.

51. Elisabeth Schüssler Fiorenza, *In Memory of Her: A Feminist Theological Reconstruction of Christian Origins* (New York: Crossroad, 1983), xxii.

52. Schüssler Fiorenza, *Bread Not Stone*, 14.

53. Schüssler Fiorenza, *Discipleship of Equals*, 254–55.

54. Schüssler Fiorenza, *Bread Not Stone*, xiv.

55. Schüssler Fiorenza, *Discipleship of Equals*, 196.

56. Schüssler Fiorenza, *Discipleship of Equals*, 327, ftnt. 16.

57. Schüssler Fiorenza, *Bread Not Stone*, 344, 349–50.

58. Schüssler Fiorenza, *Discipleship of Equals*, 229–30. Schüssler Fiorenza defines *basileia* as the commonweal or, to borrow Ada María Isasi-Díaz's phrase, the kinship of God. See Elisabeth Schüssler Fiorenza, "To Follow the Vision: The Jesus Movement as *Basileia* Movement," *Liberating Eschatology: Essays in Honor of Letty M. Russell*, ed. by Margaret A. Farley and Serene Jones (Louisville: Westminster John Knox Press, 1999), 134.

59. Schüssler Fiorenza, *In Memory of Her*, 141, 343–46.

60. Schüssler Fiorenza, *In Memory of Her*, 347.

61. Schüssler Fiorenza, *Bread Not Stone*, xiv. For a conference of Roman Catholic, American women in 1983, Diann Neu translated *ekklēsia gynaikōn* as women-church, which Schüssler Fiorenza then used in *Bread Not Stone*, published the following year. See Schüssler Fiorenza, *But She Said*, 127. Schüssler Fiorenza has always avoided the singular and essentialist term "woman-church." See Schüssler Fiorenza, *Discipleship of Equals*, 212.

62. In a 1990 address and in an article published in 1994 she omits the qualifier "of women" altogether, speaking only of ekklēsia. See Schüssler Fiorenza, *Discipleship of Equals*, 290–306; Schüssler Fiorenza, "The Bible, the Global Context," 79–98. These seem to be the only instances of this, however, as other articles and books written during the same period use the phrase ekklēsia of women. See Schüssler Fiorenza, *Discipleship of Equals*, 332–52, 353–72; Schüssler Fiorenza, *Jesus*.

63. Schüssler Fiorenza, *Discipleship of Equals*, 293.

64. Schüssler Fiorenza, *Discipleship of Equals*, 328–29.

65. Schüssler Fiorenza, "Transforming the Legacy of *The Woman's Bible*," 20–22.

66. Elisabeth Schüssler Fiorenza, *Rhetoric and Ethic: The Politics of Biblical Studies* (Minneapolis: Fortress Press, 1999); *Jesus*; *Sharing Her Word*.

67. Schüssler Fiorenza, *Jesus*, 191, ftnt. 1.

68. Elisabeth Schüssler Fiorenza, "Celebrating the Struggles, Realizing the Visions," Keynote address at "Soul to Soul: Women, Religion & the 21st Century," Graduate Theological Union, Berkeley, Feb. 26–March 1, 1998, *Journal of Women and Religion* 16 (1998): 19.

69. Donna J. Haraway, "A Manifesto for Cyborgs: Science, Technology, and Socialist Feminism in the 1980s," *Feminism/Postmodernism,* Thinking Gender Series (New York: Routledge, 1990). See an insightful critique of Haraway by Marsha A. Hewitt, "Cyborgs,

Drag Queens, and Goddesses: Emancipatory-Regressive Paths in Feminist Theory," *Method & Theory in the Study of Religion* 5, no. 2 (1993): 135–54.

70. Susan Woods, "Review of *Discipleship of Equals*," *Modern Theology*, 11 (April 1995): 281–82.

71. Schüssler Fiorenza, *In Memory of Her*, 3.

72. Elisabeth Schüssler Fiorenza, "Response to 'from Study to Proclamation' by Walter J. Burghardt," in *A New Look at Preaching*, vol. 7, ed. John Burke, Good News Studies (Wilmington, Delaware: Michael Glazier Inc., 1983), 44–45.

73. Elisabeth Schüssler Fiorenza, "Emerging Issues in Feminist Biblical Interpretation," in *Christian Feminism: Visions of a New Humanity*, ed. Judith Weidman (San Francisco: Harper & Row, 1984), 51.

74. Schüssler Fiorenza, "Transforming the Legacy of *The Woman's Bible*," 15.

75. Schüssler Fiorenza, *Bread Not Stone*, 5, 7.

76. Schüssler Fiorenza, *But She Said*, 115.

77. Schüssler Fiorenza, *Discipleship of Equals*, 344–45.

78. Schüssler Fiorenza, "Transforming the Legacy of *The Woman's Bible*," 20–21.

79. Schüssler Fiorenza, *Discipleship of Equals*, 345–47.

80. Schüssler Fiorenza, *But She Said*, 127.

81. For a critique of women-church as a "gynocentric reversal of androcentric ecclesiology" see Rosemary Radford Ruether, "Review of *Bread Not Stone*" *Journal of the American Academy of Religion* 54, no 1 (Spring, 1986): 143. For further elaboration upon Schüssler Fiorenza's ontological grounding, see Sheila Greeve Davaney, "Problems with Feminist Theory," 88. For a response to Davaney and defence of Schüssler Fiorenza's method, see Carol P. Christ "Embodied Thinking: Reflections on Feminist Theological Method," *Journal of Feminist Studies in Religion* 5, no. 1 (Spring, 1989).

82. Schüssler Fiorenza, "G*d at Work in Our Midst," 71.

83. Schüssler Fiorenza, "Transforming the Legacy of *The Woman's Bible*," 19.

84. Schüssler Fiorenza, "Celebrating the Struggles, Realizing the Visions," 23.

85. In her most recent writing Schüssler Fiorenza uses the construct "G*d" to indicate the inadequacy of our language about G*d. She had used G-d in *Discipleship of Equals* and *But She Said*, until Jewish feminists complained that the spelling "G-d" suggested to them a conservative and reactionary theological frame of reference. See Schüssler Fiorenza, *Jesus*, 191 ftnt. 3; Schüssler Fiorenza, "Feminist Liberation Theology as Critical Sophialogy."

86. Schüssler Fiorenza, *Discipleship of Equals*, 331, 347–52.

87. Schüssler Fiorenza, *Bread Not Stone*, 30–33.

88. Schüssler Fiorenza, *Bread Not Stone*, 143.

89. Schüssler Fiorenza, *Jesus*, 28; Schüssler Fiorenza, "Feminist Liberation Theology as Critical Sophialogy," xxx, xxxiv.

90. Schüssler Fiorenza, *Bread Not Stone*, xvi.

91. Schüssler Fiorenza, *But She Said*, 96.

92. Schüssler Fiorenza, *In Memory of Her*, 32.

93. Schüssler Fiorenza, *Discipleship of Equals*, 174–79.

94. See Schüssler Fiorenza, *In Memory of Her*, 286–87.

95. Schüssler Fiorenza, *Bread Not Stone*, 49. David Tracy suggests that an approach must be adequate to common human experience and appropriate to Christian tradition, especially the Christian texts. See David Tracy, *Blessed Rage for Order: The New Pluralism*

in Theology (Minneapolis: The Winston/Seabury Press, 1975), 70–73.

96. Schüssler Fiorenza, *Bread Not Stone*, 104; Elisabeth Schüssler Fiorenza, "Rhetorical Situation and Historical Reconstruction in I Corinthians," *New Testament Studies* 33, no. 3 (1987): 393.

97. Schüssler Fiorenza, *Bread Not Stone*, 58–67.

98. Elisabeth Schüssler Fiorenza, "The Ethics of Biblical Interpretation: Decentering Biblical Scholarship," *Journal of Biblical Literature* 107, no. 1 (March 1988): 14–15.

99. Schüssler Fiorenza, "Ethics," 14–15.

100. Schüssler Fiorenza, *Discipleship of Equals*, 349.

101. Schüssler Fiorenza, *Discipleship of Equals*, 348–52.

102. Schüssler Fiorenza, *But She Said*, 134–35.

103. Schüssler Fiorenza, *But She Said*, 132.

104. Schüssler Fiorenza, *Bread Not Stone*, 50.

105. Schüssler Fiorenza, *Sharing Her Word*, 29–33.

106. Schüssler Fiorenza, *Bread Not Stone*, x.

107. Schüssler Fiorenza, *In Memory of Her*, xv.

108. Schüssler Fiorenza, *In Memory of Her*, 30.

109. Schüssler Fiorenza, *Bread Not Stone*, xiii.

110. Schüssler Fiorenza, *Rhetoric and Ethic*, 38.

111. Schüssler Fiorenza, *Bread Not Stone*, 58–61.

112. Schüssler Fiorenza, *Jesus*, 75.

113. Kwok Pui-lan, *Introducing Asian Feminist Theology,* Introductions in Feminist Theology Series (Cleveland: The Pilgrim Press, 2000), 85.

114. Schüssler Fiorenza, *Bread Not Stone*, 39–40, 48–49.

115. Schüssler Fiorenza, "Response to Burghardt," 51–52.

116. Schüssler Fiorenza, *Jesus*, 89.

117. Schüssler Fiorenza, *In Memory of Her*, 34.

118. Schüssler Fiorenza, "Response to Burghardt," 51–52; Schüssler Fiorenza, *Bread Not Stone*, 40.

119. Paul Tillich, *Systematic Theology: Reason and Revelation; Being and God*, Vol. I (London: SCM Press Ltd., 1951), 34–36, 122–26, 157–59; Emil Brunner, *The Christian Doctrine of God*, Vol. I, trans. Olive Wyon (Philadelphia: Westminster Press, 1949), 22–34.

120. Schüssler Fiorenza, *Bread Not Stone*, xvi–xvii.

121. Schüssler Fiorenza, "Transforming the Legacy of *The Woman's Bible*," 8. Kwok cautions against the use of the Bible as a prototype when little mention is made in the biblical texts of non-Jewish, poor slave women. See Kwok Pui-lan, *Discovering the Bible in the Non-Biblical World*, The Bible and Liberation Series (Maryknoll: Orbis Books, 1995), 40–41.

122. Schüssler Fiorenza, *In Memory of Her*, 33.

123. Schüssler Fiorenza, *Bread Not Stone*, 10.

124. Schüssler Fiorenza, *Bread Not Stone*, 35.

125. Schüssler Fiorenza, *But She Said*, 152–54.

126. Schüssler Fiorenza does acknowledge this point in one of her latest writings, *Sharing Her Word*, 83–84.

127. Schüssler Fiorenza, *But She Said*, 138–39.

128. Schüssler Fiorenza, *But She Said*, 150.

129. Schüssler Fiorenza, *Bread Not Stone*, xv.

130. Schüssler Fiorenza, *But She Said*, 137–38.

131. Schüssler Fiorenza, *In Memory of Her*, 53–56.

132. Schüssler Fiorenza, "Transforming the Legacy of *The Woman's Bible*," 9.

133. Schüssler Fiorenza, *In Memory of Her*, 53–56.

134. Schüssler Fiorenza, *Bread Not Stone*, 36.

135. Schüssler Fiorenza, *But She Said*, 138–43.

136. Schüssler Fiorenza, *Bread Not Stone*, 92.

137. Schüssler Fiorenza, "Transforming the Legacy of *The Woman's Bible*," 9.

138. Her preference for the word "scripture" over "Bible" in the title of a book indicates her dismissal of the "Protestant notion of a revealed text or a canon of books that serve as the primary locus of authoritative teaching." See Schüssler Fiorenza, "Transforming the Legacy of *The Woman's Bible*," 8–9.

139. Schüssler Fiorenza, "Introduction: Transgressing Canonical Boundaries," 11.

140. Schüssler Fiorenza, "Struggle is a Name for Hope," 237.

141. Schüssler Fiorenza, "Changing the Paradigms," 796–800.

142. Randy L. Maddox suggests that Schüssler Fiorenza's earlier work still reflects some modern disdain for rhetorical strategies. It is not until *But She Said* that the rhetorical method becomes central to Schüssler Fiorenza's work. See Randy Maddox, "Review of *But She Said*," *Christian Scholar's Review* 24, no. 3 (March 1995): 323–25.

143. Schüssler Fiorenza, *Jesus*, 94–96, 107–09, 161–62.

144. Schüssler Fiorenza, *In Memory of Her*, 92.

145. Schüssler Fiorenza, *Bread Not Stone*, 87.

146. Schüssler Fiorenza, *But She Said*, 214–15.

147. Schüssler Fiorenza, *In Memory of Her*, 108–09.

148. Schüssler Fiorenza, *But She Said*, 54.

149. Schüssler Fiorenza, *Bread Not Stone*, 19–20.

150. Schüssler Fiorenza, *Bread Not Stone*, 171, ftnt. 39.

151. Schüssler Fiorenza, *But She Said*, 54; Elisabeth Schüssler Fiorenza, "The 'Quilting' of Women's History: Phoebe of Cenchreae" in *Embodied Love: Sensuality and Relationship as Feminist Values*, ed. Paula M. Cooey, Sharon A. Farmer, and Mary Ellen Ross (San Francisco: Harper & Row, 1987).

152. Rosemary Radford Ruether, "Review of *Bread Not Stone*," 142; Frank Witt Hughes, "Feminism and Early Christian History," *Anglican Theological Review* 69, no. 3 (July 1987): 287–99; Ross S. Kraemer, "Review of *In Memory of Her*," *Religious Studies Review* 11, no. 1 (January 1985): 6–9; Ross S. Kraemer, "Review of *In Memory of Her*," *Journal of Biblical Literature* 104, no. 4 (December 1985): 722–25; M. H. Micks, "Review of *In Memory of Her*," *Christianity and Crisis* 43 (October 17, 1983): 388–89; Leopold Sabourin, "Review of *In Memory of Her*," *Religious Studies* 4, no. 2 (May 1984): 102–04; Beverly R. Gaventa, "Review of *In Memory of Her*," *Lexington Theological Quarterly* 20 (April 1985): 58–60; Janice Capel Anderson, "Review of *In Memory of Her*," *Critical Review of Books in Religion* (1991); Leonard L. Thompson, "Review of *Revelation: Vision of a Just World*," *Catholic Biblical Quarterly* 55 (July 1993): 576–78; Esther D. Reed, "Review of *Jesus: Miriam's Child, Sophia's Prophet*," *Expository Times* 106 (September 1995): 380–81.

153. Schüssler Fiorenza, *Bread Not Stone*, 18–19.

154. Schüssler Fiorenza, *But She Said*, 54.

155. Schüssler Fiorenza, *Bread Not Stone*, 20–22; Schüssler Fiorenza, *But She Said*, 54–55.

156. Schüssler Fiorenza, *But She Said*, 52–53.

157. Schüssler Fiorenza, *Sharing Her Word*, 77, 201.

158. Schüssler Fiorenza, "Struggle is a Name for Hope," 238–40.

159. Schüssler Fiorenza, *Sharing Her Word*, 76–77.

160. Schüssler Fiorenza, *Sharing Her Word*, 112–36.

161. Schüssler Fiorenza, *But She Said*, 46.

162. Schüssler Fiorenza, "Biblical Interpretation," 11. The increasing use of critical theory, reader response criticism, and poststructural analysis, all of which have similar socio-political concerns, underlies the contemporary revival of ancient rhetoric.

163. Schüssler Fiorenza, "Biblical Interpretation," 11.

164. Her analysis of I Corinthians is an example of this rhetorical analysis. See Schüssler Fiorenza, "Rhetorical Situation and Historical Reconstruction in I Corinthians," 386–403.

165. Schüssler Fiorenza, "Text and Reality," 26.

166. Schüssler Fiorenza, "Text and Reality," 19–34; Schüssler Fiorenza, "Politics of Otherness."

167. Schüssler Fiorenza accuses Rosemary Radford Ruether of submitting to a logic of identity with her prophetic biblical principle. Schüssler Fiorenza reasons that this principle universalizes particular biblical experiences, and collapses the diversity of biblical texts under one biblical principle. However, Schüssler Fiorenza derives her own principle of liberation from the biblical experiences of the discipleship of equals in the Jesus movement. In this sense, both Schüssler Fiorenza and Ruether submit biblical texts to the judgement of biblically derived norms of justice. For a debate on this point between Schüssler Fiorenza and Ruether, see "Review Symposium," *Horizons*, 11, 1 (Spring 1984): 146–150, 154–157.

168. As examples, see Susan Brooks Thistlethwaite, "In Memory of Her: A Symposium on an Important Book," *Anima* 10, no. 2 (Spring 1984): 102–05; Kristine A. Culp, "Review of *But She Said*," *Theology Today* 50 (January 1994): 619–20+; Marie Anne Mayeski, "Review of *Jesus: Miriam's Child, Sophia's Prophet*," *Theological Studies* 57 (March 1996): 167–69.

Chapter 3

Poststructural Response:
Mary McClintock Fulkerson

"Those whose experience differs from the model of 'women's experience' are not accounted for, or constitute a lobotomized casualty of patriarchy."
—Mary McClintock Fulkerson, *Changing the Subject*

Mary McClintock Fulkerson is keenly aware of various groups of women whom feminist theologies either ignore or consider lobotomized. She mentions that her mother, a white, affluent housewife in a mainline churchwoman's organization, belongs to one of these ignored groups.[1] Fulkerson is troubled by the discounting of particular women's experiences that do not match feminist descriptions of "women's experiences." For this reason, she has intentionally studied some of these groups, such as Presbyterian housewives, Appalachian Pentecostal women, and women of Jehovah's Witness.

In these studies, Fulkerson maintains a feminist, liberationist commitment to the analysis of and resistance to gender oppression. She tries not to impose feminist understandings of resistance that are foreign to these groups, however, but to honour their own particular understandings of resistance to gender oppression. Rather than appealing to experience as the basis of feminist theology, which tends to exclude the experiences of non-feminist women's groups, she tries to explain experience.

Fulkerson acknowledges that her personal experiences of privilege as white, upper-middle class and heterosexual have limited her awareness of oppression on the basis of race, class or sexual preference. Within her Presbyterian Church, woman-church and academic communities, Fulkerson is primarily aware of the construction of dependency based upon gender.[2] Therefore, her attention in *Changing the Subject* is focused upon issues of gender, although she does give considerable attention to class analysis.

Elsewhere she has examined the issue of sexuality, including homosexuality, within Protestant churches.[3]

Fulkerson has found that poststructural analysis best helps her attend not only to the differences amongst women, but also to the production of these differences. She disputes any notion of raw, innate experiences by drawing upon poststructural explanations of their social location and construction. At the same time, Fulkerson resists poststructural tendencies of endless signifying, nihilist relativism, the potential erasure of women as the subject, and the rejection of the metaphysical.[4] She conducts her analyses from a theological perspective because of the faith commitments of herself and of the diverse women to whom she is attending.[5]

Although Fulkerson has some of the same concerns with poststructuralism as has Schüssler Fiorenza, Fulkerson has even greater concerns with modernity and liberalism. Much of her writing addresses modern and liberal problems, some of which she believes Schüssler Fiorenza does not escape. In this chapter I will be exploring the specific concerns she has with modernity and liberalism, followed by an outline of her own alternative theological approach.

Critique of Modernity and Liberalism

Fulkerson believes that feminist theologies suffer from the same modern and liberal problems that they find within "malestream" theology.[6] In her critique of modernity and liberalism, she shows how modern theologies, including feminist, contribute to the obliteration of the other. As elaborated below, she suggests that this happens primarily through representational fallacy, universalism, historical appeals, identity politics, and individualism.

Representational Fallacy

Along with Schüssler Fiorenza, Fulkerson resists the concept of a text's "real" meaning that can be unearthed through objective analysis. Both believe that an adequate, historical, contextual Christian interpretation can be ascertained, but that this does not constitute the real or original meaning of the text. An interpretation is considered adequate by locating its production within an historical community. As a community reads the text, it will read it differently than another community, and thus produce a different meaning of the text itself. Both Fulkerson and Schüssler Fiorenza agree that there is no objective text with its own meaning that stands apart from readers.[7] The Bible can only be known as it has been read by different people associated with different communities.

Drawing upon poststructural theory, Fulkerson also explains that there is no singular text. As the Bible is read by different communities, it becomes a different text. The multiple languages and translations of the Bible alone produce multiple biblical texts. And yet even the same version of the Bible, read differently by different communities, will become a different text for each community. Someone studying the Bible as a literary classic will read a different text than someone studying it as scripture within a faith community. Therefore, the social location of the readers will determine not only the meaning but the type of the biblical text brought into being. For this reason, Fulkerson notes that the Bible is not a singular text, but a multiplicity of diverse texts produced through diverse social locations.

Fulkerson notes that when the meaning of the biblical text is constructed within multiple communal readings, the text itself becomes destabilized, evoking an "infinitely open number of readings."[8] When the biblical text is understood as a destabilized text, it is no longer possible to categorize the whole of scripture or even particular passages as either oppressive or liberative. Rather, the same passage may take on an oppressive meaning in one community and a liberative one in another.

Fulkerson agrees with Schüssler Fiorenza's emphasis upon the constructive nature of biblical interpretation, and the danger of historical and biblical positivism. Both resist the modern assumption that, with the correct tools, it is possible to represent the historical reality and correct meaning of the biblical text. Fulkerson is not convinced, however, that Schüssler Fiorenza has completely abandoned representational thinking.[9] Once Schüssler Fiorenza attempts to distinguish her historical reconstructions from fiction she falls into a representational fallacy. Such a fallacy assumes one can find and represent a reality outside of our own.

Ferdinand de Saussure's work, as developed by poststructuralists, explains the representational fallacy. Fulkerson refers to his argument that "language constructs meaning out of relational differences rather than reference to extra-linguistic reality."[10] We can only speak about that which we experience. Language is a correspondence between words and things and cannot, therefore, reflect a reality that is external to our experience.

Fulkerson also refers to Charles Pierce's semiotics which, along with Saussure's work, produced sign theories. Semiosis, the making of meaning, studies the process of signification. A *sign* is a combination of *signifier*, a sound or image, with *signified*, a meaning or concept. A sign's value can only be determined in its pattern or system of use.[11] Instead of looking for meaning in the referents of language, sign theories suggest that meaning is found within language itself, in the relation of signs to each other.[12] Signs do not reflect the real world, but create it. Therefore, there is no real meaning of a text outside of discourse. Language about God is only meaningful when it refers not to an external divine reality, but to other theological terms within the discourse.[13] This does not mean that God does not exist outside of our own reality, but that language about God must relate to other words in order to have any meaning.

In order not to reduce everything to language, Fulkerson follows critics of Saussure to suggest that discourse, not simply language, produces meaning. Discourse encompasses practices, contexts, material reality, bodies, and social relations as well as language.[14] Fulkerson suggests that the very process of research is a discursive construction of reality. It is therefore impossible to step outside of our social location and discover a historical reality that can be distinguished from fiction. Attempts to uncover a pre-discursive reality inevitably reproduce the interpreter's own reflections as a false universal.[15] Representational thinking therefore leads to the positing of false universals.

Universalism

Fulkerson argues that theologians who employ ideological critique and are suspicious of neutral, impartial claims may still produce false universals. As an example, she cites the work of David Tracy, Edward Farley and Schubert Ogden, whom she calls critical modernists. They attempt to justify their work in relation to other disciplines by appealing to the abstract notions of "structures of intelligibility" and "ecclesial universals."[16] They suggest universally valid criteria to legitimate truth claims. This necessitates "universal conditions of access," which of course do not exist across the world or across the different classes within each society.[17] They also neglect the usefulness of these criteria for faith communities.[18] Even though Tracy, Farley and Ogden are aware of their own theories' fallibility, they seem unaware of the discursive formation of these theories and of themselves.

One aspect of this discursive formation entails the role of all academic theologians in the professional managerial class, and their contribution to the professionalization of knowledge. This creates a universal standard and control of knowledge. Instead of a "dialogical heterogeneity of discourses," unity is urged through a retention of modernity's "culture of certainty."[19] In other words, the experts know best, and adjudicate the work of those with less formal academic education. Theologians of all stripes, including feminist, contribute to this universal standardization and professionalization of knowledge.

Fulkerson is particularly critical of feminist theologies which employ universalizing strategies. A critique of gender domination/submission that is unmodified through history and inattentive to the particularity of discourse assumes pre-discursive agency and events.[20] This results in an external critique that stands outside of a particular community and assumes that it is capable of understanding and evaluating this community (giving this critique pre-discursive agency). This type of feminist critique usually appeals to women's experience, positing experience as a pre-discursive authority which "implicitly grants that experience the status of a universal shared consciousness."[21] However, this experience is inevitably that of the evaluator's, and does not necessarily relate to the experiences of women within other communities. By appealing to a generalized experience instead of a particular discourse, a false universal is established. Such an appeal is also oblivious to the embeddedness of this experience in dominant forms of power relations.[22]

The difficulty with appeals to women's experience is most evident when considering women who support traditional gender roles and, in some cases, oppose feminist principles. Women who do not have the same experience of gender domination are considered by many feminists to be lobotomized by patriarchal distortion, unable to recognize their own oppression. Fulkerson notes that this view strips such women of all agency, rendering them utterly passive.[23] In short, it universalizes particular experiences of feminists, thereby failing to account for "the other."

Fulkerson recognizes that a refusal to look beyond the particular towards global implications will result in a depoliticized, myopic vision. For this reason she does not dispense entirely with universality. In order to develop a feminist liberation theology that is based upon particular discourse, Fulkerson suggests that the global and historical accumulation of sexist discourses points towards the pervasiveness of sexism and its possible, even likely, universal reoccurrence. This "new universal" of sexism, a "genderization of fallibility," arises out of historical particularities as a field of risk, a likely possibility, rather than a generalized claim inattentive to diversity.[24] On the basis of historical patterns of sexist actions across the world, there is a high probability that social structures perpetuate sexism globally. This could be called a relativized universal, supported by historical particularities, but open to correction. In this sense Fulkerson appeals to the construction of discourse throughout history.

Historical Appeals

Although Fulkerson is skeptical of attempts to discover historical reality, she still insists on historically embedded discourse.[25] Christian faith, by its very nature, must be interested in the past. However, as we explore it, reconceive it, critique it, celebrate it, and are accountable to it, we must acknowledge our impact on this historical reconstruction.[26] Fulkerson draws upon reader-response theories to demonstrate this unavoidable impact. She supports Schüssler Fiorenza's rhetorical method of historical reconstruction, and her refutation of historical positivism. However, Fulkerson suggests that by referring factually to these reconstructions, such as the egalitarian Jesus movement, Schüssler Fiorenza continues to represent pre-discursive historical reality extracted from false consciousness.[27] While Schüssler Fiorenza wants to avoid historical and textual positivism, she still appeals to readings which best fit or do justice to historical settings. Fulkerson suggests that this constitutes an appeal to a pre-discursive historical reality which contradicts Schüssler Fiorenza's insistence that all interpretation is rhetorical construction.[28] However, I am not convinced that Schüssler Fiorenza, particularly in her later work, is appealing to a pre-discursive historical reality. Her ethics of historical reading limits the number of interpretations according to historical documents which have been constructed rhetorically within historic communities.

Fulkerson is concerned when appeals to the author's intention, the community of origin, or particular stages in a history's tradition, are extracted from their historical discourse to represent incorrigible data. These appeals represent natural, unshaped facts that are removed from their formative relations of power and situational knowledge. The subject position of the historian is also ignored. Fulkerson explains that when descriptions of Jesus or early Christian communities are gleaned from the text, the interests of the interpreter in the selection of these descriptors is ignored. It is assumed that anyone with the same historical-critical tools could find the same descriptions. This, of course, poses a problem for those to whom historical-critical tools are not available.[29] Would their readings and historical interpretations be any less adequate? Reliance upon historical-critical methods would dismiss these potentially liberative readings from marginalized people.[30]

These historical appeals, according to Fulkerson, contribute to the modern "sins" as elaborated by Stephen Moore, a poststructural biblical critic. He suggests that modernity brings a premature closure to the text in its search for 1) a transcendentalized textual content of ideas that can be extracted from the text and exist independently; 2) an original situation with self-contained meanings apart from its context; 3) an authorial intention that will yield the secret of the text.[31] Fulkerson suggests that all historical-critical inquiry must be understood as rhetorical construction, as refined in Schüssler Fiorenza's later work, if it is to avoid these sins of modernity.

Identity Politics and Individualism

Such modern assumptions are implicated in textual, as well as historical, appeals. If a theme or principle is identified in scripture and becomes the unifying norm for the entire Bible, it has been separated from its contextual discourse. It constitutes Moore's first sin of transcendentalized textual content where ideas are removed from their *Sitz im Leben*.[32] The theme or principle also subsumes the diversity of the biblical texts into the identity of the unifying norm. Fulkerson is in agreement with Schüssler Fiorenza on this point.

The politics of identity refers to subjects as well as texts. Fulkerson refers to the concept of the Cartesian subject which has figured prominently in modern thought. This concept connects with Moore's first sin by presuming the possibility of a neutral, autonomous and therefore transcendentalized subject.[33] Based on this presumption, one can assume that the description of a subject, such as "woman," will remain a constant regardless of context. This would preclude multiple identities of "woman" formed from different social locations and systems of meaning. It would also assume that our knowledge of ourselves reflects our true or real selves, apart from the influences of our social location.[34]

It is this universalizing Cartesian subject which Fulkerson suggests poststructuralists seek to "kill." Contrary to many critiques, Michel Foucault's understanding of "death of the subject" does not indicate the disappearance of the subject, but rather the instability of its multiple identities.[35] Similarly, Fulkerson attempts to destabilize the singular subject of "woman" in order to honour women's multiple identities and social locations. This, in turn, honours the concerns of women of colour and Third World women who protest the monolithic identification of "women" with a universal state of victimization.[36] Such destabilization of the term "women" resonates with Schüssler Fiorenza's construction of the term "wo/men." However, Fulkerson still believes that attempts of Schüssler Fiorenza to recognize the multiplicative interstructuring relations of race, class, colonialism, and sexual orientation on gender fail to destabilise the unifying subject of woman. Fulkerson suggests that these attempts still hold onto a pre-discursive notion of women that is then impacted by other sociopolitical systems of domination.[37] I am not convinced of this in Schüssler Fiorenza's later work, where I think she has sufficiently destabilized the term wo/men to respect the multiple identities of women.

In Fulkerson's investigation of American Protestant church documents dealing with sexuality, she questions the assumptions made by both sides of the debate about the stability of identity. She refers to Foucault's explanation that personal identity determined by sexuality or sexual orientation is a modern creation of science and therapy.[38] With reference to feminist theories which have long argued that masculinity and femininity are social constructions, she turns to Judith Butler's postmodern argument that "woman" is also an unstable construction. If our sex and corresponding gender are considered the core of our identity, then we are defined according to our oppositional gender differences. When our sexual orientation or desire is added to this formative core, our identity is defined out of oppositional heterosexual desires. By problematizing "woman" with multiple identities, Butler attempts to break out of this fixed, binary gender system which produces compulsory heterosexuality.

Fulkerson uses Butler's argument to resist the absolutized, sexed identity that enforces heterosexuality. She shows that both the liberal inclusion and conservative exclusion of lesbian and gay people are based upon this fixed, oppositional understanding of sexual identity. An oppositional binary gender system will inevitably create heterosexual norms against which lesbian and gay people will be measured. She calls for a new, literal interpretation of Galatians 3:28 in which sexual identity is immaterial to the requirements of membership within the Christian community. She also gives a curious appeal to history by stating that identity defined by sexuality is inconsistent with the original, biblical world views.[39]

Intimately connected with the politics of identity is essentialism. Fulkerson notes that if our core identity is defined by our sexuality, our essential self must be gendered. There must be a sexed essence that could be identified as masculine or feminine, heterosexual or homosexual.[40] Fulkerson resists this assumption that women, or lesbian and gay people share a natural essence based on uncoded aspects of their identity. Attaching natural meaning to women's bodies, as with particular racial groups, has had horrendous historical consequences.[41] Fulkerson points out that even essential, anatomical definitions of sexuality are being contested today.[42] She insists, therefore, that sexuality, as well as other aspects of our identity, must be understood as socially constructed.

Fulkerson's intent is not to eliminate the subject of woman or the biblical text, but to destabilize both with the recognition of their multiple identities and discursive formations. She is challenging not the existence of a subject, its "thatness," but the fixed character of its meaning, its "whatness."[43] Destabilizing the subject of woman and the text will honour the diversity of women's readings of scripture as well as women themselves.

Fulkerson wants to resist a feminist tendency to essentialize scripture as oppressive or liberative. She states that biblical texts are not containers of fixed meaning that can be labelled oppressive or liberative. Rather, their meanings are dependent upon the way in which communities, in their particular social locations, read the scriptures. Non-feminist women may read a passage of scripture that has been declared sexist in a non-sexist way.[44]

By setting the interpretation of biblical texts within a discursive context, Fulkerson problematizes the notion of private, individual interpretations. Individuals are not as autonomous as liberal thought would suggest. Neither are they purely passive victims of oppressive texts. Rather, individuals are discursively constructed, unstable subjects in a dynamic relationship with the multiple functions of an unstable text. Fulkerson explains that the instability of the subject is caused by various subject positions formed by social location and the impact of global infrastructures, such as capitalism.[45] Every person is shaped by many social identities that are sometimes conflicting and shifting.

This perspective challenges the Enlightenment's notion of a pre-discursive subject with free, individualistic agency. Whereas pre-Enlightenment thinking understood people only corporately, in relationship to community without separate individual identities,[46] and liberal thinking understands people individually, free from corporate control, poststructural thinking understands people discursively, in relationship to communities with multiple individual identities.

The liberal concept of pre-discursive autonomy has established experience as "an event of consciousness that precedes language and is a source of knowledge."[47] This concept of pre-discursive experience does not recognize that our experience is shaped by our economic, political and cultural systems.[48] Because of this omission, liberal attempts to empower the marginalized are frustrated. Fulkerson contends that feminist theology can be emancipatory only to the extent that it shifts its emphasis from women's experience to "women's faith practices in discursive totalities," from a politics of identity to a social construction of multiple, shifting identities. Only then will it be able to move from a realist representation of its own "ruminations" to analysis of the embeddedness of discourse in power.[49]

Fulkerson also notes that without a recognition of the social construction of individuals, the liberal solution to the exclusion of particular people is simply to include them. Inclusionary logic is based upon the equality and essential "sameness" of all people.[50] However, this logic erases multiple identities and social locations, and ignores structural systems of domination. It is ineffective and inappropriate to simply add diverse people to discussions, communities, and institutions without analyzing and transforming the structures and systems of power that exclude and silence them in the first place.

Theological Method

Mary McClintock Fulkerson's intended audience for her work is the theological academy.[51] She hopes to challenge feminist appeals to experience, liberal inclusionary politics, and the modern elevation of historical-critical methods.[52] By uncovering the emancipatory work of women who are ignored in these processes, she hopes to more adequately attend to the "concretely social other." This phrase indicates that subjects are produced in particular social locations within a particular social order (i.e. patriarchal and capitalist) and that liberation must be social. The social aspect also suggests to Fulkerson that the purpose of feminist academics is not to liberate the oppressed other, but to "liberate ourselves in relation to the oppressed other."[53]

Fulkerson raises up women who do not share feminist agendas, nor are located within academic circles, as mirrors for those of us who are academic feminists. These mirrors reveal the exclusionary aspects of our own practices, such as the professionalization of theology.[54] Her goal is therefore to liberate feminists in order to create affinities between feminist communities and women in other communities.[55] This goal is "authorized" by a vision of God's realm of justice in which all forms of domination and hierarchy are resisted and transformed.[56]

In order to reach this goal, Fulkerson tries to identify and understand women who resist patriarchal oppression within conservative faith communities, but would not call themselves feminist, or be considered feminist by outsiders. For this reason she intentionally seeks out readings that are at odds with traditional feminist interpretations but are located within sites of resistance to male hegemony. Instead of measuring their resistance against women's experience in general, or against women-church, as many feminists do, Fulkerson measures their resistance against their own faith practices and communal contexts. This allows Fulkerson to recognize particular actions, which may be seen as submissive by the outside world, as quite radical in their resistance to male hegemony within their community. For instance, a decision by women not to preach but to give testimony may not be as submissive to male authority as it may seem—it may actually be a radical and creative strategy that allows women to speak in church while remaining within the bounds of their faith tradition.

This approach avoids the universalizing problem of using "women's experience" to describe power relations. What is assumed to be the experience of all women may not be so for some, and may end up disempowering the "other" women who do not fit into that experience. What is liberating for one group of women may not be liberating for another.[57] When descriptions of other women are based on assumptions formed outside the social context of these other women (pre-discursive descriptions of reality), the danger of misrepresentation is heightened. Fulkerson considers the danger of pre-discursive descriptions of reality so great that she names representations of the "other" as "inevitable acts of violence."[58]

Instead of attempting to represent the other, Fulkerson suggests that a theo/acentric agape calls us to mediate difference. We are called to attend to differential relations, not representations, by recognizing that our accounts of difference are discursive productions, formed out of our varying social locations. We are also called to "speak for" the other through establishing affinities, not shared identities or solidarities. Fulkerson refers to this calling to "speak for" the other as a call to represent the other without attempting philosophical or cultural representation. This positive sense of representation is based upon the teachings of others that are received through political affinities. It gives us "the power to say what the other is in a way that the other does not have."[59]

Fulkerson's negative and positive uses of the term "representation" are confusing at best, and may indicate some conflict between the various theories she employs alongside poststructuralism, as will be seen in the next section.

Authority

Fulkerson's critique of representational language extends into her understanding of authority and political judgements. She is aware of the apolitical tendencies of poststructuralism, but insists that aspects of poststructuralism, such as its critique of naturalized language and its analysis of power, contribute to a political praxis. However, she realizes that she must use additional critical theories, including particular theories about ideology and culture, feminist standpoint theory, materialist and Marxist analysis, in conjunction with poststructuralism in order to sharpen her political edge. Poststructural critiques of representational language allow her to critique naturalized language, which is one function of ideology. By combining theories on ideology with poststructural analysis of power she is able to identify social sin and faithful Christian resistance. Feminist standpoint theories add a further gender specific aspect to resistance. Fulkerson's understanding of authority and limitations to endless signifying is also enhanced by her location of truth and doctrinal agency within particular faith communities. I will now elaborate upon each of these points.

By refusing a representational meaning of language, poststructuralism removes the basis for the naturalized or innate descriptions of reality.[60] Destabilizing both subjects and texts prevents the establishment of dominant discourses which presume to represent natural reality and constitute the norm against which marginalized discourses are measured. A poststructural refusal of representation is thus able to challenge underlying ideologies that are dependent upon naturalized language.[61]

Fulkerson explains how naturalization is one function of ideology. When beliefs are assumed to reflect actual reality, they are naturalized. The assumptions are themselves invisible, leaving only assertions that appear as irrefutable facts. The unnaturalness of homosexuality and the subordination of women are two examples of such assertions that flow from the ideology of naturalization.[62] In a 1991 article, Fulkerson bases her account of ideology upon the work of Louis Althusser, a Marxist theorist who has developed ideological criticism. She follows him by defining ideology as "a false understanding of one's true situation" regarding social reality which has oppressive results.[63] She recognizes the problem of this definition from a poststructural perspective and assures the reader that a "true situation" is still constructed out of signifiers and is unavailable outside of discourse. However, she is unwilling to give up the concept of ideology altogether, because it provides poststructural feminists the political basis for judging oppressive situations.[64]

Fulkerson defines oppression as a configuration of discourses which contains or suppresses fears and manipulates utopian desires. Thus, oppression is derived not from a specific content of a text, but from a configuration of discourses that ideologically manipulates fears and desires. Giving some compensatory function, such as containing or managing fears, an ideological explanation can convince women, such as those of Jehovah's Witness, to support their own submissive roles through a "false" account of their situation.[65]

Possibly because of the problems inherent with a poststructural defence of true and false situations, Fulkerson relies on a slightly different account of ideology in *Changing the Subject*. She gives more of a pragmatic definition of ideology that depends upon the oppressive effects of discourse instead of a description of true or false reality. For this account, she draws on Terry Eagleton's analysis of ideology as it functioned within the Nazi era of Germany. He suggests that ideology accounts for the massive self-deception and legitimation of human brutality that occurred. This ideology was formed not only from misinformation but also out of a complex mix of pleasures and wants, fears and guilt. Eagleton also points out that it was not absolute in its pervasiveness because of the resistance of a few people.[66]

Fulkerson adds a theological dimension to Eagleton's account by construing ideology as social sin marked by human finitude, and resistance as faithful practice in the remembrance of Jesus. Fulkerson is careful to distinguish her account of sin from the privatized, modern account of individualistic finitude. Sin is socially constructed, as are individuals.[67]

In order to analyze gender oppression and resistance to this oppression amongst different groups of women, Fulkerson combines this understanding of ideology with poststructural theories on relations of power. Discourse theory refuses to separate ideas or ideologies from the forces of production, and leads to the identification of two forms of power. Fulkerson notes that, while patriarchal capitalism exudes a hegemonic power over all women, resulting in their commodification and creating their dependency, local forms of this oppression will vary. These particular construals will offer benefits to particular women, explaining their acceptance of oppression and the variation in its effects upon different groups of women and men. Moreover, these localized forms will also tap into fears and desires, enabling potential resistance.[68]

Fulkerson connects this theory with the work of Michel Foucault. She refers to Foucault's description of modern, disciplinary power that has replaced repressive, juridical power. As a means of enforcement, disciplinary power has substituted surveillance for repressive force and violence. The success of surveillance is dependent upon its internalization, which causes women to promote their own oppression. Key to this argument is the insistence that power is not only in the hands of the oppressors but is pervasive. Everyone participates in the web of dominant power relations and cannot step outside of it to make judgements. In this sense, Fulkerson agrees with Foucault that knowledge and truth are relations of power. Fulkerson points out that this also means that the marginalized are neither without power nor are situated outside of power. Therefore, the complex interstructuring of power relations for particular groups of women includes the *potential* for both oppression and liberation, compliance and resistance. In theological terms, Fulkerson suggests that these multiple discourses provide the *possibility* for the social manifestation of both sin (the harm and denial of the goodness of creation) and grace (the recognition and transgression of hegemonic power).[69] In order to make judgements about the presence of sin or grace, issues of authority and norms must be addressed.

I have italicized the words "potential" and "possibility" above to emphasize Fulkerson's insistence upon the local, discursive formation of oppression and liberation, sin and grace. She still retains these concepts as universals, but only as universal *potentials*. This allows the retention of overarching norms and definitions of sin and grace, while insisting that the particularities of these norms and potentialities be defined within local communities. Thus, truth is relativized without being abandoned to nihilist relativism.

Fulkerson adds explicit gender analysis to this deconstruction of power with the help of feminist theories. One of these is feminist standpoint theory, also used by Schüssler Fiorenza. It promotes the epistemological privilege of the oppressed, reasoning that "the position of oppression gives women ... a special vantage on reality."[70] Feminist standpoint theory provides an interpretive grid which constructs reality out of a woman's particular context.[71] Fulkerson finds this compatible with poststructuralism because of its location within specific discourses. Elsewhere, however, she distances herself from feminist standpoint positions because of their reliance on women's experience as a natural warrant for their claims.[72] Her ambivalence over standpoint theory may be attributed to poststructural resistance to the privileging of one particular discourse over another.

In order to provide some means of feminist evaluation that does not transgress poststructural theory, Fulkerson has developed what she calls "feminist stipulations of relevance."[73] These stipulations allow assessments of particular discourses to be made concerning their ability to resist the social sin of patriarchal capitalism. They can take the form of questions regarding the effects of a particular ordering of discourse upon the marginalized, including women. They are produced, not imposed, by an "intertextual economy."

Fulkerson notes that the term "intertextual" was coined by Julia Kristeva to indicate that one structure of meaning is generated in relation to another structure. The phrase "intertextual economy" therefore indicates an exchange of relations between two structures of meaning.[74] In contrast, "intratextual" refers to relations within a community and its historical traditions without reference to the outside world. "Extratextual" refers to those who observe and analyze a community or text from the outside.

Unlike liberal extratextualism, Fulkerson's intertextual approach acknowledges its own embeddedness in relations of power. Unlike postliberal intratextualism, it examines the discursive impact of the socio-political context upon a community's reading of scripture and even upon scripture itself.[75] Fulkerson refers here to Kathryn Tanner's description of the plain sense, which will be explained in Chapter Five. As with other intratextualists, Tanner supports the notion of a core biblical text that remains unchanged and retains agency over and against the reader. Fulkerson resists this notion, because it places the text outside of discursive construction.[76]

As with Schüssler Fiorenza, Fulkerson's evaluative criteria are based upon pragmatic judgements within communal contexts. Instead of basing an assessment upon external norms or a particular way of reading scripture, Fulkerson asks how a particular performance of scripture resists and transforms the sinful distortions of the lives of certain women, thereby widening the realm of God.[77]

Fulkerson acknowledges that her position makes it difficult for past traditions to "correct" our present understandings. Any account of the past, including scripture, the events of Jesus, and doctrinal statements, has been constructed, thereby softening its critical role. This also makes it impossible to distinguish between historical reality and fiction.[78] Fulkerson does bring some stability and agency to scripture, however, by locating it within faith practices and rituals.[79] She argues that the authority of scripture can exist within the relationship of the biblical text to the faith community. As a Jesus narrative is read within the stabilizing impact of a community, it does have some critical force upon that community.[80] It must be remembered, though, that the Christian story will always be braided with other stories, such as our society's struggle to affirm the personhood of women, First Nations, lesbian and gay people, and those living in poverty. When braided with other stories, the biblical narratives and Christian traditions are being remade, not simply retold.[81] This means that the critical impact of the Christian story cannot be known in advance, but will always bring new and surprising twists.

In conjunction with a communal location of scriptural agency, Fulkerson suggests that truth can only be found within local, discursive relations of knowledge and power. Truth is situational, according to Fulkerson, and not absolute. It is dependent upon its construction within a faith community and cannot be adjudicated according to its correspondence to a total system. Totalities create closures and closures create outsiders.[82] What constitutes a liberative, and therefore truthful, practice for one community may constitute an oppressive, and therefore sinful, practice for another. However, Fulkerson insists that her concept of truth does not lead to absolute relativism. Neither does it support the absolutizing of particular communal values or beliefs.[83] Fulkerson acknowledges that she posits a "radically situational judgment about meaning." As an example, she states that she must rely upon the claim of a community as to whether or not it is Christian.[84] At the same time, she posits a universal norm of agapic care for the other, and suggests a new universalism of potentiality.[85]

A community's Christian identity will help its members to be self-critical and to discern the truth within their reasons, rules and values on the basis of pragmatic and teleological norms. Demonstrations of "visions of the good," in spite of our fractured finitude, usher in a moment of truth and grace that can identify and resist hegemonic powers. The paradox of grace is its call for God-dependence as visions of God's realm are glimpsed and partially realized in our material world, but never fully evident.[86]

It is within these events of grace that Fulkerson locates revelation. Revelation cannot constitute any special privileging of a particular discourse, but can only be found within an event or testimony of liberation.[87] In that situation, Fulkerson finds a "theo/acentric transcendence."[88] Fulkerson is cautious, however, of intimations of extratextual disclosures of revelation. While she clearly articulates her belief in God, she resists the possibility of truth that could be revealed outside of our social relations. Theological inquiry should be materialist, not idealist, by focusing upon practice, not disclosure or correlation.[89] It should also recognize that it can only be limited and partial. The paradox of grace suggests that the human transformation for which we strive is incomplete even as we "depend upon the God who is already there before us."[90]

Fulkerson declines an apology for her references to God, acknowledging that any reference to the metaphysical is at odds with poststructural denial of extratextual reality. Even her use of the term "theology" sets her against certain poststructuralists and postmodernists. Thus she concedes that her critique "is not directly postmodern."[91] Without a fuller development of her concept of revelation, however, it is difficult to ascertain how her belief in God informs her theological method. One reviewer recognizes this theological lacuna and hopes that she will develop her concepts of revelation and theological realism in further work.[92]

Canonical System

Because Fulkerson locates authoritative criteria, truth, and revelation within particular faith communities, it is crucial that she have some method of understanding and analyzing the faith practices of these communities. Fulkerson has therefore developed a brilliant system that allows scripture and doctrine to have agency within a faith community and allows both oppression and resistance to be analyzed in terms of the community's own faith system. A Christian community's faith practice is centred around particular rules or canons of tradition that constitute a reading regime. Fulkerson defines a regime as the actual way in which scripture is practised. She uses the phrase "performing scripture" to acknowledge the communication of scripture by those who are illiterate, as well as to indicate that different social practices produce different texts.[93] A community will have rules for reading or performing scripture that include formal hermeneutical regulations as well as implicit, institutionalized practices. This creates a set of norms and a stabilization of meaning which comprises the community's canon. When a biblical text is read or performed within a community, the historical and cultural conditions shaped by the community's canon and social location limit the Bible's potential meanings, thereby bringing stability to it.[94]

Fulkerson proposes that the Christian canon be understood as a Christian community's allegiance to theological norms, creeds or doctrines, as well as to a broader, denominational tradition.[95] This tradition establishes legitimate translations and interpretations as well as experts, such as feminist theologians, who produce certifying discourses. The canon also includes the goals of the community's practice, such as saving souls or creating justice. This canonical system is the primary organizer of the biblical text.[96] As such it creates an ideal reading regime.

Up to this point Fulkerson agrees with postliberals, who contest the monopoly of historical-critical studies over "correct" interpretation by focusing upon the ecclesial community's reading of scripture.[97] However, in distinction to a formal communal hermeneutic, such as that adopted by postliberals, she warns against the uncritical acceptance of ecclesial readings. Dominant reading regimes may well silence the marginalized voices and readings within that community. She also challenges the tendency of communal hermeneutics to ignore the wider social formation of that community and to view the community as a stable, unified constant. This would constitute representational thinking.[98]

Unlike postliberals, Fulkerson contrasts the ideal regime of the community's canonical system with the resisting reading regimes of women, both of which are influenced by their social location. These resisting regimes find ways to lessen oppressive aspects of the dominant, ideal reading regime, while still remaining within the bounds of their faith community's traditions. The intertextual weaving of the ideal regime with the resisting regime produce meaning and bring stability to the biblical text.[99]

While Fulkerson wants to initially destablize subjects, such as women and the biblical text, she prevents the endless process of signifying by temporarily re-stablizing these subjects within particular communities. The interstructuring of the canonical system with the resisting regime is the means by which this stability occurs. Fulkerson uses Laura Donaldson's term *graf(ph)ting* to indicate how women produce meaning as they read texts. Donaldson derives this term from Jacques Derrida's expression *engraf(ph)ting*, which combines *graphion*, meaning stylus, with the horticulture term *graft*. This evokes the material creation of a text written anew within the relation of text and context.[100] This new text brings a temporary closure and stability within the discourses of a particular group of women.

Let us recall that Fulkerson is interested in women's subordinated discourses which identify particular problems of gender oppression and render some resistance within their faith communities. An analysis of their canonical system interacting with the social location of the women provides a means for determining: 1) the patterns of meaning created by a faith community; 2) subordinated and resisting discourses to the dominant patterns; and 3) the relation of these patterns of discourse with the hegemonic social orderings of patriarchal capitalism.[101]

Fulkerson suggests that canonical systems both limit the possibilities of resistance and provide rules for ordering this resistance. A feminist analysis should therefore not begin with a pre-formed notion of sexist texts or practices, but examine the change or challenge of a faith practice within the limits of a particular canonical system.[102] In order to identify moments of resistance, she recommends dispensing with traditional indicators of feminist liberation theology. Instead she suggests looking for practices supported by their Christian faith that reject certain dependencies generated by patriarchal capitalism. These rejections will appear as strains or contradictions within their discursive situation and may not be named by the women as resistance or as feminist.[103] However, Fulkerson urges feminists to recognize these practices as liberative.

Although Fulkerson's intent is to respect the diversity of women who do not identify as feminist, her analysis of the discourse of these women through her feminist grid, and her naming their discourse as feminist at one point is problematic.[104] Her feminist analysis appears to challenge, not respect, their objection and possible antagonism to feminism. She also names their liberative actions as resistance, even though she also acknowledges that they, themselves, may refuse to see these actions as resistant to male hegemony.[105] One woman responded to the results of a study used by Fulkerson: "I was afraid someone like you ... an outsider ... would misunderstand."[106] Fulkerson justifies this "misunderstanding" by explaining that she is analyzing their discourse, not the women themselves with their intentions and self-interpretations.[107] Yet how can an intertextual analysis, which asserts the historically and culturally grounded character of discourse, ignore a community's intentions and self-interpretations? This has implications for Fulkerson's call for a representation of the other through political affinities. Granted, the interpreter's own grids will produce a different picture of a people than the people's own interpretation.

Yet, I would risk representational fallacy along with Schüssler Fiorenza in order to find some criteria that will encourage the interpreter's picture to more closely resemble that of the people. Otherwise, there could be no basis of respect or trust that would allow political representation, affinities, or mediation of difference.

Because Fulkerson's study of the Presbyterian Women[108] has direct implications for United Church of Canada documents on sexuality which I will be examining in the second part of this book, I will give a brief outline of the Presbyterian Women's canonical system and resisting regime. Fulkerson first explains the canonical system of Reformed confessions. Central to this system is the belief that the Protestant Bible is foundational for faith, doctrine and life. This belief is based upon Luther's emphasis upon justification by grace through faith according to the rule of *sola scriptura*. Because this emphasis was meant to refute the authority of the Catholic Magisterium, Fulkerson identifies this as an iconoclastic and evangelical reading regime. These characteristics, together with the Reformed motto "the church reformed and always reforming," lead to a refutation of any absolute authority other than the living Word. While scripture alone provides communal norms, bibliolatry is condemned. Fulkerson notes that Calvin, in contrast to Luther, held the entirety of scripture to be revelatory for the purposes of individual and societal salvation. The underlying conviction of both Calvin and Luther was that scripture was to be read by believers for salvific purposes. Anything that was unclear in scripture was to be interpreted by other parts of scripture which were deemed clear.[109]

More recent confessions from the Presbyterian Church (USA), based on historical Calvinist Confessions, have proposed seven rules for interpreting scripture: 1) Jesus Christ is the central subject and hermeneutical key; 2) the plain text, with its historical meaning, is to have precedence; 3) the Holy Spirit confirms scripture; 4) doctrines offer guidance; 5) love for God and neighbour is another hermeneutical key; 6) study and scholarship are important; and 7) scripture should be interpreted in light of scripture.[110] Fulkerson notes that these principles provide flexibility for the interpretation of specific passages of scripture. She also notes that the rule regarding plain sense can either support or refute women's subordination in the church.[111] Influential in this decision are the other intersecting discourses, such as the certifying discourses produced by "reading experts" from the church administration and the seminaries.

After giving a brief historical overview, Fulkerson shows how the formal Presbyterian theology "ordered the authority of God's Word as a written, christological, and transforming presence of God through the Holy Spirit, by its doctrine of justification by grace through faith."[112] Although these elements allowed for change and self-critique, they were joined by less explicit rules for reading, such as how to read the Bible, who may read it publically, and who may interpret it. These rules discouraged any change which might be liberative for women. Gender discourses of the early twentieth century were also influential. They proposed a gender complementarity which justified the restriction of women to domestic spheres. The formal theology, together with the informal rules and gender discourses, contributed to the Presbyterian canonical system.[113]

When the formal theology began to change, gender discourses and the rules for reading remained entrenched for a much longer period, explaining the Presbyterian Women's unquestioning acceptance of gender prohibitions long after formal theology began to question it. However, even though the women did not protest their prohibition from authoritative reading by the canonical system, they were able to resist their subordination through their own reading regime. This resisting regime was ordered by the biblical injunction of love for God and neighbour, which allowed them to provide "women's work for women," expanding their roles beyond domesticity into mission work. They were therefore able to read, interpret and preach Scripture in their meetings and in their own literature, while still abiding by the gender restrictions within the wider work of the church.[114]

In order to better understand the ways in which particular readings of scripture offer resistance within a canonical system, Fulkerson refers to the concept of register. According to semiotic analysis, register indicates "that *what* is said and *how* it is said are inseparable."[115] Three variables constitute a register: field or subject matter; tenor or quality of social relations; and mode or medium of communication. Fulkerson further divides tenor into four types, each of which can be found in the Presbyterian Women's literature: 1) personalized mutuality, found in face-to-face conversations;

2) objective, egalitarian didacticism, found in field-dominant registers; 3) authoritarian or benevolent patriarchy, found in expert addresses; and 4) interrogation.[116] These variables demonstrate that register is "the content function of language, its interpersonal or social function, and its rhetorical or textual function" which together produce meaning.[117] As an example, Fulkerson discusses the register of a mother's game-playing with her child. The field is the ideas discussed, the tenor is the tone of the dominant-subordinate relationship, and the mode is the spoken, dialogical form of communication.[118]

Along with the identification of the types of register employed, Fulkerson also examines which variable is given more weight by the community. The Pentecostal women whom Fulkerson studies appear to emphasize the tenor and mode of their faith practices more than the field or subject of their preaching. A woman's choice of words, intensity of presentation, gestures, and personalized address are crucial for her success as a preacher. In contrast, she suggests that feminist theology is a field-dominant register in which its ideas and subject are much more important than its mode or tenor of presentation.[119] While I agree with Fulkerson that some feminist theologies are field-dominant, I have found other feminist theologies to intentionally focus upon the mode and tenor of embodied theology.

Employing this concept of register in an analysis of discourse unites form and content and explains how variations in the tenor or mode of a reading-performance of scripture can alter its meaning. This refutes the notion of a fixed text that has one "correct" meaning, and moves beyond authorial intention as the source of this meaning. It will also better enable the judgement of non-feminist women's reading-performance regimes as resistant within their own faith communities.[120]

Conclusion

The overall goal of Mary McClintock Fulkerson's feminist theological method is to take seriously the multiple forms of gender oppression and resistance within diverse faith communities. By destabilizing both the biblical text and subject, she hopes to honour their diversity and recognize their social construction. Fulkerson also hopes to demonstrate the impact of one's social location upon one's description of "the other." This will allow her to better "attend to the other," helping her to fulfill the Christian vision of agapic care for the stranger.[121] It must be remembered that Fulkerson's phrase "attending to the other" indicates a willingness to listen to and be challenged by the other. It does not mean a patronizing attitude of help that can be given from a place of privileged stability.[122]

We have seen that Fulkerson seeks to accomplish these objectives with the help of poststructural analysis. There are several implications of this approach for feminist theology. One is that critiques of either the biblical text or the subject position of women within faith communities cannot be made apart from these communities and their intertextual formation. An external analysis that does not take into account the multiple "differential networks"[123] of a community, including its interaction with the wider social reality, cannot honour the women or their readings of scripture. In opposition to postliberal intratextual approaches which try to maintain a closed discourse, Fulkerson insists that discourses that shape communal readings are intersected with those of the larger society.[124]

A second implication is that the boundaries between disciplines are blurred through this intersection. Theological and scientific knowledge cannot be correlated, as each does not exist as a pure entity. Although Fulkerson admits that distinctions can (and should?) be made between discourses, they cannot be completely disjunctive. Rather, they find meaning within their intertextual or dialogical relationship.[125]

Thirdly, a poststructural approach also helps to identify both the dominant and the resisting discourses within a faith community. These can be described theologically as discourses concerning sin and grace. Fulkerson departs from Foucault by insisting that discourses of power and knowledge demonstrate not only human finitude and fallibility, but also provide space for practices of resistance.[126]

A fourth implication of poststructuralism is that accounts of human finitude and sin must include the embeddedness of social relations in ideologies. Fulkerson emphasizes that everyone, including women who resist their own oppression, is intricately situated within these social relations. Thus, even resistance constituted as a faithful remembrance of Jesus can only be partial. Fulkerson is careful to note that this account of human finitude does not support an "essential humanness" but only the potential for sin and redemption.[127]

The partiality of and potential for redemption has an eschatalogical emphasis upon the "not yet." It acknowledges the need for us to help create God's realm of justice, while knowing that our finite role in this creation will always bring potential distortion. For this reason, both our present interpretations and past traditions must not be given absolute status, but understood as contributing to "a redemptive traditioning process."[128]

This leads to a fifth implication regarding the place of tradition. Since Fulkerson does not believe that there is a correct, and therefore authoritative, reading of scripture and tradition, she insists that the past is to be re-membered and reconstructed.[129] In fact, Fulkerson states that "without our interests and their conflicts with hegemonic discourses, there *is* no scripture."[130] This statement does not indicate a rejection of scripture, but an acknowledgement that scripture produces meaning only through its use and temporary stabilization within faith communities.[131] She also acknowledges that this stabilization of scripture and tradition within a community's canonical system grants both of them agency. In this sense, the biblical text makes claims upon the community.[132]

Sixthly, resisting regimes must be judged liberative for women not by outside feminist standards, but by the extent to which they protest patriarchal capitalist hegemony within their own canonical system. The concept of register helps Fulkerson to identify the connections between the reading-performance regimes and the canonical system, and to understand how variations in the tenor or mode of an interpretation of scripture can provide a resisting, altered meaning.

A final implication of poststructural analysis is that Fulkerson is not attempting to represent the women whom she studies. She is well aware that her own feminist grid affects her analysis. Rather, she is attempting to "mediate difference" in her production of the other that challenges herself and other feminist theologians. She hopes that this will lead to a respect of differences based on a theology of affinity.[133]

Notes to Chapter 3

1. Mary McClintock Fulkerson, *Changing the Subject: Women's Discourses and Feminist Theology* (Minneapolis: Fortress Press, 1994), 3.

2. Fulkerson, *Changing the Subject*, 378–79. Fulkerson's Presbyterian identity is named in *Grace Upon Grace: Essays in Honor of Thomas A. Langford*, ed. by Robert K. Johnston, L. Gregory Jones, and Jonathan R. Wilson (Nashville: Abingdon Press, 1999), 10.

3. Mary McClintock Fulkerson, "Gender—Being It or Doing It? The Church, Homosexuality, and the Politics of Identity," *Union Seminary Quarterly Review* 47, no. 1–2 (1993): 29–46; Mary McClintock Fulkerson, "Church Documents on Human Sexuality and the Authority of Scripture," *Interpretation* 49, no. 1 (January 1995): 46–58.

4. For further elaboration see Fulkerson, *Changing the Subject*, 64–66.

5. Fulkerson, *Changing the Subject*, viii–ix.

6. The term "malestream" originates with Dorothy Smith and is also used by Schüssler Fiorenza.

7. Fulkerson refers to Stanley Fish's work at this point. See Mary McClintock Fulkerson, "Contesting Feminist Canons: Discourse and the Problem of Sexist Texts," *Journal of Feminist Studies in Religion* 7, no. 2 (Fall 1991): 59–60.

8. Fulkerson, *Changing the Subject*, 63–64.

9. Fulkerson, "Contesting Feminist Canons," 66–67. See Schüssler Fiorenza's response in Elisabeth Schüssler Fiorenza, *But She Said: Feminist Practices of Biblical Interpretation* (Boston: Beacon Press, 1992), 133–34, ftnt. 5. Fulkerson responds to this response in *Changing the Subject*. Later in this chapter this debate will be discussed more fully.

10. Mary McClintock Fulkerson, "Sexism as Original Sin: Developing a Theacentric Discourse," *Journal of the American Academy of Religion* 59, no. 4 (Winter 1991): 654.

11. Fulkerson, "Contesting Feminist Canons," 55.

12. Fulkerson, *Changing the Subject*, 69.

13. Fulkerson, "Sexism as Original Sin," 654–55.

14. Fulkerson, "Sexism as Original Sin," 655–56; Fulkerson, *Changing the Subject*, 164–65.

15. Fulkerson, *Changing the Subject*, 115.

16. Fulkerson, *Changing the Subject*, 36.

17. Fulkerson, *Changing the Subject*, 310.

18. Fulkerson, *Changing the Subject*, 304–12.

19. Fulkerson, *Changing the Subject*, 313–18, 322, 338.

20. Fulkerson, "Sexism as Original Sin," 668.

21. Fulkerson, *Changing the Subject*, 56.

22. Fulkerson, *Changing the Subject*, 102–03.

23. Fulkerson, *Changing the Subject*, 56–57.

24. Fulkerson, "Sexism as Original Sin," 671–73.

25. Fulkerson, *Changing the Subject*, 29.

26. Fulkerson, *Changing the Subject*, 128, ftnt. 20.

27. Fulkerson, *Changing the Subject*, 129.

28. Fulkerson, "Contesting Feminist Canons," 66.

29. Fulkerson, *Changing the Subject*, 126–29.

30. Fulkerson, *Changing the Subject*, 133.

31. Fulkerson, *Changing the Subject*, 124.

32. Fulkerson, *Changing the Subject*, 130–32.

33. Fulkerson, *Changing the Subject*, 112.

34. Fulkerson, *Changing the Subject*, 27–28.

35. Fulkerson, *Changing the Subject*, 79–81.

36. Fulkerson, *Changing the Subject*, 63–64.

37. Fulkerson, "Contesting Feminist Canons," 66.

38. Fulkerson, "Church Documents," 58, ftnt. 6; Fulkerson, "Gender," 30.

39. Fulkerson, "Gender," 29–46.

40. Fulkerson, "Gender," 33.

41. Fulkerson, *Changing the Subject*, 8–9.

42. Mary McClintock Fulkerson, "Women, Men, and Liberation: Old Issues, New Conversations," *Quarterly Review* 8, no. 4 (Winter 1988): 86.

43. Fulkerson, *Changing the Subject*, 88.

44. Fulkerson, *Changing the Subject*, 9, 41, 105.

45. Fulkerson, "Contesting Feminist Canons," 56–58.

46. Fulkerson, "Gender," 33.

47. Fulkerson, "Sexism as Original Sin," 654.

48. Mary McClintock Fulkerson, "Theological Education and the Problem of Identity," *Modern Theology* 7, no. 5 (October, 1991): 472–75.

49. Fulkerson, *Changing the Subject*, 112, 115.

50. Fulkerson, *Changing the Subject*, 5–6.

51. Fulkerson, *Changing the Subject*, viii.

52. Fulkerson, *Changing the Subject*, 4, 355, 389–90.

53. Fulkerson, *Changing the Subject*, 3–4.

54. Fulkerson, *Changing the Subject*, 389–92.

55. Fulkerson, *Changing the Subject*, 4.

56. Fulkerson, *Changing the Subject*, 25.

57. Fulkerson, *Changing the Subject*, 177.

58. Fulkerson, *Changing the Subject*, 377.

59. Fulkerson, *Changing the Subject*, 383–85.

60. Fulkerson, *Changing the Subject*, 67.

61. Fulkerson, *Changing the Subject*, 67.

62. Fulkerson, *Changing the Subject*, 67.

63. Fulkerson, "Contesting Feminist Canons," 57.

64. Fulkerson, "Contesting Feminist Canons," 57.

65. Fulkerson, "Contesting Feminist Canons," 58.

66. Fulkerson, *Changing the Subject*, 19–20.

67. Fulkerson, *Changing the Subject*, 20–25.

68. Fulkerson, *Changing the Subject*, 10, 92–98.

69. Fulkerson, *Changing the Subject*, 99–106.

70. Fulkerson, *Changing the Subject*, 53; Fulkerson, "Women, Men, and Liberation," 83.

71. Fulkerson, *Changing the Subject*, 54.

72. Fulkerson, *Changing the Subject*, 85.

73. Fulkerson uses Stanley Fish's phrase "stipulations of relevance." See Fulkerson, *Changing the Subject*, 155.

74. Fulkerson, *Changing the Subject*, 156–57.

75. Fulkerson, *Changing the Subject*, 156–64.

76. Fulkerson, *Changing the Subject*, 162–63.

77. Fulkerson, *Changing the Subject*, 164.

78. Fulkerson, *Changing the Subject*, 369.

79. Mary McClintock Fulkerson, "Feminist Exploration: A Theological Proposal," *International Journal of Practical Theology* 2, no. 2 (1998): 216–219.

80. Mary McClintock Fulkerson, "Toward a Materialist Christian Social Criticism: Accommodation and Culture Reconsidered," *Changing Conversations: Religious Reflection & Cultural Analysis*, edited by Dwight N. Hopkins and Sheila Greeve Davaney (New York: Routledge, 1996), 55.

81. Mary McClintock Fulkerson, "*Theologia* as a Liberation *Habitus*: Thoughts Toward Christian Formation for Resistance," *Theology and the Interhuman: Essays in Honor of Edward Farley*, edited by Robert R. Williams (Valley Forge, Pennsylvania: Trinity Press International, 1995), 172–73.

82. Fulkerson, *Changing the Subject*, 370–71.

83. Fulkerson, *Changing the Subject*, 372–74.

84. Fulkerson, *Changing the Subject*, 365, ftnt. 7.

85. Fulkerson, *Changing the Subject*, 25.

86. Mary McClintock Fulkerson, "Grace, Christian Controversy, and Tolerable Falsehoods," *Grace Upon Grace: Essays in Honor of Thomas A. Langford*, ed. by Robert K. Johnston, L. Gregory Jones, and Jonathan R. Wilson (Nashville: Abingdon Press, 1999), 251.

87. Fulkerson, *Changing the Subject*, 372–77.

88. Fulkerson, *Changing the Subject*, 361, ftnt. 3.

89. Fulkerson, *Changing the Subject*, 26.

90. Fulkerson, "Grace, Christian Controversy, and Tolerable Falsehoods," 251.

91. Fulkerson, *Changing the Subject*, 63.

92. Graham Ward, "Review of *Changing the Subject*," *Modern Theology* 11, no. 4 (October 1995): 478.

93. Fulkerson, *Changing the Subject*, 147.

94. Fulkerson, *Changing the Subject*, 122.

95. Fulkerson, *Changing the Subject*, 167.

96. Fulkerson, *Changing the Subject*, 167–73, 303.

97. Fulkerson identifies scripture as "the sacred text of a community." See Fulkerson, *Changing the Subject*, 148.

98. Fulkerson, *Changing the Subject*, 148–50.

99. Fulkerson, *Changing the Subject*, 173–75.

100. Fulkerson, *Changing the Subject*, 152–53.

101. Fulkerson, *Changing the Subject*, 167.

102. Fulkerson, *Changing the Subject*, 173–77.

103. Fulkerson, *Changing the Subject*, 177.

104. Fulkerson, *Changing the Subject*, 179, ftnt. 87.

105. Fulkerson, *Changing the Subject*, 177.

106. Fulkerson bases her analysis of Pentecostal women on different studies, one of which was conducted by Elaine Lawless, a folklorist. Lawless recorded the reaction of the women to her study, and this quote is one of the reactions. See Fulkerson, *Changing the Subject*, 289, ftnt. 89.

107. Fulkerson, *Changing the Subject*, 179, ftnt. 87.

108. The term "Presbyterian Women" refers to an official organization of women within the Presbyterian Church (USA). See Fulkerson, *Changing the Subject*, 183, ftnt. 1.

109. Fulkerson, *Changing the Subject*, 186–90.

110. Fulkerson, *Changing the Subject*, 190.

111. Fulkerson, *Changing the Subject*, 190–91.

112. Fulkerson, *Changing the Subject*, 196.

113. Fulkerson, *Changing the Subject*, 196–200.

114. Fulkerson, *Changing the Subject*, 229–38.

115. Fulkerson, *Changing the Subject*, 178.

116. Fulkerson, *Changing the Subject*, 217.

117. Fulkerson, *Changing the Subject*, 178.

118. Fulkerson, *Changing the Subject*, 178.

119. Fulkerson, *Changing the Subject*, 282–85, 301–02.

120. Fulkerson, *Changing the Subject*, 178–79.

121. Fulkerson, *Changing the Subject*, 7–8.

122. Fulkerson, *Changing the Subject*, 4–5.

123. Fulkerson prefers the phrase "differential networks" to "system," because system implies a cohesiveness and totality of discursive relations that may not exist. On the other hand, differential networks indicate an openness to the signifying process. She does, however, use the term "system" in reference to a community's functional canon (its canonical system). See Fulkerson, *Changing the Subject*, 78.

124. Fulkerson, *Changing the Subject*, 362–65.

125. Fulkerson, *Changing the Subject*, 362–65.

126. Fulkerson, *Changing the Subject*, 366–67.

127. Fulkerson, *Changing the Subject*, 19–21.

128. Fulkerson, *Changing the Subject*, 369.

129. Fulkerson, *Changing the Subject*, 369–70.

130. Fulkerson, *Changing the Subject*, 369.

131. Fulkerson, *Changing the Subject*, 370.

132. Fulkerson, "Church Documents," 50–57.

133. Fulkerson, *Changing the Subject*, 377–86.

Chapter 4

Postcolonial Response: Kwok Pui-lan

> "Feminist theology in Asia is not written with a pen,
> it is inscribed on the hearts of many who feel the pain,
> and yet dare to hope."
> —Kwok Pui-lan, "God Weeps with Our Pain"

Kwok Pui-lan was born and raised in Hong Kong. Although she grew up within the Confucian tradition, as an East Asian she was also influenced by a dynamic interaction with Taoism and folk Buddhism.[1] When she was a teenager she attended the Anglican Church in Hong Kong, which further extended her religious diversity. Today she identifies herself as an Anglican, a Chinese, a woman, a mother, a feminist, a Christian theologian and a participant in the ecumenical movement.[2] Kwok refers to herself as a feminist, in spite of its association with white, middle-class western women, because of its political significance in the Chinese language. In addition, she doesn't think any group should have a monopoly on the use of the term "feminist."[3]

This multiple identity contributes to Kwok's feelings as an "outsider-within" regarding her relationship with both her non-Christian family of origin and the Christian community.[4] The complexity of the construction of national, religious and cultural identity is thus demonstrated.[5] It is from these margins that Kwok approaches the Bible, articulates her theology, nourishes her faith and connects with other Christian feminists who also live in the margins.[6]

Kwok has an ambivalent attitude towards the Bible. It has been used as a colonizing tool to legitimate Eurocentric superiority. It has also been a resource for Asian Christians struggling against oppression. Drawing upon an extensive Asian hermeneutical tradition, and utilizing new paradigms for biblical interpretation, she hopes to honour liberative readings and confront hegemonic readings of the biblical text.[7]

Kwok's theological method has been deeply affected by the colonization of Asia, and especially of Hong Kong where English was the only official language until 1971. Such legislation forced most residents to rely on English speakers to interpret government documents and file tax forms.[8] One of her first political actions was to join the student movement in Hong Kong to fight for Chinese as an official language.[9]

Out of this experience of colonization she draws upon postmodernists, such as Michel Foucault, Jacques Derrida, and Jean-François Lyotard, as well as postcolonialists, such as Gayatri Chakravorty Spivak, Trinh T. Minh-ha, Edward Said, and R. S. Sugirtharajah to deconstruct "Eurocentric hegemony and the colonization of the mind."[10] The term "postcolonial" does not refer to a period after colonization, notes Kwok, but to a period since colonization began and is continuing into the present. It identifies the cultural practices and reading strategies emerging in colonized societies.[11]

Kwok's critique of colonialism encompasses a critique of modernity and its elevation of the historical-critical method. She is interested in the development of theological methods that offer an alternative to the western male approach, particularly regarding biblical interpretation and its traditional reliance upon historical criticism. She hopes to give greater attention to the voices of those marginalized by Euro-American scholarship, especially Asian women living in poverty. Along with Fulkerson, she wants to honour biblical interpretation conducted in communities where there is little or no access to western, academic tools of analysis. In addition to Fulkerson, she exposes the destructive colonialist implications of these tools.

In order to best honour the multiple identities of marginalized people, Kwok takes an interfaith, interdisciplinary approach. In her later work, beginning with *Discovering the Bible in a Non-Biblical World*, she refines this with a more explicitly postcolonial approach.[12] Within the Asian context, boundaries between cultures and religions are blurred. Kwok suggests that this ingrained resistance to rigid separation is helpful in overcoming the dichotomy between East and West, and the increasing isolation amongst academic disciplines.[13] This has led her to develop "multifaith hermeneutics," a term she has borrowed from R. S. Sugirtharajah, from a postcolonial perspective. She suggests that a multifaith hermeneutic is valid not only for Asian Christians but for all Christians with a global awareness.[14] After all, colonization affects colonizers as much as the colonized.[15] At the same time, she cautions Caucasian women and men to question their use of postcolonial analysis. Are we using this material as allies in the postcolonial struggle, or are we once again appropriating resources and scholarship from marginalized communities? Is it possible for Caucasian women and men to contribute to postcolonial discussion?[16] Those of us who are Caucasian must take these questions very seriously.

Critique of Colonialism

While Schüssler Fiorenza and Fulkerson focus their critiques upon modernity, Kwok critiques modernity within a broader critique of colonialism. The debates between modernity and fundamentalism were transported by missionaries to Asia.[17] These debates argued about what was true and what was nominal for Christian belief, thereby introducing concepts of doctrinal exclusiveness. In an Asian context exclusivity was an anomaly to their "multiscriptural ethos," where many scriptures from different religions were interwoven together.[18] Adoption of Christianity according to these modern understandings therefore meant adoption of this narrow and exclusive, western interpretation of doctrines and scripture that conflicted with a more inclusive Asian culture.

The majority of the missionaries in Asia were ethnocentric, believing both western culture and Christianity to be a superior form of evolution from the less developed eastern culture and religions.[19] The eastern oppression of women was given as an example of eastern inferiority, and yet Kwok notes that female missionaries sent to Asia achieved an independence and power denied them in western society.[20] She also notes that in some Asian cultures, such as the Philippines, women were afforded higher status before the introduction of Christianity.[21]

As a result of this ethnocentrism, it was assumed that Christianity could best be studied or adopted through western philosophy and languages. This assumption created a dependency upon western scholarship and western churches, and largely neglected the critical contributions that eastern philosophy and culture could have made to the study and practice of Christian beliefs.[22] Thus, Christian debates within Asia replicated western modern concerns within an overall hegemony of Eurocentrism. The following section will elaborate on this colonial impact of modernity, with particular attention given to modernity's elevation of the historical-critical method.

Historical-Critical Method

Kwok acknowledges the contribution of the historical-critical method in its challenge of the dogmatic interpretation of scripture. However, she questions its usefulness for racial and ethnic minority churches. African American biblical scholars, she notes, complain that the readings of marginalized communities are judged superfluous and biased against the more objective, and therefore normative, historical-critical readings.[23] Kwok refers to R. S. Sugirtharajah's observation that Asian readings of the Bible involve intuition, imagination and free association of ideas. These approaches are often dismissed when measured against logical, sophisticated and internally coherent western scholarship.[24] Kwok notes that such evaluation is based upon the norms and standards of western biblical criticism which elevates abstract, deductive, one-dimensional thought indicative of the west.[25]

As with all generalizations, I would add that this distinction is limited by the definition of the west, and the impact of the global, free market economy. If the west includes First Nations people, and the capitalist markets of the east are acknowledged these distinctions between eastern and western thought force an false, artificial polarity between the east and west. For instance, First Nations traditions and western feminist thought emphasize holistic embodiment, while technological expertise from in Japan and Korea involve linear, abstract logic. However, the predominant thought in the west still prioritizes linear, abstract, and objective empiricism.

By viewing the Bible as objective, value-neutral history accessible only through "sophisticated technical analyses," academics view the Bible as past history, limit its contemporary power for liberation, and keep it locked away from faith communities.[26] Kwok joins with Schüssler Fiorenza to reveal the partiality of historical criticism and to suggest that, while it can still be taken seriously, it is necessary to move beyond it to a dialogical relationship with contemporary communities.[27] Along with Fulkerson, she presses for the recognition of communal readings of the Bible that may not draw upon modern methods.

The historical-critical method was developed in the midst of the rise of white supremacy and territorial expansion. Kwok refers to Edward Said's connection of western thought with an underlying colonialist consciousness.[28] Kwok contends that the nineteenth century search for the historical Jesus was a quest both for Jesus and for land and people to conquer.[29] She argues that this quest was greatly influenced by Europe's "empire-building ethos" and the European projection of "natives." Drawing upon Gayatri Chakravorty Spivak's work, Kwok uses the term "natives" to mean a "eurocentric construction of the peoples conquered or colonized by Europe."[30]

Assumptions of the superiority of the Greek language and the ensuing development of western thought were held by biblical scholars into the 1970s.[31] This was contrasted with the supposedly more primitive language and thought of "natives." Modern approaches attempted to divest Christianity of myth and miracle in order to present it as a more highly evolved, rational religion. This too was contrasted with the "superstitious primitive beliefs" of colonized people, thereby justifying their need for Christian conversion and western "civilization."[32]

Kwok joins with Schüssler Fiorenza to critique the newest quest of the historical Jesus, arising during the Reagan-Bush era. The images of Jesus arising out of this newest quest are described by Kwok as the "Noble Savage par excellence." Jesus is portrayed as foreign and yet tameable, similar to the European descriptions of the First Nations of North American. Kwok suggests that the historical positivism of this quest must be viewed in light of the anti-immigrant ethos and belittling of "natives" who live within the borders of western society. Kwok notes that the Enlightenment's quest for common identity (i.e. the Aryan race) and objectivity was fuelled by anxiety over identity in the midst of a rapidly changing Europe. As a parallel, she observes that the contemporary emphasis on objectivity is accompanied by an identity crisis of middle-class, white America.[33]

Kwok does not want to reject entirely the historical-critical method but rather to view it with suspicion as a modern project.[34] It is the interpretive communities which must judge the historical-critical method, and not vice versa. While this method may be inconsequential to illiterate Third World women primarily concerned about their survival, it is of some help to Third World and African American biblical scholars. However, even for them it is limited because of its refusal to entertain certain questions or perspectives.[35] Kwok insists that the European positivist approach to history and historiography not be the sole norm of interpretation. Otherwise history becomes reified, glorified or portrayed as a unifying totality. The contrasting Asian view of history, together with the readings of local religious communities, offer additional norms and critiques of biblical interpretation.[36]

While Kwok acknowledges that her critiques of modernity have been enhanced by feminist and postmodern critiques, she remains suspicious of both. She has recently become aware of the need to view European and North American feminist biblical scholarship critically. While Asian women theologians have realized the need to develop their own theologies apart from western feminist theologies, they have often depended upon western feminist biblical scholarship. "There is the assumption that Asian women can analyze our socio-political situation, whereas western feminist scholars can tell us what the Bible means."[37] If questions concerning colonization and white supremacy are not addressed by western feminists and postmodernists, they remain as Eurocentric as the modern historical-critical method. "The postmodern emphasis on deconstructing the subject, indeterminacy of language, and excess of meaning will not be helpful at all if it does not come to grips with the colonial impulse and the sense of white supremacy which make 'modernity' possible in the first place."[38]

Kwok recommends a reading strategy of "parallel processing" by which various western methods, including historical-critical and postmodern, be read simultaneously with postcolonial, literary, sociological, and reader-response criticisms.[39] She stresses that theological professors must "catch up with the times" and teach students both "the master's texts" and the tools to critique them.[40] As these various methods are explored, she suggests that another time-frame on the margins of both modernity and postmodernity must be entered in order to attend to the differentiations of gender, race, class, ethnic groupings, sexual orientation, age, and disabilities.[41]

Identity Politics

Kwok suggests that in its contact with the East, western Christian thought posited Asia as the essence of the Other. Asian women and men were defined by western constructions.[42] Colonization enforced this essentialized difference between westerners and Asians which objectified colonized people and constructed them as appendages to western history.[43] Kwok refers to Trinh T. Minh-ha's thesis that hegemony separates the colonizer from the colonized by superimposing irreconcilable essences of differences while not acknowledging the diversity of social construction. This is an "ideological construction of sameness and difference" that does not "respect diversity in terms of race, gender, class, culture, and religion."[44] As a result, an artificial polarity between colonized and colonizing women is enforced while diversity amongst each group is flattened.[45] Kwok notes that this prevents female bonding and masks white privileges and power, thereby supporting white male supremacy.[46]

The converse side of essentializing differences is the western liberal notion that all humans are equal and the same. This notion discounts power and privilege afforded particular groups. It overlooks the critique of ideological domination and socio-political differences between people, and assumes that western categories and socio-political systems work for everyone. "The sad truth is that a small group of white people have always functioned as the spokespersons for all."[47]

Neocolonialism has ushered in a different set of problematics concerning identity. Kwok notes that it is influential not through force and coercion, indicative of past colonial powers, but through the power of seduction, persuasion, and the production of desire, as promoted through the western mass media. As a result an Asian woman is torn between stereotypical images of the past constructed by Asian males, and western images of the ideal woman of the future. She is neither Asian enough nor western enough. However, Kwok finds hope in this "in-between" space, for it is here that identity can be negotiated through cultural hybridity and different social locations.[48]

In order to develop their own theologies, Asian theologians must deconstruct these western views and claim their own identities. These identities are based on "shared colonial history, multiple religious traditions, rich and diverse cultures, immense suffering and poverty, a long history of patriarchal control, and present political struggles."[49] Kwok notes that these dynamics are contextualized within political engagement and are not concerned with a particular essence of gender or culture. She locates the essentialist debate within Greek metaphysics, universalizing colonialist discourse, and the present western controversy with language and representation. These are culturally specific for the west, and have little relevance for Asia. Instead, she defines an Asian woman with multi-layered, fluid descriptions that are partial, situated, and context-bound. This allows her to retain gender, race, and culture as political categories without reverting to universalizing, objective discourse.[50] It also necessitates the weaving of various different narratives arising out of multiple identities. She refers to Jean-François Lyotard's observation that, as our roles shift in each narrative, the interaction of our shifting roles produces new meanings, and alternate narratives. Thus, Kwok challenges the concept of an isolated, monolithic identity. Rather, multiple subject positions produce multiple identities within multilevel discourses.[51] Identity is therefore not static, but ever shifting. As an example, Kwok notes that, prior to July 1, 1997, she was a British subject. After that date, when Hong Kong returned to the sovereignty of China, her national identity changed. Out of this experience, Kwok has begun to use the verb "identifying" rather than the noun "identity" in order to emphasize the shifting, multiple nature of identity.[52]

With this understanding of political identity, Kwok demonstrates that feminist biblical interpretation is largely based upon white western male scholarship and white feminist theory, and emerges within the western women's movement and women-church movement. In contrast, she calls for the development of indigenous Asian biblical hermeneutics that will honour the multiple identities of Asian women and expose the intersection of anti-Judaism, sexism, and cultural and religious imperialism in historical interpretations.[53]

Theological Method

Kwok Pui-lan proposes a multifaith hermeneutics appropriate for the multiple identities of Asian Christians. Because of their multifaith context, Asian people are more apt to incorporate a variety of faith traditions within their own perspectives and beliefs. This is particularly true of adherents of Chinese folk religions, such as her parents.[54] Asian Christians therefore realize that the Bible must be interpreted for people of other faith traditions. When the Bible is read along side other scriptures, new insights into the biblical texts and ourselves as Christians will be gained. In order to receive "divine disclosure" from other faith traditions, Kwok stresses the importance of Christian humility and radical openness.[55] After exploring the multifaith and multicultural data used by Kwok, I will examine its implications for truth and authority. Following this, I will look at Kwok's proposals for new faith communities, dialogical imagination, and the performance of scripture.

Theological Sources

In her article defending the "syncretism" of Chung Hyun Kyung's address at the World Council of Churches meeting in Canberra, Kwok points out Rudolph Bultmann's assertion that Christianity is a syncretic religion, formed out of a synthesis of Judaism, Gnosticism, Greek philosophy, and Hellenistic religions.[56] Western philosophies and religions contributed to the formation of early Christian doctrines and biblical interpretations in the western world. Thus, Christianity has always been a syncretic mix of various western philosophies and religions. In a similar syncretic manner, Kwok draws upon eastern philosophy and religions to discern the Gospel within eastern contexts.

The reference to eastern philosophy and religions for Asian Christians is unavoidable in the translation of certain biblical words and doctrines which must use terms and concepts from Asian religions. As an example, Kwok cites the 300-year Chinese Christian controversy over the name for God. One of the difficulties missionaries encountered was the translation of a monotheistic, masculine and transcendent God into a pluralistic, polytheistic society which accepted both female and male principles within the deities. In contrast to western perceptions of God as supreme over creation, indigenous Chinese thinking perceived cosmogony as dynamic and continuous with no creator standing outside of it. Different Chinese terms for God reflected different aspects of the divine, none of which fully captured the western concept, and all of which gave different additional meanings. The missionaries' choices of Chinese terms reflected their contrasting doctrinal emphases and cultural biases, differentiating between British and American culture, as well as amongst Roman Catholic, Protestant and evangelical traditions.[57]

Kwok notes with irony that by adopting the philosophy of the west and ignoring that of the east, Asians have been "busy solving other people's theological puzzles—and thus doing a disservice to our people and the whole church by not integrating our own culture in our theology."[58] If Asian cultures were used as sources for Christian theology, some of the most heated debates within western Christianity, such as *homoousia* and the present-day controversy over female images for the divine, might be avoided.[59] Thus, Kwok emphasizes the importance of Asian theological sources for everyone, not just for those within Asian contexts. With reference to Chung's presentation in Canberra, she lauds the contribution of Asian theologians to "intrafaith" dialogue, moving from insular Christian introspection to a "survival-liberation centred syncretism."[60]

For these reasons Kwok utilizes a variety of Asian resources as "theological data."[61] She suggests that "Asian cultural and religious symbols are adequate vehicles to express the divine."[62] In addition to Asian philosophical and religious traditions, including Confucianism, Taoism, folk Buddhism, and goddess-worship, she also uses songs, performances, writings and experiences as sources for her theological method. These include lullabies, poems, dances, rituals, songs, myths, stories, letters from political prisoners, historical events, and obituary notices.[63] Kwok notes that the legends and the social biographies of Asian people have provided theological data for many Asian theologians.[64]

Kwok interweaves both Asian and western sources of theological data into a holistic framework of "correlative thinking." By this term she refers to the Chinese belief that everything is connected with the whole, a belief which challenges the western dualistic separation of immanence from transcendence, material from spiritual, and human from cosmological.[65] However, at the same time she does not advocate indiscriminate use of these resources, nor of western traditions. She does not want to romanticize Asian culture by overlooking socio-political struggles and patriarchal biases.[66] Like Schüssler Fiorenza, she approaches all theological sources with a hermeneutics of suspicion.

Truth and Authority

The use of multifaith and multicultural theological data for interpreting Christianity has important implications for the concepts of truth and authority, some of which I will now explore as they relate to revelation, the characteristics of Asian scripture, the biblical canon, the diversity of biblical texts and global authoritative criteria. Kwok states that western missionaries assumed there was an essence of Christianity contained in particular doctrines and biblical teachings that could be extracted from western traditions. The challenge was to present this "body of theological truths" in ways acceptable to Asian people. Attempts to introduce the Gospel "Asian style," however, have been unable to escape the imposition of particular western imperialist assumptions and standards.[67] These methods of accommodation, according to Kwok, view scripture and the "core symbolism of Christianity" uncritically, without a realization of the androcentric bias inherent within these western sources. They also view Asian cultures uncritically, adopting cultural expressions without a realization of their patriarchal nature.[68] In addition, they assume that western traditions contain the truth, while eastern traditions are mere vehicles for this truth.[69] "If other people can only define truth according to the western perspective, then christianization really means westernization!"[70] The Bible played an integral role in this colonization, and was used to signify the superiority not only of Christianity, but also of western culture.[71]

As an alternative, Kwok suggests that the primary concern should not be the *presentation* of a fixed Gospel, but the *discernment* of a living Gospel within the contemporary life and struggles of Asians. "Instead of adapting a colonial, western Christianity to Asia, [Asian theologians] now see the task of theology as reconceptualizing and reformulating the meaning of Christian faith."[72] As previously noted, this task draws heavily upon Asian resources, including indigenous Asian religions, in the discernment of the Gospel and truth.

In her later work, Kwok forms a more complex analysis of truth with the help of Michel Foucault's "political economy of truth." Foucault connects truth with power in his study of the societal production and repression of truth. From this analysis, Kwok asks what truth is, who owns it and who is given authority to interpret it.

Kwok also draws upon the work of Charles Peirce to explain the difference between eastern and western perceptions of truth. Peirce proposes three ways of theorizing language: relating it to the world (semantics); relating it to itself (syntax); and relating it to its social context (pragmatics). Kwok explains that "Chinese philosophy focuses more on pragmatics – on the correct use of language to provide guidance for action, to shape social relations, and to transmit a moral vision of society."[73] Because of its pragmatic and relational emphasis, Kwok refers to Chinese thought as "correlative-logic." In contrast, western philosophy has tended to focus upon existential issues relating to semantics. For this reason, Kwok refers to the "identity-logic" of the West.[74]

Postmodernism demonstrates such western biases. Kwok suggests that postmodern concerns about the representation of language, its truth claims, and the relation between its sign and referent are indicative of western anxiety and mistrust about language. They arise out of a separation of the transcendent from the immanent, the human from the natural, and the historical from the cosmological. Chinese philosophical traditions do not acknowledge such separations. The purpose of learning is not to grasp an intellectual concept of abstract, eternal truth. Rather, according to Confucius, the purpose is for the "self-cultivation" of the individual within an ordered society of "human relatedness." Instead of searching for absolute truth, Chinese hermeneutics seeks "wisdom for practical living."[75]

In contrast with postmodern concerns about language, the concern of Chinese philosophers, such as Confucius, is with the abuse and distortion of language arising out of selfish and ulterior motives. Kwok notes that this approach welcomes dialogue, difference and multiplicity.[76] It also provides an alternate understanding of truth from that of the west. Within Chinese traditions, truth is constituted by the "integral relationship between knowing and doing." Therefore, greater emphasis is placed upon "moral and ethical visions of a good society" than upon metaphysical or epistemological questions.[77]

Kwok extends this analysis to biblical revelation. Instead of accepting the Bible as the revealed Word of God, Kwok suggests that revelation be discerned by the manner in which the biblical tradition is enacted within the Christian community. She refers to Katie Geneva Cannon's questioning of a Christianity which supported the rape, lynching, and castration of Black people whose basic human rights were denied. Along with African Americans, she states that people of the Third World are more concerned about God's truth that is revealed through an enacted biblical tradition, than about a hidden, metaphysical truth contained within the Bible. "The politics of truth is not fought on the epistemological level."[78]

A contextual approach to the Bible in Asia will dismiss not only an abstract, western metaphysics but also an exclusive concentration upon the Bible as scripture. To demonstrate this, Kwok examines the use of the Word of God as a traditional, Protestant hermeneutical key. A logocentric interpretation of scripture assumes a univocal Word of God that can be found within the biblical text which establishes a foundational truth or meaning. Kwok develops Jacques Derrida's critique of this "false assumption" of a prior, unmediated presence behind the text. She insists that it is in the interaction between text and community where truth is found. God's revelation occurs not within the Bible itself, but within the *enacted* biblical tradition. She therefore dismisses a logocentric positioning of the Word of God within the text and agrees with Derrida's rejection of a prior unmediated presence behind the text.

If one agrees with her premises, however, is this conclusion necessary? While Fulkerson also insists that revealed truth can only be found within social interactions, she still upholds a belief in a divine reality that is both within and supercedes our material reality. If divine truth can be found in the interaction of text with community, I assume that there must be a prior unmediated presence behind both the text and the community. Derrida may well dispute this because of his atheistic stance, but from a Christian perspective, I do not believe that revelation can occur without this unmediated presence. At the same time revelation cannot occur apart from the community. If the Word of God is understood as the pre-existent *logos* of John 1, with reference to both Sophia and the Christ as suggested by Schüssler Fiorenza, the Word of God is not equated with the text.[79] It can, however, be revealed within the text AND the community as they engage in dialogue and faithful response.

This view of revelation can be enhanced by Kwok's understanding of the biblical text as one language system amongst others that designates the sacred. Rather than viewing different scriptures as sacred in themselves, Kwok understands them as interplaying signs that point towards the sacred.[80] This necessitates a multifaith hermeneutics.

Kwok's Chinese multiscriptural context has taught her that "scripture is a very fluid and dynamic concept." This has led her to four observations about the character of scripture. The first is that scripture is relational. A text only becomes scripture through its particular relationship with a community. Its status may also change over time. As an example, she explains the shifting views towards the Confucian classics throughout the centuries. Secondly, within China one encounters many different scriptures, each with their own claims to authority. The Chinese are accustomed to weighing the authority of one tradition against another, thereby relativizing all claims, and allowing for creative, new syntheses. This enabled the birth of Zen Buddhism and Neo-Confucianism. Thirdly, there are no rigid canonical boundaries of scripture. Because the canons are immense, few have access to all of the texts. There are also few Asian religions which have a regulative body to uphold the authority of a particular canon.[81] Lastly, scripture is not necessarily limited to a written text. Kwok demonstrates the importance of the oral tradition within Hinduism, Confucianism, and Buddhism, as well as Christianity. Along with Fulkerson, Kwok notes the importance of the performance of scripture, especially amongst poorer communities which have less accessibility to the written texts. Kwok also notes that the performance of scripture places less emphasis upon a canonical body of texts and more upon oral and aural interpretations.[82] Further discussion about the oral transmission of scripture will occur later in this chapter.

These four characteristics of scripture within the multiscriptural Chinese context have made most Chinese people suspicious of any religious group, such as the Christian missionaries, who claim that their scriptures alone contain the truth and hold ultimate authority.[83] Kwok refers to the late nineteenth century missionary movement, epitomized by John R. Mott, as an example of an exclusive, biblical claim for truth and revelation. She states that such a claim posited the Bible as a "signifier" of the superiority of western beliefs and the deficiency of "heathen" culture. This construction made western culture normative and inherently superior. Kwok draws a parallel between this and Jacques Lacan's poststructural description of the phallus signifying female deficiency. This parallel is emphasized through missionary literature describing its work with words such as "aggressive," "intrusion," and "penetration."[84]

Kwok quotes Zhao Zichen who questions this exclusive view of revelation. There is no time or place when God has not been breaking into the world, nor can it be denied that God has inspired eastern sages.[85] As an example she mentions the Beijing massacre where she discerned God's presence with the students.[86] Kwok equates revelation with truth in her insistence with "many other" Chinese Christians that the Bible is not the only source of truth.[87]

Kwok is uncomfortable not only with exclusive views of revelation, but also with traditional descriptions of Christian revelation as unique or special. These descriptions contain imperialist overtones which implies the superiority of Christian revelation over other religions.[88] Is it not possible, though, to refer to Christian revelation as unique while resisting any exclusive claims to revelation or imperialist overtones of superiority? Different religions do consist of beliefs that are unique in their content and practice. Kwok would not want to deny any religion its unique *différance*, as long as each one is understood as unique and as important as any other one. However, it must be granted that the difficulty with using the term "unique" in reference to Christianity has been its historic association with the superior, "special" revelation found in Jesus in contrast to the inferior "general" revelation found in nature and other religions.[89]

Perhaps because of this association, Kwok cautions against recognizing the particularity of the Jesus event and the unique contribution of

Christianity.[90] At the same time, she does not dispense with Christology. She encourages an organic model of Christ which emphasizes Jesus embracing eco-justice for all of creation, not only for humans. She also draws upon the work of Schüssler Fiorenza and Elizabeth Johnson to support the concept of Jesus as the Wisdom of God. This concept works well with the wisdom traditions of Asia. Kwok can accept God's revelation through Jesus as long as it is understood as one amongst many revelations of the divine. Within Christianity the christic presence can be affirmed through acts of compassion and solidarity, in movements of people who are bearers of hope, and in rituals that celebrate life and evoke the power of the divine.[91]

Kwok's discomfort with the special nature of Christian revelation is connected with her concern about the closed biblical canon. She echoes Schüssler Fiorenza's critique of the formation of the canon. She notes the particular voices which were excluded both from the texts and from the process of transmission of the written text.[92] In order to rectify this, the biblical canon could be opened to include other texts and traditions. She refers to Bo Chenguang who argued in 1927 that, just as the Bible contains the Jewish classics which preceded Jesus, the Chinese Bible should contain Confucian, Daoist and Buddhist classics.[93] The definition of canon could also be expanded, as both Schüssler Fiorenza and Fulkerson have suggested. However, Kwok is considering dispensing with the concept altogether. She points out the connection of canon with power. It is formed by those who are dominant within a religious community and it is used to control those who are marginalized within the community and those whose cultures differ from the dominant. Out of Kwok's personal experience she notes that the biblical canon has been used to control and denigrate Asian cultures and women. Under the pretext of protecting the truth, the closure of the biblical canon has functioned to repress truth.[94]

While Kwok rejects the canon and the sacrality of the biblical text, she still emphasizes the importance of the Bible for faith communities. It is not the biblical text which she rejects, but the authoritative status given it. As with Schüssler Fiorenza, she does not accept the normativity of the Bible or of biblical critical principles. She agrees with both Schüssler Fiorenza and Fulkerson that authoritative criteria must lie within the faith communities as they each arrive at their own biblical interpretations.[95] "Biblical truth cannot be pre-packaged ... [but] must be found in the actual interaction between text and context in the concrete historical situation."[96]

One of the reasons she locates authoritative criteria within faith communities is because the meaning of biblical texts is dependent upon communal performance. Like Schüssler Fiorenza and Fulkerson, she believes that a biblical text has multiple meanings that are constructed within the community. Because of her use of the Chinese theory of language, with its emphasis upon a pragmatic, dialogical approach, she is not interested in a free-floating text whose meaning can be traced to divine or authorial intent, or to the original context. Rather, "multiple meanings are created in public discussion, creative dialogue and sometimes heated controversy."[97] The more diverse the interpretive communities, the richer and fuller the interpretive dialogues can be. As communities become more inclusive, the voices of the Other will be able to contribute to these dialogues and not be subsumed into dominant voices.[98]

Along with Schüssler Fiorenza and Fulkerson, Kwok is careful to honour the diversity of the biblical texts. It is for this reason that she does not want to posit any biblical critical principles as the norm. This would create a coercive hierarchy of truth that would obliterate the plurality of the texts under the guise of unity. She recognizes that different communities will establish different norms for interpretation according to their own situations. She also recognizes the importance of intercommunal relationships and suggests that each community must be accountable to others, tested through public discourse.[99]

Although Kwok is wary of universal norms, she also realizes the need for global criteria that can assist in the public accountability of each community. She insists that Christians must be accountable not just to the world-wide Christian community, but to the global human community. "The question shifts from how the Bible can be normative for the Christian community to how it can bear meaning for the survival of human beings and the planet."[100] Instead of extracting biblical principles as prescriptions for this task, she suggests drawing upon the particularity of biblical stories with their insights into common human issues. These insights can then be contrasted and enriched by stories and insights arising out of other faith traditions. The criteria by which these insights can be tested concern the lessening of human suffering, the resistance to oppression within the church, academy and society, and the liberation of the disadvantaged, particularly women and children.[101] More specifically, Kwok gives a number of theses to guide biblical interpretation. It must not be anti-Semitic and must not oppress or discriminate against any race or ethnic group. Further, issues of racism, ethnocentrism, sexism, and the politics of difference must be examined by everyone, not just Third World or minority women. Also, the cultural complexity within the biblical texts should be examined in order to better understand contemporary cross-cultural interpretations. Lastly, the Bible must be interpreted through a multifaith hermeneutics.[102] In sum, Kwok posits ethical criteria, as do Schüssler Fiorenza and Fulkerson, to judge biblical interpretations and theological methods. They must contribute to the liberation and humanization of the global community, emphasizing freedom, justice, peace, and reconciliation.[103]

Community and Diversity

The *minjung* communities have helped to shape Kwok's ethical criteria. *Minjung* is a Korean term consisting of two Chinese characters which mean the common people, or the masses, who are subjugated or ruled. By focusing on the *minjung* communities, Kwok is able to highlight the biblical interpretations of women and ethnic minorities.[104] They have also helped her to realize a significant difference in her ethical criteria from those of Schüssler Fiorenza and Fulkerson. While Kwok is careful to honour groups of people who are most vulnerable and silenced, she takes issues with the epistemological privilege of the oppressed and feminist standpoint theory.

In her later work she challenges the belief that Third World people, the poor and the marginalized have an *a priori* privilege of biblical interpretation. This concept of epistemological privilege assumes that the marginalized or contemporary "natives" share common experiences with the marginalized or "natives" of the biblical texts, thereby increasing the ability of today's marginalized to understand and identify with these texts. Kwok suggests that such identification fails to appreciate the construction of the "native," overlooks the dissimilarities between the historical development of the Palestinian societies and our own, assumes that only authentic "natives" can understand the Bible, and claims a fundamental distinction between Caucasian societies and "native" societies. These problems "commit the sin of Orientalism" by collapsing "native" into one category and ignoring the varied social and historical constructions of each society. They also perpetuate the sharp and false distinction between Caucasian and all other societies. Although Caucasian cultures constructed white supremacy, they are not "fundamentally different" from all others. This assumption only serves to strengthen the "we-they dichotomy that has given such power to the white people."[105] The epistemological privilege of the oppressed also assumes that one is either the oppressed or the oppressor, without realizing that multiple identities create a mix of privilege and marginalization. "The Other is never a homogeneous group; there is always the Other within the Other."[106] Full appreciation of the diversity of the marginalized means that we will need to move beyond this type of identification.

As an alternative, Kwok agrees with Fulkerson and Rebecca Chopp that knowledge and experience be understood through social construction, rather than through standpoint theory. This places an emphasis upon the communal construction of knowledge and experience.[107] On this basis, Kwok calls for new faith communities which will honour inclusivity, mutuality and solidarity. Together with Chopp, she challenges the church to model such communities for the sake of the world.[108] These communities are not to remain isolated in their diversity, however. Kwok refers to John S. Pobee's process of building a community of communities. In order to have a global consciousness, diverse communities must also envision and work towards a wider community constituting the body of Christ.[109] Thus, the plurality which her method celebrates serves not to thwart Christian unity, but enrich it with more genuine authenticity.[110]

According to Kwok, solidarity is one of the means by which this global community can be formed. Through an etymological study of the word "solidarity," Kwok demonstrates the combined influence of western and eastern connotations of this term. The French word, *solidarité*, originally meant a natural bonding of people from the same background. Marx introduced a political twist by defining it as the self-organization of the oppressed. European and North American usages have continued to stress its connotation of justice. The Indonesian term means "faithful to a friend." In Korean it means "binding everyone in a circle" and in Chinese it means "identifying as the same." Thus, the Asian usages have stressed the interconnection of everything. Building upon these Asian usages, Kwok calls the Church to be in solidarity with the people and all of creation. At the same time she cautions against the "clichéd rhetoric of solidarity" which does not put speech into action.[111]

With her call to solidarity, she stresses that the Church and theological institutions must shift their theological orientation from ecclesial-centered to people-centred.[112] In a later writing Kwok shifts her position slightly by suggesting that Christianity should move from anthropocentrism to bio-centrism.[113]Kwok challenges the Church to enter into an ecological solidarity which will observe the goals of the World Council of Churches' (WCC) Ecumenical Decade of Churches in Solidarity with Women In Church and Society, and the WCC's call for justice, peace, and the integrity of creation. Through these goals diversity will be recognized and mutual responsibility will replace scapegoating and victimization. The interconnection of multiple oppressions and identities will also be made, thus envisioning the unity of the global Christian community amidst the diversity of the local communities.

Dialogical Imagination and the Performance of the Talking Book

Within these justice-seeking faith communities, Kwok proposes a model of biblical interpretation. With reference to the critical role Schüssler Fiorenza gives ekklēsia of wo/men, Kwok locates the "critical principle of interpretation" not in the Bible, but in the communities of women and men who are reading the Bible with "dialogical imagination" for their own liberation.[114] Influenced by M. M. Bakhtin's *Dialogic Imagination*, Kwok has coined the term "dialogical imagination" to describe her method of biblical interpretation that honours intra- and intercommunal dialogue.[115] The Chinese characters for dialogue imply "mutuality, active listening, and openness to what one's partner has to say."[116] By imagination Kwok means "a consciousness of conflict ... a pause, the finding of a new image, the repatterning of reality, and interpretation."[117] Conflict is inevitable for Asian Christians because of the clash between the western imbued biblical interpretation that they have inherited and their own Asian reality. Therefore new images and interpretations forged through an imaginative dialogical process between biblical traditions and people with other religious and cultural traditions are necessary.[118]

Kwok's process of dialogical imagination considers not only the written text, but the discussion of it in different dialects. It invites dialogue with many different scriptures and takes a "multiaxial" approach that analyzes the intersection of race, class, gender, culture and history. This approach emphasizes a democratic process that welcomes the voices of the marginalized and works towards a just and inclusive community.[119] Bakhtin's work on dialogism and heteroglossia gives a helpful basis for this approach. He explains that the internal divisions of one language into social dialects are dependent upon class, religion, generation, region, and profession. His term "dialogism" refers to the mixing of the speakers and listeners' intentions within the mix of social dialects.[120]

By expanding this concept to the church and biblical interpretation, a dialectical approach, indicating discourse between polarities, is replaced by a dialogical one, indicating multiple discourses which are both convergent and disparate.[121] Kwok suggests that a dialogical model of biblical interpretation will examine the multiplicity of interpretations that arise out of particular communities which in turn are differentiated by identities such as race, class, culture and sexual orientation. She refers to Fulkerson's insistence that certain groups of people, such as women, do not speak with one voice.[122] A dialogical model listens to marginalized voices and insists that dialogue must take place not only amongst Christian communities but with *human* communities of all faiths. This will more accurately reflect the multiple identities of all people, and particularly Asians who live in a multiscriptural context. Instead of approaching biblical interpretation from a singular perspective, such as gender, race or class, Kwok insists that the intersection of multiple identities and contexts be considered. In sum, her dialogical model "emphasizes plurality of meanings, multiplicity of narratives, and a multiaxial framework of analysis."[123]

Based on this dialogical model, Kwok suggests viewing the Bible as a "talking book." She borrows this term from Henry Louis Gates who uses it to describe African American literature. He demonstrates how African Americans used the same language and books, including the Bible, as the white "masters" used, but changed the signifying practices in a subversive way. By referring to the Bible as a talking book, Kwok emphasizes the subversive and imaginative readings of the Bible by marginalized and colonized communities.[124]

Kwok distinguishes this image of the Bible from others that have been prominent at different times. The doctrinal model views the Bible as the Word of God, emphasizing verbal inspiration and the revelation of God speaking through the text. Interaction with the Bible becomes a monologue of listening and obedience with no allowance for historical and communal constructions of meaning. Another image given by the historical-critical method views the Bible as an historic document which allows dialogue, but is more concerned with the past than the present. It focuses more upon "diachronic dialogue"(historical development) than "synchronic" (thematic development). Elisabeth Schüssler Fiorenza's image of the Bible as an historical prototype recognizes the historical context of the Bible while shifting concern to a contemporary liberationist reading. However, Kwok wonders if her debate with historical positivists and apolitical postmodernists is relevant for people from other cultural contexts. Asian peoples have been more interested in religious and moral insights gleaned from scriptures than historical truth. African American women have been more concerned with the relation of the Bible to their daily lives than its historical context. Kwok also questions Schüssler Fiorenza's inattention to the participation of poor women and slave women in the "discipleship of equals."[125] Without this information, Kwok cautions against using the Bible as a historical prototype.[126]

In contrast to these images of the Bible, the concept of a talking book emphasizes the oral transmission of scripture. Kwok notes that this mode has been prevalent not only in Asia but, until the last two centuries, in the West as well. Before Gutenberg's invention of movable type, accessibility to the biblical text was restricted to ecclesial leaders who alone produced its meaning within the interests of their privileged positions. While the common people engaged in oral transmission of the texts, the official and thereby correct interpretations and meanings were produced apart from these common transmissions. The people would also have been limited in their aural reception of the text by the liturgical readings. They would only hear parts of scripture chosen to support particular doctrines or principles.

Even though there has been a rise in literacy in the west, I hunch that the oral transmission of scripture is becoming once again the dominant mode within mainstream Protestant churches. I have found that the more liberal western Protestant churches are reverting back to the oral transmission of scripture as the primary mode, in part because of little interest in Bible Study or devotions. The Bible as talking book is therefore an apt description for western, mainstream Protestant churches.

Kwok's term "talking book" intentionally shifts authority away from the written text to the interpretive community. They now control the production and evaluation of its meaning. Emphasis upon the oral transmission of the talking book also better enables marginalized voices to contribute to its meaning and evaluation.[127] Along with Fulkerson, Kwok realizes the importance of the performance of scripture through oral transmission for marginalized communities.[128]

Kwok is not rejecting a focus upon the written text, but simply wants to affirm the importance and validity of oral transmission. She observes a class difference in the particular approaches Asian women take towards the Bible. Women who have received theological training tend to focus upon the written text and western hermeneutical methods while the majority of Asian women focus upon oral transmission, using "free association and creative retelling of biblical stories to appropriate the Bible in their life situations."[129] Kwok acknowledges that both approaches are important. Academic study of the written text helps to unveil its androcentric bias, while a recognition of oral transmission and performative reconstruction of scripture allows the interpretations of the *minjung* communities to be heard.

In order to honour the oral reading traditions of Third World people who have little access to the written text, Kwok develops three strategies of oral hermeneutics for Asian women.[130] All require a "passionate spirituality" that is embodied, politically active, erotic, and awe-struck before the wonders of God's creation.[131] The first strategy is to re-imagine and dramatize women of the Bible as speaking subjects. Another strategy is to expand upon these stories and reconstruct them. This is common for folk traditions in India, in which epics put to song add characters and incidents to the stories in the Sanskrit texts. The third strategy blends different narratives to construct a new meaning. Biblical stories are read simultaneously with other narratives. Kwok gives an example of her transposition of the biblical stories of women in Jesus' ministry and passion with the story of the students massacred at Tiananmen Square. These three strategies of oral representation retell the story "in *one's own words*, transforming an external authoritative discourse into an internally persuasive discourse."[132]

Along with Schüssler Fiorenza, Kwok names this approach as rhetorical. She agrees with both Mieke Bal and Schüssler Fiorenza in their insistence that the text is not a window to reality, but is a narrative construction. The goal of biblical hermeneutics is therefore not to uncover historical reality and the truth, but to determine colonialist biases, and uplift interpretations that have emerged from *minjung* communities. From these marginalized interpretations comes the radical call to discipleship and to the transformation of our global community. Third World women and men who have heeded this biblical call and endured tremendous suffering ask all of us: "What price have you paid in your study of the Bible?"[133]

Conclusion

Kwok convincingly demonstrates the colonizing impact of modernity, especially through its historical-critical method, and of liberalism, both of which have contributed to identity politics. As an alternative she proposes a multifaith hermeneutics that can best address the multifaith context of Asian people. This involves the use of multicultural and multifaith theological data, impacting the conception of truth and authority which in turn impacts her understanding of revelation and the biblical canon. Kwok prefers the eastern, pragmatic conception of truth over against the western, ontological controversies. By extension, she suggests that revelation be understood as God's truth revealed through an enacted biblical tradition, rather than as a hidden, metaphysical truth contained within the Bible. She also suggests that revelation be centred on the interpretive community, rather than the biblical text. This emphasizes the interaction of the community with the Bible as well as with the scriptures from other faith traditions. Because of her concern with marginalized voices excluded from the formation of the biblical canon, and with the historical use of the canon to control and denigrate Asian cultures and women, she suggests dispensing entirely with this concept. At the same time, she recognizes the importance of the Bible for *minjung* communities. Thus, it is not the biblical text which she rejects, but the authoritative status given it.

Kwok draws on postcolonial and postmodern theories to expose the imperial interests of universalizing, western hermeneutics, and to underscore the multiple, shifting identities of faith communities, as well as the diverse, multiple meanings that each community constructs out of their interaction with scripture. While she respects the diversity of the communities and the texts, she is critical of an absolute relativity of their faith practices and interpretations. She realizes the need for global, ethical criteria that can assist in the public accountability of each community as it works toward solidarity for the liberation and humanization of the global community. As a postcolonial feminist, Kwok is particularly concerned with the multiple intersection of oppressions based on gender, race, class, militarism, and colonialism.[134]

Within these justice-seeking communities, Kwok proposes a model of dialogical imagination that will engage the multiple identities of people and communities around the world with their multiplicity of biblical interpretations. She suggests that the Bible be viewed as a talking book in order to highlight the subversive and imaginative readings of the Bible by marginalized and colonized communities, and to emphasize the importance of its oral transmission and performance.

Like Schüssler Fiorenza and Fulkerson, Kwok is dancing on the edge of modernity and postmodernity. She is calling for a new time frame on the margins of both that will more adequately address postcolonialist concerns and bring forth a plurality of meanings, a multiplicity of narratives and a multiaxial framework of analysis.

Notes to Chapter 4

1. Kwok Pui-lan, "The Emergence of Asian Feminist Consciousness of Culture and Theology," in *We Dare to Dream: Doing Theology as Asian Women*, ed. Virginia Fabella and Sun Ai Lee Park (Hong Kong: Asian Women's Resource Centre for Culture and Theology, 1989), 97.

2. Kwok Pui-lan, *Discovering the Bible in the Non-Biblical World*, The Bible and Liberation Series (Maryknoll: Orbis Books, 1995), ix, 6; Kwok Pui-lan, "The Global Challenge," in *Christianity and Civil Society: Theological Education for Public Life*, ed. Rodney L. Petersen (Maryknoll: Orbis Books, 1995), 138.

3. Kwok Pui-lan, "The Future of Feminist Theology: An Asian Perspective," in *Feminist Theology from the Third World*, ed. Ursula King (London: Society for Promoting Christian Knowledge, 1994), 65; see also Kwok Pui-lan, *Introducing Asian Feminist Theology*, Introductions in Feminist Theology Series (Cleveland: Pilgrim Press, 2000), 9–10.

4. Kwok borrows the term "outsider-within" from African American feminist theorist Patricia Hill Collins. See Kwok Pui-lan, "Speaking from the Margins," *Journal of Feminist Studies in Religion* 8, no. 2 (Fall 1992): 103–04.

5. Kwok, *Discovering the Bible*, 6.

6. Kwok, "Speaking from the Margins," 104.

7. Kwok, *Discovering the Bible*, 1–2.

8. Kwok, *Discovering the Bible*, 4.

9. Kwok, *Introducing Asian Feminist Theology*, 27.

10. Kwok, *Discovering the Bible*, 4.

11. Kwok Pui-lan, "The Sources and Resources of Feminist Theologies: A Post-Colonial Perspective," in *Sources and Resources of Feminist Theologies*, ed. Elisabeth Hartlieb and Charlotte Methuen, Yearbook of the European Society of Women in Theological Research, vol. 5 (Kampen: Kok Pharos Publishing House, 1997), 6.

12. See in particular "The Sources and Resources of Feminist Theologies," and Kwok Pui-lan, "Jesus/The Native: Biblical Studies from a Postcolonial Perspective," in *Teaching the Bible: The Discourses and Politics of Biblical Pedagogy*, edited by Fernando F. Segovia and Mary Ann Tolbert (Maryknoll: Orbis Books, 1998).

13. Kwok, *Discovering the Bible*, 3.

14. Kwok, *Discovering the Bible*, 8.

15. Kwok, *Introducing Asian Feminist Theology*, 35.

16. Kwok Pui-lan, "Response to the *Semeia* Volume on Postcolonial Criticism," *Semeia* 75 (1996): 215–216.

17. Kwok Pui-lan, "Mothers and Daughters, Writers and Fighters," in *Inheriting Our Mothers' Gardens: Feminist Theology in Third World Perspective*, ed. Letty Russell, Pui-lan Kwok, Ada María Isasi-Díaz and Katie Geneva Cannon (Louisville: The Westminster Press, 1988), 31.

18. Kwok, *Discovering the Bible*, 23.

19. Kwok, "Emergence of Asian Feminist Consciousness," 93.

20. Kwok, "Emergence of Asian Feminist Consciousness," 93–94.

21. Kwok refers to Mary John Mananzan's assertion that Philippine women received a higher societal status before the introduction of Catholicism. See Kwok Pui-lan, "The Image of the 'White Lady:' Gender and Race in Christian Mission," in *The Special Nature of Women?* ed. Anne Carr and Elisabeth Schüssler Fiorenza, Concilium Series (London: SCM Press, 1991), 25.

22. Kwok, "Mothers and Daughters," 30–31.

23. Kwok refers to Renita Weems and Brian Blount. See Kwok, "Jesus/The Native," 8.

24. Kwok, *Discovering the Bible*, 27.

25. Kwok, *Discovering the Bible*, 27.

26. Kwok Pui-lan, "The Feminist Hermeneutics of Elizabeth Schüssler Fiorenza: An Asian Response," *East Asia Journal of Theology* 3, no. 2 (October 1985): 148.

27. Kwok, "The Feminist Hermeneutics of Elizabeth Schüssler Fiorenza," 148.

28. Kwok, "Jesus/The Native," 75.

29. Kwok, "Jesus/The Native," 70.

30. Kwok, "Jesus/The Native," 70.

31. Kwok, "Jesus/The Native," 71–72.

32. Kwok, "Jesus/The Native," 76–79; Kwok, *Introducing Asian Feminist Theology*, 45.

33. Kwok, "Jesus/The Native," 81.

34. Kwok, "Jesus/The Native," 82.

35. Kwok, *Discovering the Bible*, 86.

36. Kwok, *Introducing Asian Feminist Theology*, 45.

37. Kwok, *Discovering the Bible*, 2–3.

38. Kwok, "Jesus/The Native," 83.

39. Kwok takes the term "parallel processing" from computer systems. See Kwok, "Jesus/The Native," 80.

40. Kwok, "Jesus/The Native," 80.

41. Kwok, "Jesus/The Native," 83.

42. Kwok, *Discovering the Bible*, 24–25.

43. Kwok, "The Image of the 'White Lady,' " 25; Kwok, *Discovering the Bible*, 25.

44. Kwok, *Discovering the Bible*, 79.

45. Kwok, "The Image of the 'White Lady,' " 26.

46. Kwok, "The Image of the 'White Lady,' " 26.

47. Kwok, "Jesus/The Native," 81.

48. Kwok, *Introducing Asian Feminist Theology*, 19.

49. Kwok, *Discovering the Bible*, 24.

50. Kwok, *Discovering the Bible*, 25–26.

51. Kwok, *Discovering the Bible*, 38.

52. Kwok, "Response to Archie Lee's Paper on 'Biblical Interpretation in Postcolonial Hong Kong,' " *Biblical Interpretation* 7 (April, 1999), 186.

53. Kwok, *Discovering the Bible*, 26–27, 79.

54. Kwok, "Mothers and Daughters," 21, 31.

55. Kwok, *Discovering the Bible*, 92–93.

56. Kwok Pui-lan, "Gospel and Culture," *Christianity and Crisis* 51, no. 10/11 (July 15 1991): 223.

57. Kwok Pui-lan, *Chinese Women and Christianity: 1860-1927*, ed. Susan Thistlethwaite, American Academy of Religion Academy Series, No. 75 (Atlanta: Scholars Press, 1992), 31–38.

58. Kwok, "Mothers and Daughters," 31.

59. Kwok, "Mothers and Daughters," 31.

60. "Survival-liberation centered syncretism" is Chung Hyun Kyung's term used in her book *Struggle to Be the Sun Again*, quoted by Kwok. See Kwok, "The Global Challenge," 142.

61. Kwok, "Mothers and Daughters," 27.

62. Kwok Pui-lan, "The Mission of God in Asia and Theological Education," *Ministerial Formation*, no. 48 (January 1990): 21.

63. Kwok, "Mothers and Daughters," 27–30; Kwok, "Emergence of Asian Feminist Consciousness," 97–98; Kwok, *Discovering the Bible*, 14. For a detailed elaboration of these sources see Kwok Pui-lan, "Chinese Women and Protestant Christianity at the Turn of the Twentieth Century," In *Christianity in China: From the Eighteenth Century to the Present*, edited by Daniel H. Bays (Stanford: Stanford University Press, 1996), 196–99.

64. Kwok gives examples of these sources used by C. S. Song, Archie Lee, Padma Gallup, Nantawan Boonprasat Lewis, Cyris H. S. Moon, Ahn Byung Mu and Lee Sung Hee. See Kwok, *Discovering the Bible*, 13–16.

65. Kwok Pui-lan, "Meditation," *One World*, no. 155 (May 1990): 15.

66. Kwok, *Discovering the Bible*, 67; Kwok, "Emergence of Asian Feminist Consciousness," 98.

67. Kwok, *Discovering the Bible*, 57–58.

68. Kwok, "Emergence of Asian Feminist Consciousness," 98.

69. Kwok, "Mothers and Daughters," 29–30.

70. Kwok, *Discovering the Bible*, 11.

71. Kwok, *Introducing Asian Feminist Theology*, 43.

72. Kwok, *Discovering the Bible*, 57–58.

73. Kwok, *Discovering the Bible*, 35.

74. Kwok, *Discovering the Bible*, 34.

75. Kwok, *Discovering the Bible*, 35–36.

76. Kwok, *Discovering the Bible*, 36.

77. Kwok, *Discovering the Bible*, 11.

78. Kwok, *Discovering the Bible*, 12.

79. For a helpful delineation between the Word of God and the word of God, see the second chapter of Sandra M. Schneiders, *The Revelatory Text: Interpreting the New Testament as Sacred Scripture* (San Francisco: Harper, 1991).

80. Kwok, *Discovering the Bible*, 16–17.

81. Kwok, *Discovering the Bible*, 21–23.

82. Kwok, *Discovering the Bible*, 44–56.

83. Kwok, *Discovering the Bible*, 23.

84. Kwok, *Discovering the Bible*, 9.

85. Kwok, *Discovering the Bible*, 10.

86. Kwok, *Discovering the Bible*, xiii.

87. Kwok, *Discovering the Bible*, 10.

88. Kwok, "The Sources and Resources of Feminist Theologies," 15; and Kwok, "The Future of Feminist Theology," 68.

89. Kwok, *Introducing Asian Feminist Theology*, 79–80.

90. Kwok, "Ecology and Christology," *Feminist Theology* 15 (May, 1997).

91. Kwok, "Ecology and Christology," 121–25.

92. Kwok, *Discovering the Bible*, 17, 49.

93. Kwok, *Discovering the Bible*, 10.

94. Kwok, *Discovering the Bible*, 17–18.

95. Kwok, *Discovering the Bible*, 18–19.

96. Kwok, *Discovering the Bible*, 11.

97. Kwok, *Discovering the Bible*, 39–40.

98. Kwok, *Discovering the Bible*, 40.

99. Kwok, *Discovering the Bible*, 19.

100. Kwok, *Discovering the Bible*, 23.

101. Kwok, *Discovering the Bible*, 31.

102. Kwok, *Discovering the Bible*, 84–95.

103. Kwok, "Mothers and Daughters," 32–33.

104. Kwok, *Discovering the Bible*, 15–16, 18–19.

105. Kwok, "Jesus/The Native," 82.

106. Kwok, *Discovering the Bible*, 82; Kwok, "The Sources and Resources of Feminist Theologies," 78.

107. Kwok, *Introducing Asian Feminist Theology*, 39.

108. Kwok, "The Global Challenge," 141.

109. Kwok, "The Global Challenge," 141.

110. Kwok, "Mothers and Daughters," 32–33.

111. Kwok, "The Sources and Resources of Feminist Theologies," 13.

112. Kwok, "The Mission of God in Asia," 21, 23.

113. Kwok Pui-lan, "Ecology and the Recycling of Christianity," in *Ecotheology: Voices from South and North*, ed. David G. Hallman (Geneva: World Council of Churches, 1994), 110–11.

114. Kwok, *Discovering the Bible*, 19.

115. See Chapter Three, especially footnote 11 of Kwok, *Discovering the Bible*, 32–34, 108.

116. Kwok, *Discovering the Bible*, 12.

117. Kwok derives this process of creative imagination from Sharon Parks. See Kwok, *Discovering the Bible*, 13.

118. Although Kwok uses the term "dialectical" in one chapter of *Discovering the Bible*, she recommends replacing it with the term "dialogical" in another chapter of the same book, as I indicate in the following paragraph. This confusion may have resulted because the chapters were written at different times as separate articles, and later complied into one book. See Kwok, *Discovering the Bible*, 12–13, 37.

119. Kwok, *Discovering the Bible*, 36.

120. Kwok, *Discovering the Bible*, 37.

121. Kwok refers to Evelyn Brooks Higginbotham's extension of Bakhtin's work to the church as a dialogical model. See Kwok, *Discovering the Bible*, 37.

122. Kwok, *Discovering the Bible*, 37.

123. Kwok, *Discovering the Bible*, 37–40.

124. Kwok, *Discovering the Bible*, 42.

125. Kwok, "The Feminist Hermeneutics of Elizabeth Schüssler Fiorenza," 147–53.

126. Kwok, *Discovering the Bible*, 40–42.

127. Kwok, *Discovering the Bible*, 42.

128. Kwok, *Discovering the Bible*, 51.

129. Kwok, *Discovering the Bible*, 48–49.

130. Kwok, *Discovering the Bible*, 52–56.

131. Kwok, "Ecology and the Recycling of Christianity," 110.

132. Kwok describes this process in Bakhtin's terms. See Kwok, *Discovering the Bible*, 55.

133. Kwok, *Discovering the Bible*, 95.

134. Kwok, *Introducing Asian Feminist Theology*, 46.

Chapter 5

Postliberal Response: Kathryn Tanner

"The Moderns quarrel with the Ancients because of what now seems to be the latter's intolerable and offensive penchant for the dark density of ambiguous and polysemous discourse, for the concentric circularity and random inclusiveness of orderings according to resemblance ... The task of the new philosophy is to shear through with quick, clean strokes the 'cunning cobweb contextures' which traditional learning spins, circle inside circle."

—Kathryn Tanner, *God and Creation in Christian Theology*

Kathryn Tanner is an American Episcopalian theologian who studied and taught at Yale University before moving to her current teaching position at the Divinity School of the University of Chicago. Her work shows influences of the "Yale School,"[1] as espoused by Hans Frei and George Lindbeck whose works have been described by many as "postliberal,"[2] or in one case as "post-postmodern."[3] As with postliberals, Tanner is primarily concerned with mainstream Christian beliefs as they are practised within faith communities. She entertains an internal critique in which she uses certain Christian beliefs and the biblical canon to critique other Christian beliefs and practices. To conduct this internal critique, she employs the use of grammatical rules, as developed by Lindbeck. Because of these similarities with postliberalism, I have called Tanner's approach postliberal, even though she does not use this term to describe her own work. In her more recent work dating back to 1997, with the exception of one article, she has distanced herself from some aspects of postliberal approaches, and from her own use of rules to determine proper Christian belief.[4] Although she is beginning to identify herself more closely with postmodern approaches, I am still retaining postliberal as a description of her work in order to highlight her continued emphasis on an internal critique within mainstream Christian beliefs and her use of canonical criticism, as will be explained below.

Even though I am convinced that postliberal aspects in Tanner's work continue to distinguish her work from the other three feminists, it bears repeating that all four feminists transgress boundaries in their interdisciplinary approaches and cross over into each other's categories. Thus, even in her earlier work, Tanner refers to postmodern criticism of modern philosophical approaches. In this respect, she intimates some affinity with Michel Foucault, Jacques Derrida, and Richard Rorty.[5] She is also very clear that social location and cultural production inform the theology of both faith communities and academic theologians (popular and elite theologies).[6]

As with Schüssler Fiorenza, Fulkerson, and Kwok, Tanner brings a deep concern for justice and liberation to her work. Unlike Schüssler Fiorenza and Kwok, her focus is not on communities marginalized from the dominant Christian traditions, nor is it on Fulkerson's emphasis on communities marginalized by feminist theologies. Rather, she has made a political choice to concentrate on mainstream Christian traditions in order to demonstrate their radical, liberative potential in challenging the political status quo. Her own personal involvement in the feminist and gay liberation movements attests to her political commitment.

One of Tanner's concerns is with the tendency of modern theologies to misinterpret Christian beliefs. As a result, minority opinions have been sacrificed and colonialist theology has been perpetuated. Although she recognizes the history of abuse accompanying the Christian tradition, she is convinced that a Christian theology advocating social justice is best supported by using Christian traditions to critique the abuses instead of revising the traditions themselves.

If Christian beliefs are interpreted and enacted "properly,"[7] Tanner suggests they will be "self-critical, pluralistic, and viable across a wide range of geographical differences and historical changes of circumstance."[8] The role of diverse Christian communities is integral in this interpretive task. In order to examine this role, Tanner emphasizes the importance of interdisciplinary analysis, giving particular attention to sociology and anthropology as they inform cultural theory.

Critique of Modernity and Liberalism

Tanner believes that modern approaches to theology have contributed to the apparent incoherence of traditional Christian beliefs, as well as factionalism between Protestants and Roman Catholics.[9] Differences of belief have been challenged to a contest of the most objective and therefore the most factual and true account. By exposing certain modern assumptions as historically and culturally conditioned, Tanner hopes to recover the coherence and "correct assessment"[10] of Christian traditions, and establish their political support for diversity and the liberation of the oppressed. She does not accept traditional theology uncritically, as she believes that pre-modern theology should not be privileged, nor viewed as pure.[11] In fact she speaks strongly against the abuses towards which pre-modern theologies have contributed. While recovering the coherence of traditional Christian theology, she wants to challenge both the closure of modern viewpoints and the common pre-modern alignment of traditional beliefs with conservative politics of domination.

Decontextualization and Referentiality

One of the difficulties with modernity is its tendency to decontextualize beliefs and view them as referential descriptions of reality. Tanner takes issue with modern philosophical tendencies to isolate a particular belief "for identification of its meaning or reference, experiential expressiveness, rational justification, or evidential support."[12] The assumption behind these tendencies is that it is possible to remove oneself and the subject matter from prejudice and past traditions. Tanner believes, along with Schüssler Fiorenza, Fulkerson and Kwok, that this is impossible and undesirable. She, too, reveals the fallacy of a neutral and objective Cartesian standpoint.[13] By separating individuals from their "social, cosmic and divine relationships" modern approaches set them against their social and historical contexts. "Persons are no longer essentially parts of a whole society, no longer reflections of a world formed by repeated patterns of resemblance."[14] The intent of the modern interpreter, strongly influenced by Descartes and Locke, is to strip away the incidentals and uncover "the facts" or core elements. It is to discover and represent the world in itself, as it really is, free from the biases of traditional beliefs and external authorities. The desire to control and predict phenomena encourages universal generalizations and principles, and minimizes or eliminates varying particularities. Subjects of inquiry are stratified into primary essences and secondary variables of human affection, volition and relations. Clear, linear, stratified abstractions replace complex, holistic ambiguities. In these empirical abstractions modern methods of analysis are also deemed neutral.[15]

Tanner suggests that these characteristics of the modern scientific method have contributed to the distortions of Christian theology. These include mind/body, fact/value dualisms and the belief that certain domains are autonomous and separate from divine power. Divine order is separated from the natural order, and individuals are considered independent from external powers and constraints. Traditional rules about the sovereignty of God and human agency are subverted. They can no longer be held together; belief in one can only be affirmed at the expense of the other.[16]

When theological rules are decontextualized, their historical and geographical location, as well as their communal use, is ignored. Statements of belief tend to be viewed as simple references to reality, rather than rhetorical responses to particular situations. In this aspect, Tanner supports Schüssler Fiorenza's rhetorical approach to early Christian texts. Rather than providing a simple description of reality, theological statements reflect the concerns of a particular community or theologian. They often arise as a corrective to theological trends deemed heretical. Tanner suggests that if these statements are separated from this context, they cannot be held in tension with the opposing trends, and may well become heretical in themselves. For instance, if an emphasis made upon God's sovereignty is absolutized as an ontological, referential description and removed from its rhetorical tension with human agency, it may never be possible to speak coherently of human freedom and power.[17]

Two consequences of referentiality are positivism and reification. Tanner defines positivism as the identification of *de facto* norms (acceptable behaviour within a particular situation) with *de jure* norms (what is genuinely right).[18] Little attention is given to the social location of norms, leading to universal pronouncements that may prove injurious in other locales. Humanly created, situation-specific statements become God-given ontological descriptions that are then considered beyond critique. Moral realists have attempted to avoid positivism by basing universal norms upon areas outside of human variability, such as the created order or natural law. However, Tanner notes that these areas are also influenced by humanity.[19] Moral realists simply contribute to positivism by identifying certain orders of human relations, such as the family or the state, or certain "natural human tendencies" with divinely-created reality.[20]

The second consequence of referentiality is reification. When certain norms, relations, behaviours or theological statements are understood as ontological descriptions of divinely-created reality, they are separated from other aspects of human existence. By isolating particular elements as independent units of analysis, modern theology tends to reify these elements into essentialized categories. Each category is viewed as complete in itself and only secondarily related in a linear fashion to the others. Thus, creatures are understood as independent beings related only externally to God. They are identified by their core essence and roles, and are only secondarily affected by God's actions. As an example, Tanner cites a Protestant tendency to separate the utterly corrupt human order from God's transcendent realm. While this was indicative of some of the early reformers, I would add that liberal Protestantism has countered this with an elevation of human goodness. In both cases, however, there is a tendency to separate the human domain from the divine. Tanner also refers to the common "distortion" of modern theologians who claim that God works alongside humanity as a partial, not complete, cause. All of these examples are instances of Pelagian distortions claiming some degree of independence from God.[21]

When theological statements are understood as ontological descriptions of a reified essence, combining the two problems of referentiality and reification, theological distortions are intensified. If humanity's sinfulness is understood as an ontological statement of the essence of human nature, humanity will be essentially corrupt. No remedy is possible even by God, as the removal of sin will remove a necessary part of that which defines humanity as human.[22]

Totalitarianism

Essentialism is particularly problematic regarding diversity and domination. Universalism and essentialism negate the diverse identities of minorities.[23] Standards posited as universals reflect the identity of the group positing them, which is usually straight, white, middle-class and male. This becomes apparent when other groups, such as people of colour, gay men, or women, need to deny their own particularity in order to appropriate these standards. Anything deemed characteristic of marginalized identities is considered peripheral at best. Thus, an inner essence of human quality is distinguished from non-essential qualities, which all but the original group need to renounce. Only the original group's particularity converges with the inner essence that they have reified and raised to a universal standard. Others are accepted only when they conform to this identity of the dominant group. Any difference between them and the dominant group is absolutized and devalued while differences amongst the non-dominant groups are ignored.[24] Tanner names this as a "peculiar dialectic of identity and difference,"[25] or more specifically as totalitarianism.[26] This is similar to the identity politics and the logic of identity described by Schüssler Fiorenza, Fulkerson and Kwok.

One aspect of this dialectic of identity and difference that Tanner examines is colonialism. She suggests that the liberal, pluralist approaches to inter-religious dialogue are colonialist. The generalized commonalities from which they begin their dialogue with others face the same problems arising from universalized norms. Both emphasize conformity to universal standards and devalue difference. Both arise out of particular interests and identities of a dominant group, but are assumed to represent all people and their religions around the globe. Even though pluralists attempt to choose standards of respect that are found in every religion, their choice is influenced by their own historical, religious and cultural location. Commonalities which should only arise out of dialogue are preformed as conditions for dialogue with no attention to power imbalances between dialogue partners. Tanner notes that this is particularly problematic for Christians, as we have been most at fault historically for imposing our assumptions and will upon others, thus contributing to imperialist and colonialist abuses.[27]

Edward Said, whose work has been instrumental for postcolonialists such as Kwok, is also influential in Tanner's work. Accordingly, Tanner's postcolonial critique of liberal, modern approaches is similar to Kwok's. Tanner echoes Kwok's concern that western Christian proposals of universal standards of respect for dialogue force others to conform to these standards, thereby "meeting a condition of sameness or identity." Any divergence from these standards is consequently ignored or disparaged. People and their opinions are differentiated on the basis of these standards and thus on their similarity to those who have proposed them. We are all forced into "us" and "them" categories, which absolutizes particular differences and occludes others. Assumed commonalities are essentialized. Such an approach also justifies aggression, based upon moral superiority, towards those who do not exhibit these particular standards. Beneath the guise of moral superiority lies a superiority of power that enables dominant groups to establish universal standards against which others are measured.[28]

This unacknowledged power differential is characteristic of what Tanner refers to as "a liberal theory of rights."[29] An emphasis on equal treatment of every individual assumes everyone has equal access to this treatment. It assumes that oppression will be eliminated if the personal spaces of the oppressed are protected from willful interference. Such assumptions ignore the institutionalized sources of oppression and their internalized perpetuation within the lives of the oppressed. They also ignore the diversity of the oppressed and the oppressor. In addition, they ignore the impact of social relations. Liberal approaches emphasize the individual at the expense of the community.[30]

While Tanner emphasizes equal rights due each individual as a creature of God, she is careful to avoid these liberal pitfalls. Her theological method attends to the diversity of individuals as well as their communal identities. Their social location and welfare are integral to her theological claims.

Theological Method

As with Schüssler Fiorenza, Fulkerson and Kwok, Tanner takes an explicitly liberationist tack in her work. By incorporating mainstream Christian beliefs into a liberation theology, she counters the alliance of mainstream Christian beliefs with right-wing agendas and the patriarchal status quo.[31] Should she be accused of "tampering with the faith for political ends" she can "claim to be at least as conservative of that faith as they are."[32] Thus, Tanner seeks to demonstrate the radical political import of traditional Christian doctrine. While this goal is not new, as evidenced by the social gospel movement amongst others, Tanner's approach attempts to correct the modern and liberal fallacies of previous prophetic challenges to injustice.[33]

Rules and Style

There has been a noticeable shift in Tanner's work concerning the method by which she examines traditional Christian doctrine. In her earlier work she recommends doctrinal rules by which the proper interpretation of Christian belief and practice can be assessed. In her later work she questions this postliberal approach and suggests that the style or manner in which Christian material is used replace the concept of rules. Instead of focusing on the meaning of fundamental beliefs or rules, she is now beginning to focus on the manner in which these beliefs are incorporated with other beliefs and practices. In order to demonstrate this shift, I will first describe Tanner's earlier emphasis upon grammatical rules. Following this, I will describe her shift to style.

In Tanner's earlier work, she upholds two doctrines that she considers "fundamental" to the Christian faith and social justice: God's transcendence and God's universal providential agency. She agrees with Ian Ramsey, Bernard Lonergan and George Lindbeck that there are additional Trinitarian and christological rules from the early church's creeds and conciliar formulas but she chooses to limit her focus to these two rules.[34] She chooses these because she considers them to be presupposed by most other Christian beliefs and because they have great practical potential for challenging the status quo.[35]

Throughout Tanner's work she emphasizes the transcendence of God the Creator with little mention of the incarnation. Perhaps this is to counterbalance modernity's overemphasis on the immanence of God at the expense of God's transcendence. However, in an attempt to recover a coherent core of the Christian tradition in support of social justice, it seems strange to ignore christological beliefs. Is Christianity coherent without the centrality of the Christ?[36] Perhaps in response to critiques similar to mine, Tanner has given more emphasis to Jesus, the Word of God in her most recent book, *Theories of Culture.* She has also written a recent article on christology.[37]

Tanner takes a pragmatic approach to the recovery of fundamental Christian beliefs. Her concern is less with the referents of these beliefs than with their coherence and pragmatic implications.[38] She does not deny their referentiality to God, for "what would be the point of doing theology if one were not really talking about God?"[39] However, her argument is less concerned with what God is like than with the practical effects of certain beliefs within Christian communities. A theologian's primary task is not to quibble about the ontological veracity of particular beliefs, but to reflect and correct a community's practices. It is to organize in coherent form their talk about God and the world. It is to provide "a logic or grammar covering Christian linguistic competency."[40]

This grammar is not to be constructed in isolation from the wider Christian community. Rather, a local community's practices must be viewed in light of its historical traditions. This enables Christian tradition to provide a critical role in theological reflection. Such a role will help to identify four problems common to Christian communities: 1) misstated Christian beliefs; 2) the inappropriate use of well-formed statements of belief; 3) the inability to articulate beliefs in novel circumstances; and 4) the incompatibility of Christian beliefs.[41]

In order to discern and rectify these problems, Tanner follows George Lindbeck's rule theory of doctrine to suggest two linguistic rules for the construction of statements of belief.[42] The first concerns God's transcendence. Language about God must not identify God with particular attributes, nor contrast the divine with non-divine predicates. God's transcendence lies beyond identity and opposition. The second rule concerns God's creative agency. No limitations in the scope or manner of God's creative agency must be made. God's creative agency is universal and immediate.[43]

Tanner also offers derivative rules that uphold the coherence between these two foundational rules. She suggests that every created cause is ultimately determined by God as the primary creative agent. There is, therefore, no created cause that is outside of God's agency, as this would compromise God's transcendence and pose opposition between divine and non-divine agency. Thus, God is not a secondary agent, influencing and changing human direction into God's direction. Rather, human direction always operates within God's overall direction. At no time have created causes been separated from God's overall intent and influence. Conversely, no created cause, as an outside element, can influence God. God can only be influenced by causes that are already predetermined by God.[44]

Tanner outlines these derivative rules with extensive reference to Karl Barth and Thomas Aquinas in order to demonstrate that representative Protestant and Roman Catholic positions can both adhere to the same rules. That Karl Barth is used as the representative of Protestantism may give some Protestants a cause for concern. I suspect that the same would be the case with Thomas Aquinas for some Roman Catholics. However, in her political choice to be as conservative in faith as any, she has wisely chosen representatives of both Protestant and Roman Catholic traditions who are respected by those holding conservative beliefs.

These "meta-level" logical rules restrict and direct the formation of theological statements, but allow a diversity of statements according to their context. With reference to the functionalist sociological approach of Emile Durkheim,[45] Tanner suggests that diverse, even conflicting, theologies formed in different contexts according to these rules will be functionally equivalent: they will all "show the coherence of Christian talk about God and creation."[46]

One aspect of these rules which encourages theological diversity is their two-sided character. They can be expressed positively and negatively. Positively, creatures could be viewed as everything with God. All that we do is an important part of God's overall plan for the world. God has bestowed upon us immeasurable gifts and capacities through our dependence upon God. We are valued. Negatively, creatures are nothing without God. We are dispensable in God's realm and cannot change what God has ordered.

Different contexts will determine which side of the rules should be emphasized. In order to retain the coherent balance of these rules, Tanner suggests that theologians assess current "illicit" tendencies and stress the opposite side. For instance, if a community or culture emphasizes divine sovereignty at the expense of human capacities, the theologian should stress the positive side of the rules.[47]

In the modern context, Tanner suggests that modern theologies have perpetuated rather than corrected modern illicit tendencies to overstate human power and freedom. They perpetuate the Pelagian heresy of human autonomy, and exclude it from God's sovereignty.[48] In order to protect this misconstrual of free, human agency, the transcendence of God is also compromised. Thus, Tanner concludes that modernity has rendered God's transcendence and human agency incompatible. If the closure rendered by modernity's verdict of incoherence is opened, and modern approaches are understood as fallible, these two fundamental rules may once again coexist coherently.[49] Tanner believes that if Christians reclaim the "ruled relations" of Christian tradition, an internal coherence of Christian theology, marred by modern approaches, will be regained.[50]

In her later work, Tanner does not dispense with her two fundamental beliefs or with her emphasis on coherence. What changes is the form in which she presents these as guidelines. With the help of postmodern theory, she gives greater emphasis to the discursive construction of meaning for traditional Christian doctrine. Similar to Fulkerson's intertextual approach, Tanner explains that the same doctrinal statements used within diverse communities throughout history will have different meanings, according to the relation of the statements to other Christian materials and varying cultures.[51] This disrupts postliberal proposals of grammatical rules that remain constant in meaning, underlie Christian traditions and provide cohesive regulation of correct interpretations.[52] No such consistency in meaning exists, nor can such internal organization and unity amongst the diversity of Christian materials be found across space and time.[53] Tanner joins Fulkerson in acknowledging that postliberal rules were originally socially constructed within Christian communities, but by raising them to universals, postliberals lift them from "the ongoing historical processes that formed them, as if, once produced, they could not be altered by the same processes in the future."[54]

Tanner also points out the danger of rules usurping the Word of God.[55] Following Barth's clear distinction, Tanner identifies the Word of God with the person Jesus Christ. She warns that "the Incarnate Word is only at best indirectly identifiable with even those human words of the Bible that Christians believe effectively witness to him."[56] In this sense, Tanner is concerned that rules of faith *about* the person of Jesus Christ become more important *than* Jesus the Christ.

Another difficulty Tanner has with postliberal rules concerns what Fulkerson calls the professionalization of knowledge. By suggesting that rules allow Christian consensus, postliberals infer that those trained in and knowledgeable of the rules are best able to judge correct interpretation. With the proper training, they assume that people will come to the same conclusions. This understanding negates postliberal attempts to *reflect* Christian practice and instead privileges the evaluation of a minority of "well trained" Christians to decide what all Christians *should* practice.[57] I will add that it also commits the same modern fallacy associated with the historical-critical method: with the proper training and methodology it is possible to find the singular, correct meanings of historical texts. Thus, academic training is privileged over communal practice. In addition, this postliberal approach subsumes the diversity of Christian interpretations into meta-level rules. Any interpretations which differ with the rules, no matter how integral they are to a particular community's traditions, are dismissed as incorrect or incoherent. Tanner makes this same modern fallacy in her earlier work, particularly in the development of her derivative rules. Even though her intent is to allow diversity within the overarching guidance of meta-level rules, she alienates many diverse traditions and theologies. This is apparent from the multiple critiques of this aspect of her work.

For example, by stressing that humanity can never act outside of God's pervasive will, she limits human freedom and incorporates human acts of atrocity into the overall purpose of God. Any theologies which insist on human freedom, however partial, and separate human sin from God's will are accused by Tanner of incoherence and interpreting Christian beliefs improperly. Such judgement effectively condemns many theologies across the centuries that have contributed to our Christian traditions. Although Tanner suggests that doctrinal statements should be held in tension with their originating rhetorical context, she does not keep in dialectical tension the theologies which uphold human freedom. Nor does she hold the radical transcendence of God in dialectical tension with God's radical immanence. To have drawn upon the immanence of God through the person of Jesus may have helped to alleviate her difficulty with the subsumption of sin and evil into God's will as a corollary of God's transcendence.[58]

As an alternative to rules, Tanner suggests in her later work that style be used to identify Christian practices and uses of materials. Instead of determining a common meaning of Christian materials, as postliberal rules attempt, Tanner proposes a common use of borrowed Christian materials to determine Christian identity. Tanner stresses that there is nothing inherently Christian about materials Christians share in common. The materials are a hybrid mixture of various cultures, religions, and philosophies. In this sense, they are borrowed materials. What identifies them as Christian is not a common Christian *resemblance* of the materials, but common *use* of the materials, such as a reference of all materials to God in service of the Word.[59] Tanner suggest that some postliberals defy this relativization by subordinating all borrowed, cultural material to Christian material, even though Christian material is itself borrowed material. They are guilty of subordinating the Word to a particular choice of human words declared to be inherently Christian. "Christianity does not need to keep the upper hand when using borrowed materials; the Word does."[60]

Christian identity is therefore based not on agreement of *meaning*, but agreement of *investigation* of particular materials and practices.[61] For example, Christians may share common material and practices, such as the Bible, creeds, baptism, and communion, but they may also differ widely in their selection and organization of material, traditions and practices. A common use of materials also indicates a common purpose for their use, such as the worship of God, the discernment of the Word of God, the recognition of the crucial significance of Jesus, and the ritual celebration of biblical stories. It is the common use of materials, practices, and beliefs, and not their common meaning, that distinguishes Christian identity.[62]

Does Tanner's revised methodology radically subvert her earlier work? Has she removed the possibility for traditional Christian doctrine to retain agency and critical distance from contemporary Christian beliefs and practices? The preceding description of her use of style indicates that this may be the case. However, she interweaves into this revised methodology aspects of her earlier work that reveal a greater consistency, and still allow her work to be distinguished by a postliberal emphasis upon a core, Christian narrative.

As an example, when characterizing the Christian use of materials, Tanner equates the manner in which they are used with her earlier rule of God's transcendence: a Christian use of materials refers all things to God, thereby relativizing them. However, instead of elaborating derivative rules that must be followed in order to allow coherence with other traditional Christian beliefs, she now suggests that common theological purposes can be described only in very general terms.[63] Even when agreement has been reached on the manner in which Christian materials are used, such as their reference to God, and the purpose for their use, such as a concern for true discipleship, these points of agreement must remain intentionally vague and undefined.[64]

Another consistency within Tanner's work is her emphasis upon contextuality and pragmatic ethical criteria. Theology properly formulated must attend not only to traditional Christian doctrine, but also to its historical, cultural, and geographical location. The practical effects of theological statements will also help to determine their validity. Thus, their function within particular communities must be considered. In this sense, Tanner, Schüssler Fiorenza, Kwok, and Fulkerson share a similar pragmatic orientation in their methods.

In the following sections I will explore the implications of both her earlier and later approaches as they affect doctrinal and scriptural agency, authoritative criteria, revelation, and the diversity and solidarity of faith communities.

Plain Sense of Scripture

Tanner's analysis of scripture gives evidence of her pragmatic, functional concerns. She takes a socio-cultural approach in order to heighten the importance of the communal reading of scripture. It is not the text itself upon which Tanner focuses, but the way in which a text is read by a particular community. This is similar to Fulkerson's poststructural emphasis upon the communal use of scripture. In fact Tanner refers to Foucault and Derrida in support of her thesis.[65]

One of the factors pertaining to the use of scripture is its plain sense. She defines this with reference to David Kelsey's functional definition of scripture and canon. There is no inherent property of the biblical text that makes it scriptural or canonical. Rather, a text becomes scripture through its function within community to "shape, nurture and reform" the church's identity.[66] A set of texts becomes a canon when these texts alone are declared sufficient for these purposes. Likewise, the plain sense is not an inherent characteristic of the biblical text. It cannot be described by philosophical, ontological statements such as "what the text simply says," "the text's own immanent sense," "the text's sense when the expositor is a purely passive or transparent recorder of objective meaning," or "the text's sense without the imposition of extratextual categories."[67] Rather, the plain sense is "the obvious or direct sense of the text" according to communal agreement. It is the basic, traditional, normative sense of the text as established by consensus. It is the exposé that needs no additional warrants for its authority. It is the familiar and therefore authoritative meaning according to a particular community's conventions for reading. When a text is read as scripture, its plain sense is the normative and definitive meaning which shapes, nurtures and reforms the community's identity.[68]

This functional definition does not imply that a community agree with the norms established by the plain sense. Tanner suggests that communities usually do *not* agree with these norms, even though they agree that they represent the familiar, traditional reading. However, in order to introduce alternative readings and norms, they must challenge the norms of the plain sense and give additional warrants for their alternatives. Such a challenge would only be necessary if the traditional reading was considered authoritative for the community.[69] As an example, a community may support the ordination of women but also agree that the traditional reading of I Corinthians 14:33–35 prohibits women from speaking publically in church. They will then give additional warrants to justify their alternative interpretation of this passage.

The use of key phrases by a community may help to identify the plain sense within their conventions of reading. These include "the sense the author intended," "the verbal or grammatical sense," "the sense for the writer's public," "the sense that God intends," "the sense a text has when included in the canon," "the sense Church authorities designate," and "what the text itself says."[70] Tanner is not equating the plain sense with these phrases. For instance, she would not want to equate the intention of the author with the plain sense. Nor, as already mentioned, would she want to create an ontological definition of "what the text itself says." What the phrases indicate is the community's understanding of the traditional meaning of the text. Because the plain sense is not *the* "proper" meaning, but is one amongst many that is privileged by a particular community, it will vary across communities as well as within the same community across a span of time.

Tanner's understanding of the plain sense, as described up until this point, coheres with her later work. It also complements and enhances Fulkerson's notion of the canonical system. However, Tanner gives additional descriptions that confuse and possibly contradict this initial understanding.[71] Although Tanner acknowledges that the plain sense "is itself the product of an interpretive tradition,"[72] she distinguishes it as the exposition of the text from subsequent interpretations. In other words, she separates the text and its plain sense from interpretations and applications in order to allow the text and its plain sense to stand against the community as a source of internal critique. In order not to privilege conservative, traditional interpretations over liberative ones, yet still retain the normative power of the plain sense, Tanner prefers the plain sense to remain vague. Even though she equates the plain sense with the traditional meaning of the text, she is uncomfortable with its explicit association with any particular meaning. In this way, she can separate plain sense from interpretation and say that the text and its plain sense do not change, while interpretation does. She can also acknowledge that any attempt to formulate the plain sense will, in itself, constitute an interpretation, thereby nullifying its privileged status. Even though she suggests that a plain sense can only be found within communal practice, she tries to retain the notion of plain sense that is "irreducible to the community's specifications of it."[73] It is only the text itself and its accompanying, undefined plain sense that retains normative, critical status:[74]

> The general consequence of such a radical distinction between text and interpretation is an authoritative plain sense that is unavailable in any form distinct from the text itself. The plain sense of the text becomes an independently unspecifiable locus of meaning, something that transcends any and all attempts to reformulate it. As such it functions critically even with respect to consensus readings of a text; it works to evacuate the pretensions of communal discourse generally.[75]

Although Tanner has not written further on the plain sense, I suspect that she would distance herself in her later work from this undefined, pre-discursive notion of the biblical text's plain sense. There are two basic problems with this undefined, pre-discursive notion of plain sense. First, if the plain sense constitutes a normative standard which can never be articulated, it becomes an undefined entity, whose elusive quality lessens its critical impact. The text will be less able to stand against the reader. Secondly, if the plain sense is understood as the communal consensus of a text's traditional meaning, it cannot exist apart from interpretation. Rather, it constitutes one traditional interpretation preferred over others. It will also differ amongst communities. This diversity of constructed meanings becomes more apparent, and better coheres with her later work, as she associates the plain sense with narrative and canon.

In order to give a more concrete, critical force to the text and its plain sense, and to be able to challenge rigid, conservative uniformity in community life, Tanner leans heavily upon Hans Frei's emphasis on narrative and the biblical canon. She believes that if the plain sense is identified in light of the biblical canon as a narrative, especially as the story of Jesus Christ, it will allow numerous variations of the material specifications of Christian identity. To understand the Bible as a set of texts sufficient "in all times and places for the formation and regulation of community life is to force a certain degree of interpretive license in the use of them."[76]

In some respects Tanner posits the biblical canon against the plain sense, if plain sense is taken to be the traditional reading of scripture, because the universal relevance of the canon calls for innovative interpretations that may challenge previously established ones (i.e. the plain sense).[77] Tanner still insists on the priority of the plain sense, but she gives it a further definition that identifies it with "the narrative depiction of the identity of Jesus Christ."[78] This new definition hints at a christological norm against which communal practices can be measured.

Because the gospel narrative does not prescribe univocal communal beliefs, attitudes, and behaviours, a diversity of interpretation and application will result. Tanner refers to this characteristic of narrative as "structural indeterminacy in Christian conventions of appealing to texts."[79] In a later article Tanner extends this notion of structural indeterminacy to the texts themselves. She proposes that the Bible be viewed as a popular, common text, and not as a "high-culture work of literary artistry." She then draws upon a poststructural insistence of the text's indeterminacy to emphasize the multiple meanings of the text as constructed by reader response.[80]

As with Fulkerson, Tanner believes that the text becomes stabilized or determinative for a particular community only in its interpretation and application within that community. The structural indeterminacy of the text requires "exegetical ingenuity" within the particularity of a communal context for this to happen. As this ingenuity will differ amongst communities, so will the resulting readings. Thus, the universal application of such a "narrative plain sense of scripture" will promote Christian communities open to change and welcoming of difference.[81] The multiple, disparate meanings of the Bible will also challenge any particular meaning from claiming singular authority. It would challenge those who "dissolve the Bible into themselves."[82]

Authority

In this tension amongst competing interpretations and communal practices, Tanner is aware that traditional readings of scripture and adherence to traditional Christian beliefs have often promoted conservative preservation of the status quo. In order to counteract the authoritative status of conservative interpretations of traditional doctrines, she suggests that "proper" interpretations will challenge their conservative support of the status quo of injustice. While Tanner acknowledges that these doctrines have been used to support oppressive actions, she reminds her readers along with Fulkerson that the liberative potential of these doctrines is partially dependent upon the way in which they are interpreted in a particular context. Unlike Fulkerson, however, Tanner insists that their liberative potential is not completely context dependent. Tanner argues that the doctrines themselves necessitate "progressive" interpretations if they are understood "properly."[83] She draws on sociocultural theory and philosophical logic to insist that, although attitude and action cannot be separated from religious belief, they are logical consequences of belief.[84] Certain Christian beliefs "with a definite meaning"[85] will therefore necessitate "proper attitude and action."

This premise is clearly at odds with the poststructural opposition to a fixed, universal meaning of any text or tradition. Tanner avoids such language in her later work. However, Tanner adds a spin to her premise which accounts for a belief's variation in meaning without removing its political import, a goal shared with Schüssler Fiorenza. Tanner agrees with Fulkerson that a number of contextual variables determine a subject's specific meaning:

1. The meaning of a belief's central terms may vary in their usage. "Meaning, whether of religious beliefs or otherwise, is ... a product of language use by real people in the course of historically specific and politically charged interactions."[86]
2. The selective combination of one belief with others will privilege certain meanings.
3. The life situation of those considering the belief will affect their consideration.
4. The socio-political situation will determine the scope of the belief's application.[87]

Tanner interprets the latter two situation-specific variables in terms of relations of power in order to emphasize the belief's political implications.[88]

Tanner admits that variation in meaning is endless. However, she suggests that certain Christian beliefs about God and the world only uphold a limited range of variability. In themselves they have "a general practical import" that poses guidelines restricting this variability.[89] For instance, actions and attitudes which provide "active resistance to a status quo of injustice" would be considered proper responses while other "conservative, oppressive, and passive" responses would be improper.[90]

Tanner's later work can be used to critique this earlier notion of the general practical import of Christian beliefs. As she more closely aligns herself with postmodernism, she resists any sense of a pre-discursive meaning contained within Christian beliefs. It is not the beliefs, themselves, which carry a general practical import, but the manner in which they are selected and organized with other beliefs and practices. Their endless variation in meaning is limited not by their own internal meanings, but by their particular placement alongside other Christian materials and cultural contexts. Again, we find similarities with Fulkerson's stabilization of meaning within a canonical system.

Tanner still upholds the criteria of coherence in her later work, but uses it in a different way. Instead of measuring the coherence of a particular belief or practice with certain fundamental rules, she now measures its coherence with its relation to the selection and organization of other Christian materials. A belief can be judged correct or proper if it coheres not with particular rules, but with a variety of different configurations of Christian materials. While this is similar to Fulkerson's canonical system, Tanner does not limit the judgement of Christian practices to particular faith communities. She suggests that academic theologians can interact with popular theologies to introduce Christian materials or practices not previously considered. In other words, the selection and organization of Christian materials is not fixed within particular Christian communities, but is continually evolving in their interaction with other faith communities, various cultures and academic theologies.[91]

With Tanner's postmodern corrections in mind, we could look at her earlier work not as definitive prescriptions governing all Christian belief and practice, but as an example of a certain selection and organization of Christian materials that produces a general practical import. If Christian practice is viewed in light of Tanner's two fundamental beliefs, what would be the pragmatic outcome? Such an approach to her earlier work would also leave open the possibility of contrasting meanings and conclusions within a different ordering of Christian materials. Although this was not her intention in her earlier work, *Theories of Culture* encourages this reading.

As noted previously, the two primary beliefs which Tanner emphasizes in her earlier work are the transcendence of God and God's providential agency. If God's transcendence is understood in the manner specified by Tanner, any equation of socio-economic political orders with God's intent is ruled out. Natural forces and human roles are distinctly separate from the divinity. This means that they cannot be placed beyond critique through divine justification. Divine transcendence affords a critical distance from both. It also allows a distinction between "a social world and a world of individual experience."[92] In other words, individuals do not have to go through a particular social order or have a particular social identity in order to enter into a relationship with God. Lastly, Tanner draws on Jürgen Habermas' concept of transcendent truths to suggest that divine transcendence enables a distinction to be made between ideal values and social norms, ultimate reality and the appearance of reality, truth and the perception of truth.[93] This distinction insists that human ideas, proposals, and norms are limited, finite, fallible, and socially located within history.[94] "The transcendence of God functions as a protest against all absolute and unconditioned claims."[95] Tanner suggests that this protest is particularly relevant against religious claims. Belief in a transcendent God will necessitate critique of non-religious and religious claims, including one's own. Tanner does admit that this critical potential of God's transcendence is ambiguous. While it prevents anyone from establishing their own beliefs or values as absolute, it also inhibits the political impact of standards that are potentially fallible or limited by their social location. It is on this point that Tanner's second belief in God's intimate involvement with the world is helpful.

As the world's creator, guide and redeemer, God is actively working in the world as it is dependent upon God. God's presence can be found in the continuous process of "moral ordering," but not in a static "moral order." The specifics of this moral ordering can be suggested by biblical injunctions and "Christian moral heritage," but these must be interpreted in light of contemporary events. Such interpretation must be viewed as fallible, as humanity's sinful nature permeates all decisions, social structures and moral orders. Thus, decisions and standards can only be tentative and relative. Specific, universal pronouncements of judgment are ruled out.[96] To move beyond general proposals into specifics requires a recognition of their potential fallibility and limitations. It also requires interdisciplinary work, including political and economic analysis.[97]

In the book *Sexual Orientation & Human Rights in American Religious Discourse*, Tanner's response to a theological disagreement over homosexual marriage demonstrates the liberative impact of her theological method. She takes issue with Max Stackhouse's opposition to church-sanctioned homosexual marriages on the basis of her criteria of theological coherence and the general practical import of God's transcendence and creative agency. First, Tanner points out the inconsistencies of Stackhouse's argument in relation to his own choice of theological principles. His norms of fidelity, fecundity, and community, as based on one of the Genesis stories, can be met within lesbian and gay relationships as well as heterosexual. Thus, his opposition to homosexual marriage is incoherent with his selection of biblical passages and theological principles. Secondly, in terms of God's creative agency, respect for all of God's creation means to be aware of and resistant to unjust treatment towards any of God's creation. This includes an openness to self-critique, as a recognition of God's transcendence requires. As a Protestant, Stackhouse would presumably honour the Protestant principle, which encourages constant criticism of anything that presumes absolute truth or authority. These would both call for a willingness to consider changing any of our actions that discriminate and oppress others simply because of who they are, regardless of historical church precedents. Tanner suggests that Stackhouse's refusal to consider his own perpetration of injustice towards a segment of the population betrays his attempt to be a faithful proponent of prophetic witness.[98]

Another example of Tanner's theological method involves canonical criticism. Canonical criticism reads the Bible against itself, carefully considering the ordering of books within the whole Bible, and passages within each book. In a recent article she uses Old Testament descriptions of justification, righteousness and justice to explain the New Testament use of justification. Although canonical criticism is clearly involved in this method of reading the Bible against itself, she also employs historical-criticism to look at specific word usages. Like Kwok, she is not adverse to using historical-critical methods, as long as they are informed by other methods. Tanner weighs her study of Old Testament terms against the gospel narrative of Jesus. She offers this "biblical theology" as a modification of later Christian theologies which ignore the relational nature of justification and its social justice implications.[99]

Community, Diversity and Solidarity

The general guidelines and directives emerging from belief in God's transcendence and providential agency have a tremendous impact upon human relations with one another, all living creatures, and the earth.[100] As God has created creatures in all their diversity, each creature requires respect based upon its creaturehood. Humans are not to be respected because of any defining feature other than their created status. This places all creatures, including humans, on a level plane.[101] In light of this, Tanner calls for an opposition to fixed hierarchies of subordinates and superiors, to oppressive relations of domination or exploitation and to intolerance of others. Instead, equal respect for others within their diversity should be promoted.[102] These guidelines entail a number of rights due all creatures: to be oneself in all one's diversity; self-development; self-determination; minimum standards of well-being; participation or influence in social processes that govern one's fate; access to necessary sources for development.[103]

These rights are not based upon a liberal theory of individualism, but entail a social dimension in relationship with others. They are also not based upon a liberal toleration of largesse, where everyone is permitted to be without interference.[104] Rather, they are based upon a toleration of respect for all creatures of God. This creates a liberty of conscience, in which attitudes or behaviours that promote intolerance are not tolerated.[105] Toleration based upon this respect also allows for better understanding of the other. The negative traits one sees in the other must also be seen in oneself, and the positive traits one sees in oneself one must also see in the other. Tanner calls this "nonidolatrous esteem," where humble acknowledgement of sinful finitude is balanced with self-affirmation of creaturely value.[106] The inflated self-esteem of oppressors prevents them from acknowledging how they benefit from oppressive institutional structures. The lack of self-esteem of the oppressed prevents them from acknowledging how they are deprived by these structures. Tanner suggests that both are guilty of sloth in their complacent acceptance of the status quo, although to avoid blaming the victim I would suggest that it may well be more a lack of energy and resources, rather than sloth, that prevents the oppressed from actively resisting their own oppressive structures.

Tanner suggests that if the oppressors accepted their own finitude and fallibility, and the oppressed accepted their own value, both would have a nonidolatrous esteem. This would enable the oppressed to claim basic rights and the oppressor to forego privileges.[107] A nonidolatrous esteem would also counteract a tendency to reify the other as utterly different from oneself. It will respect the actual differences that exist and work against assimilation of the other into one's own identity. Belief in the creaturehood of humanity will allow the other to be genuinely other. Tanner notes some similarities of this relationship of otherness to our relationship with God as genuinely other.[108]

Tanner concludes that a community founded upon values of creaturehood will be pluralistic and radically inclusive. It will allow a solidarity of respect for diversity within and outside particular groups. It will discourage any essentializing tendencies of communities to ignore their own diversities in the midst of particular identities.[109] If any communities are formed around collective identities such as gender, they must be particularly sensitive to the diversities within that identity. In order to respect the particularities of each person within the community, Tanner eschews communitarian goals which sacrifice individual needs for the sake of the larger community. For instance, the consensus model of decision-making often restricts the free expression of difference.[110] Relationships with others will focus upon understanding the other and will avoid coercive forms of interaction such as debates and persuasion. The least powerful will have the greatest right to be heard.[111] As everyone, oppressed and oppressor alike, is a creature of God, all should be accorded value and respect. All should also realize their own finitude and fallibility. Activists will admit that they also may be mistaken in some ways; that they, too, may oppress others. This will allow a solidarity even between oppressor and oppressed as activists forgive and refuse to demonize those they oppose.[112]

Tanner's call for solidarity with the oppressor, her analysis that both the oppressed and the oppressor are guilty of the same sin of slothfulness, and her call to forgive the oppressor will be questioned by many. Kwok's definition of solidarity will help to refine Tanner's understanding. By stressing the interconnection of multiple oppressions and identities, simple identification as the oppressor or oppressed is no longer possible. A recognition of the multiple sources of oppression will also challenge Tanner's gross characterizations of sloth and premature calls for forgiveness.

Up to this point, this discussion of Tanner's views on community, diversity and solidarity has concentrated on her earlier material. Her later material does not argue with these views, but rather understands them as logical, coherent results of her particular ordering of Christian material. She continues this discussion with additional thoughts on solidarity that have emerged from her more explicitly postmodern approach. One of her concerns in this later material is with the implications of the diversity of Christian belief and practice for solidarity. She is only too aware of the divisive and destructive results of Christian disagreement that often impact marginalized people, such as lesbian and gay Christians, and people of diverse cultures and faiths. At the same time, she recognizes the inevitability of disagreement on the variable meanings of Christian materials.

Tanner's solution to this dilemma is to call for a solidarity based upon formal agreement of the use and purpose of Christian materials without requiring agreement on their meaning.[113] For instance, all could participate in a communal meal without requiring consensus of belief as to its meaning. There could be a unity of task, such as a common reference of all things to God or the proclamation of God's Word, without requiring agreement on the content of the task.[114] Instead of uniting around rules that specify the shape of Christian belief, Tanner suggests that the creeds, by virtue of their ambiguities, "are the grounds around which opposed factions unite in argument."[115]

Tanner does not dismiss the possibility of agreement on meaning. As an example, she says certain practices, such as slavery, can be ruled out of bounds when these practices are clearly considered to contravene Christian beliefs. Such agreement on uncontroversial issues could be considered part of the *regula fidae* (rules of faith, which are determined by general agreement in the church and evolve over time). However, she cautions against efforts to rule certain controversial practices out of bounds and thereby silence opposition.[116] Forced compliance often subsumes the marginalized into the dominant identity. Only on the basis of such a "weak" consensus on form, and not content, does Tanner believe solidarity to be possible amongst the widest diversity of people.[117]

Solidarity can also be furthered by honouring, and not preventing, disagreement in order to avoid divisiveness. Tanner encourages "a genuine community of argument" that is "marked by mutual hearing and criticism among those who disagree, by a common commitment to mutual correction and uplift, in keeping with the shared hope of good discipleship, proper faithfulness, and purity of witness."[118] While this seems to contradict her earlier statements eschewing coercive forms of interaction such as debates and persuasion, I believe that she is primarily concerned about manipulation. She encourages argument and debate only if they are respectful and give voice to the voiceless.

Conclusion

Kathryn Tanner's theological method exhibits similar concerns to those of Schüssler Fiorenza, Fulkerson, and Kwok. Issues of social justice, community, diversity, and solidarity are central in her work and she critiques elements of modernity and liberalism which present obstacles to these issues. In addition, Tanner is concerned about modernity and liberalism's distortions of traditional Christian belief.

Modern decontextualization, according to Tanner, has produced the fallacies of neutrality and referentiality. Two consequences of referentiality are positivism, with its identification of *de facto* norms with *de jure* norms, and the reification of rhetorical norms into ontological descriptions. When the two problems of referentiality and reification are combined, theological statements are understood as ontological descriptions of a reified essence. Essentialism is particularly problematic regarding diversity and domination. It leads to totalitarianism and colonialism in which marginalized identities are subsumed into the dominant identity. This unacknowledged power differential also results in a liberal individualism which fails to acknowledge institutionalized oppression.

As an alternative method to modernity and liberalism, Tanner presents a revision of postliberalism with the help of postmodern theory. She chooses to speak not from the margins, but from the heart of the Christian tradition. In order to challenge politically conservative Christian movements, Tanner convincingly demonstrates the support of traditional Christian beliefs for social justice. Her exposé on the transcendence of God precludes any theological or political position from self-justification by identifying itself with the divine. Reminiscent of Paul Tillich's Protestant Principle, Tanner counters that the transcendence of God should remind all of us of the limitations and fallibility of our positions.[119] The creative agency of God provides incentive to respect the diversity of all creation.

In order to distance herself from the problems of the postliberal use of rules, she prefers the use of style to determine the common usage, rather than common meaning, of Christian materials. This allows her to have a pragmatic focus on the results rather than the referents of Christian beliefs. This concept of style respects the diversity of doctrine and scripture, as well as the diversity of faith communities. Style emphasizes the social construction of Christian material within the diverse cultural contexts of the communities. It also allows the material's multiple possibilities of meanings to be limited by their organization with other Christian materials, including the community's traditional interpretation, or plain sense, of scripture.

The use of style has implications for solidarity. It encourages Christian communities to unite over the use and purpose of Christian beliefs and practices rather than over their meaning. It also allows them to enter into a community of argument that unites them in their disagreements. Tanner proposes a "politics of solidarity"[120] not only amongst Christian communities, but also amongst Christian theologians. Although her theological critique is drawn from within the boundaries of traditional Christian doctrines, she does admit that these boundaries are not fixed. Perhaps in an indirect reference to the work of Schüssler Fiorenza, she acknowledges the importance of historically marginalized voices and Christian discourse. Because these have been excluded from mainstream Christian tradition, Tanner does not deal with them in her internal critique. However, she does suggest that, "in the service of greater justice," her internal critique could supplement other methods of analysis which explore these marginalized traditions and experiences.[121]

Tanner lists a number of ways in which internal critique, as a supplement to revisionist theologies, could strengthen their political impact. First, an internal critique could help these alternative methods avoid making totalistic critiques of mainstream Christian theology. Secondly, it could help them to be more attentive to diversity. Where their communal values might exclude individuals who do not hold those values or where their emphasis on consensus might be at the expense of ethnic and racial diversity, an internal critique might check this tendency towards "totalistic holism." Thirdly, it provides a reminder that all methods are fallible and must be open to critique and constant review. Thus, it keeps theological methods from identifying their norms and beliefs with divine will and merely reflecting in theology what one already believes. It also warns against a theological identification with political recommendations. Instead, it necessitates the need for interdisciplinary, sociopolitical analysis to flesh out theological analysis. Tanner believes that if different theological methods committed to social justice work together, critiquing and therefore strengthening each other, they would afford a much more effective coalition of solidarity in the struggle for justice.[122]

Notes to Chapter 5

1. Others who have noted this same Yale school influence in Tanner's work include Randy L. Maddox, "Review of *God and Creation in Christian Theology: Tyranny or Empowerment?*" *Christian Scholar's Review* 21, no. 2 (December 1991): 216–17; John E. Theil, "Review of *God and Creation in Christian Theology: Tyranny or Empowerment?*" *Theological Studies* 51, no. 1 (March 1990): 140–41.

2. For a helpful explanation of the postliberal attributes of Frei and Lindbeck's work, see William C. Placher, "Paul Ricoeur and Postliberal Theology: A Conflict of Interpretations?" *Modern Theology* 4, no. 1 (1987): 33–52.

3. Paul Schwartzentruber, "The Modesty of Hermeneutics: The Theological Reserves of Hans Frei," *Modern Theology* 8, no. 2 (April 1992): 181.

4. See in particular Kathryn E. Tanner, "Social Theory Concerning the 'New Social Movements' and the Practice of Feminist Theology," in *Horizons in Feminist Theology: Identity, Tradition, and Norms*, ed. Rebecca S. Chopp and Sheila Greeve Davaney (Minneapolis: Fortress Press, 1997); Kathryn E. Tanner, *Theories of Culture: A New Agenda for Theology*, Guides to Theological Inquiry (Minneapolis: Fortress Press, 1997); Kathryn E. Tanner, "Scripture as Popular Text," *Modern Theology* 14, no. 2 (April 1998): 278–297. These are the works to which I refer when I distinguish her later work from her earlier work. The one exception to this diachronic ordering is an article of Tanner's published in 1997 which retains her previous use of postliberal grammatical rules to judge the coherence and proper interpretation of Christian beliefs. See Kathryn E. Tanner, "Jesus Christ," in *The Cambridge Companion to Christian Doctrine*, ed. Colin E. Gunton, Cambridge Companions to Religion (Cambridge: Cambridge University Press, 1997).

5. Kathryn E. Tanner, "Theology and the Plain Sense," in *Scriptural Authority and Narrative Interpretation*, ed. Garrett Green (Philadelphia: Fortress Press, 1987), 60.

6. See Kathryn E. Tanner, "Theology and Popular Culture," in *Changing Conversations: Religious Reflection & Cultural Analysis*, edited by Dwight N. Hopkins & Sheila Greeve Davaney (New York: Routledge, 1996).

7. Kathryn E. Tanner, *The Politics of God: Christian Theologies and Social Justice* (Minneapolis: Fortress Press, 1992), 7, 28–31.

8. Tanner, "Theology and the Plain Sense," 60.

9. Tanner, *God and Creation in Christian Theology*, 1–9.

10. Tanner, *God and Creation in Christian Theology*, 8.

11. Tanner, *God and Creation in Christian Theology*, 8.

12. Tanner, "Theology and the Plain Sense," 61.

13. Tanner, *God and Creation in Christian Theology*, 7.

14. Tanner, *God and Creation in Christian Theology*, 124–25.

15. Tanner, *God and Creation in Christian Theology*, 124–32.

16. Tanner, *God and Creation in Christian Theology*, 129, 134, 143–44, 152–53.

17. Tanner, *God and Creation in Christian Theology*, 155–56.

18. Kathryn E. Tanner, "A Theological Case for Human Responsibility in Moral Choice," *Journal of Religion* 73 (October 1993): 592–612. For Tanner's further distinctions between *de facto* and *de jure* norms see Tanner, *The Politics of God*, 54–55, 86.

19. Tanner, "A Theological Case for Human Responsibility in Moral Choice," 598–99.

20. Tanner, "A Theological Case for Human Responsibility in Moral Choice," 592–612.

21. Tanner, *God and Creation in Christian Theology*, 156–60.

22. Tanner, *The Politics of God*, 110–11.

23. Tanner refers to the postcolonialist work of Edward Said, and Tzvetan Todorov, as well as the feminist work of Elizabeth Minnich, Martha Minow and Elizabeth Spelman in her elaboration of this point. See Tanner, *The Politics of God*, 204, ftnt. 11.

24. Tanner, *The Politics of God*, 205–08.

25. Tanner, *The Politics of God*, 208–19.

26. Tanner, "A Theological Case for Human Responsibility in Moral Choice," 603–09.

27. Kathryn E. Tanner, "Respect for Other Religions: A Christian Antidote to Colonialist Discourse," *Modern Theology* 9 (January 1993): 3–4.

28. Tanner, "Respect for Other Religions," 1–18 ; Tanner, *The Politics of God*, 62, 194.

29. Tanner, *The Politics of God*, 184.

30. Tanner, *The Politics of God*, 169–70, 180–81, 184; Tanner, "A Theological Case for Human Responsibility in Moral Choice," 606–07.

31. Tanner, *The Politics of God*, ix.

32. Tanner, *The Politics of God*, viii.

33. Tanner, *The Politics of God*, x.

34. Tanner, *God and Creation in Christian Theology*, 50.

35. Tanner, *The Politics of God*, 1, ftnt. 1; 31, ftnt. 14.

36. Others have made this same critique. See Carter Heyward, "Review of *The Politics of God: Christian Theologies and Social Justice,*" *Journal of Church and State* 36, no. 1 (Winter 1994): 166–67; David F. Ford, Review of *God and Creation in Christian Theology: Tyranny or Empowerment? Religious Studies* 26, no. 4 (December 1990): 550–52; Theil, Review of *God and Creation*.

37. Tanner, "Jesus Christ."

38. Tanner draws on the philosophical "linguistic turn" to non-referentiality as expressed in the 1960s and 1970s by people such as Richard Rorty, Rudolf Carnap, Willard Van Orman Quine, David Burrell, and Victor Preller. See Tanner, *God and Creation in Christian Theology*, 11, 171, ftnt. 3–6.

39. Tanner, *God and Creation in Christian Theology*, 12.

40. Tanner, *God and Creation in Christian Theology*, 15.

41. Tanner, *God and Creation in Christian Theology*, 16–17.

42. George Lindbeck, *The Nature of Doctrine: Religion and Theology in a Postliberal Age* (Philadelphia: Westminster Press, 1984).

43. Tanner, *God and Creation in Christian Theology*, 47.

44. Tanner, *God and Creation in Christian Theology*, 90–104.

45. Tanner, *God and Creation in Christian Theology*, 27–32.

46. Tanner, *The Politics of God*, 83.

47. Tanner, *God and Creation in Christian Theology*, 105–19.

48. Tanner, *God and Creation in Christian Theology*, 120–23.

49. Tanner, *God and Creation in Christian Theology*, 6–7.

50. Tanner, *The Politics of God*, 5.

51. Tanner, *Theories of Culture*, 105.

52. Tanner, *Theories of Culture*, 74–75, 78–79.

53. Tanner, *Theories of Culture*, 76.

54. Tanner, *Theories of Culture*, 139; Fulkerson, *Changing the Subject: Women's Discourses and Feminist Theology* (Minneapolis: Fortress Press, 1994), 162–63.

55. Tanner, *Theories of Culture*, 149–51.

56. Tanner, *Theories of Culture*, 126.

57. Tanner, *Theories of Culture*, 141–42.

58. For further discussion see William Hasker, David Burnell, and Thomas Tracy in *The God Who Acts: Philosophical and Theological Explorations*, ed. Thomas F. Tracy (University Park, Pennsylvania: The Pennsylvania State University Press, 1994). See also Maddox, "Review of *God and Creation in Christian Theology*," 216–17; Ford, "Review of *God and Creation in Christian Theology*," 550–52; Incandela, "Review of *God and Creation in Christian Theology*," 66–69; Tracy, "Review of *God and Creation in Christian Theology*," 120–24; Tracy, "Acknowledgments," vii; Tracy, "Divine Action, Created Causes, and Human Freedom," 77–102; Wiles, "Review of *God and Creation in Christian Theology*," 322–24.

59. Tanner, *Theories of Culture*, 106, 114, 144–51.

60. Tanner, *Theories of Culture*, 149.

61. Tanner, *Theories of Culture*, 125.

62. Tanner, *Theories of Culture*, 152–53.

63. Tanner, *Theories of Culture*, 145–46.

64. Tanner, *Theories of Culture*, 152–54.

65. Tanner, "Theology and the Plain Sense," 64.

66. Tanner, "Theology and the Plain Sense," 62.

67. Tanner, "Theology and the Plain Sense," 62.

68. Tanner, "Theology and the Plain Sense," 63.

69. Tanner, "Theology and the Plain Sense," 65.

70. Tanner, "Theology and the Plain Sense," 65, 69.

71. Although this summary of Tanner's approach to scripture is based only upon one article, the article is divided into two sections. Tanner's understanding of the plain sense, as described so far, comprises the first section (p. 59–66). The second section (p. 66–75), which we will now be looking at, appears to be a response to critiques of the first section and an incorporation of some of these alternative views.

72. Tanner, "Theology and the Plain Sense," 64.

73. Tanner, "Theology and the Plain Sense," 75.

74. Tanner, "Theology and the Plain Sense," 66–75.

75. Tanner, "Theology and the Plain Sense," 72.

76. Tanner, "Theology and the Plain Sense," 73.

77. Tanner, "Theology and the Plain Sense," 73.

78. This definition is taken from Hans Frei's *The Eclipse of Biblical Narrative*. See Tanner, "Theology and the Plain Sense," 59.

79. Tanner, "Theology and the Plain Sense," 74.

80. Tanner, "Scripture as Popular Text," 294.

81. Tanner, "Theology and the Plain Sense," 74–75.

82. Tanner, "Scripture as Popular Text," 289–91, 294.

83. Tanner, *The Politics of God*, 1–8.

84. Tanner, *The Politics of God*, 8–17.

85. Tanner, *The Politics of God*, 20–21.

86. Tanner, *The Politics of God*, 19.

87. Tanner, *The Politics of God*, 17–22.

88. Tanner, *The Politics of God*, 27.

89. Tanner, *The Politics of God*, 30–31.

90. Tanner, *The Politics of God*, 28.

91. Tanner, *Theories of Culture*, Chp. 4.

92. Tanner, *The Politics of God*, 68.

93. Tanner refers extensively in this area to Jürgen Habermas' concept of transcendent truths in his *Theory of Communicative Action*. See Tanner, *The Politics of God*, 51–60.

94. Tanner, "A Theological Case for Human Responsibility in Moral Choice," 604.

95. Tanner, *The Politics of God*, 69.

96. Tanner, *The Politics of God*, 98–107.

97. Tanner, *The Politics of God*, 120.

98. Kathryn Tanner, "Response to Max Stackhouse and Eugene Rogers," *Sexual Orientation & Human Rights in American Religious Discourse*, edited by Saul M. Olyan & Martha C. Nussbaum (New York: Oxford University Press, 1998), 166–168.

99. Kathryn Tanner, "Justification and Justice in a Theology of Grace," *Theology Today* 55, no. 4 (January, 1999).

100. Although Tanner focuses primarily upon human relations, she has written an article which extends this concern to all creatures on earth. See Kathryn E. Tanner, "Creation, Environmental Crisis, and Ecological Justice," in *Reconstructing Christian Theology*, ed. Rebecca Chopp et. al. (Minneapolis: Fortress Press, 1994).

101. Tanner, *The Politics of God*, 165–70.

102. Tanner, *The Politics of God*, 130–31.

103. Tanner, *The Politics of God*, 179; Tanner, "A Theological Case for Human Responsibility in Moral Choice," 610–11.

104. Tanner, "A Theological Case for Human Responsibility in Moral Choice," 606.

105. Tanner, *The Politics of God*, 195–205.

106. Tanner, *The Politics of God*, 228–29.

107. Tanner, *The Politics of God*, 236–42.

108. Tanner, *The Politics of God*, 208–19.

109. Tanner, *The Politics of God*, 219–23.

110. Kathryn E. Tanner, "The Care That Does Justice: Recent Writings in Feminist Ethics and Theology," *Journal of Religious Ethics* 24, no. 1 (Spring 1996): 184–85.

111. Tanner, *The Politics of God*, 219–23.

112. Tanner, *The Politics of God*, 246–50.

113. Tanner, *Theories of Culture*, 122.

114. Tanner, *Theories of Culture*, 136.

115. Tanner, *Theories of Culture*, 140.

116. Tanner, *Theories of Culture*, 173–74.

117. Tanner, *Theories of Culture*, 122; For an extensive discussion of the nature of weak consensus, see Kathryn Tanner, "Public Theology and the Character of Public Debate," *The Annual of the Society of Christian Ethics* (1996), 79–101.

118. Tanner, *Theories of Culture*, 123–24.

119. Paul Tillich's Protestant Principle "contains the divine and human protest against any absolute claim made for a relative reality." Indeed, Tillich names as demonic any attempt to claim ultimacy for a human construction. See Paul Tillich, *The Protestant Era*, originally published in 1948, trans. by James Luther Adams (Chicago: The University of Chicago Press, 1957), 163; *Systematic Theology: Life and the Spirit; History and the Kingdom of God*, vol. III (London: SCM Press Ltd., 1963), 98.

120. Tanner, *The Politics of God*, 257.

121. Tanner, *The Politics of God*, 257.
122. Tanner, *The Politics of God*, 150–257.

Chapter 6

Critical Comparison of Feminist Theological Methods

Each of the preceding four feminist methods critiques modern and liberal approaches to theology and offers an alternative that is attentive to issues of diversity and marginalization within Christian communities. In this chapter I will compare these methods critically by using each approach to critique the other three. First, I will summarize their similarities of response to modernity and liberalism. Following this, I will highlight the four primary areas in which their alternative theological methods differ: historical adequacy, scriptural and doctrinal agency, subjecthood and community, and revelation and authority. I will show how these four different methods can complement and strengthen each other in both their similarities and differences. At the conclusion of this chapter I will indicate the type of community that is best served by each method. As will be seen in Part Two, the braiding of these four different methods significantly aids the development of a feminist theological method that more adequately addresses diversity and marginalization within Protestant denominations.

Response to Modernity and Liberalism

Each of the four feminists disputes the impartial objectivity claimed in modern methods. They challenge modern assumptions that reality can be discovered with the proper historical-critical tools. Singular meanings of biblical and historical texts are contested. Universal claims made on the basis of historical-critical methods only serve to hide the interests and ideologies of the modern researcher. These claims are decontextualized and assumed to represent the reality and interests of others in different social settings and power relations. Instead of representing the other, however, these claims subsume the identity of the other into the identity of the researcher. Certain differences are essentialized and others are occluded.

Power differentials are ignored, further marginalizing those who are colonized or dominated by multiplicative, systemic structures of oppression. Liberal attempts to include without addressing these power relations merely perpetuate the oppressive status quo. A liberal emphasis upon the autonomy of the individual overlooks their social construction. Singular interpretations of scripture are not as individualistic as they first appear, but are formed out of a complex web of significations within their social location.

These points of agreement concerning the problem of modern and liberal approaches leads each of the four feminists to develop alternatives, which share some similarities. They each use the rhetorical method to explain the formation of the biblical and doctrinal texts and/or to reconstruct these texts with contemporary faith communities. All draw upon poststructural theory to acknowledge the diversity of texts and communities, and to explain how the multiple meanings of texts and multiple subject identities can be limited and stabilized by their use within faith communities. Christian texts cannot be dismissed in a totalistic critique that collapses this diversity. They each believe that different liberative strands within the biblical texts and Christian traditions can be found by different Christian communities.

To varying extents they also recognize the limits of poststructural theory. In order to develop an emancipatory edge, additional methods are needed. Schüssler Fiorenza relies upon historical criticism from a rhetorical perspective as well as social critical theory. Fulkerson depends primarily upon poststructuralism, with the addition of Marxist analysis and narrative theory. Kwok refers primarily to postcolonial theory. Tanner combines postmodernism with a revised postliberalism. Within each of these approaches, they each establish pragmatic, liberationist norms. I will examine the similarities and differences of these norms later in this chapter.

Alternative Theological Methods

In order to contrast the different theological methods that the four feminists propose as alternatives to modern, liberal approaches, it is helpful to review their purposes, communal foci, and overall method.

Schüssler Fiorenza wants to recognize the women and men who have been marginalized in historical and contemporary Christian communities.

Therefore, she concentrates on the faith communities of marginalized women and men who struggle against oppression. Her rhetorical reading strategies allow her access to the marginalized and silenced voices within the early Jesus movement.

Fulkerson wants to recognize women whose faith traditions and commitments place them outside the realm of traditional feminist practice. Therefore, she concentrates upon the women who belong to politically and religiously conservative faith communities. Her intertextual analysis and the notion of a canonical system enable her to attend to the liberative aspects of their faith practices within their own faith traditions.

Kwok wants to recognize the women and men who have been colonized by western, Christian traditions. Therefore, she concentrates upon Asian Christian communities with their multifaith and multicultural context. Her multifaith hermeneutics and process of dialogical imagination reveal the multiple, shifting identities of Asian Christians that shape the multiple meanings of scripture and Christian traditions.

Tanner wants to recognize the liberative potential and diversity of traditional Christian beliefs. Therefore, she concentrates upon historically dominant Christian communities and their use of Christian materials. Her analysis of style allows her to construct liberative guidelines from her selection and organization of Christian doctrines, while recognizing the fluidity and diversity of these constructions within different Christian traditions.

These differences in purpose, communal focus, and method have implications for their approach to history, for the critical force which they give to scripture and Christian doctrine, for the social construction of identity, for their choice of community, for their authoritative criteria, and for their understanding of revelation. Each of these areas will now be discussed.

Historical Adequacy

Although all four feminists resist textual and historical positivism, they each attempt to take history and the Bible seriously. The extent to which they do so without falling into modern positivist fallacies is debated amongst them.

Historical and textual positivism, according to Schüssler Fiorenza, assumes one can uncover the hidden reality behind and in the biblical text. Once uncovered, these established facts help ascertain the original meaning of the text. Schüssler Fiorenza suggests that these assumptions ignore the rhetorical nature of the texts. They are not a direct correspondence with reality, but a reflection of the power and privilege of the writers. Her rhetorical approach to the text takes this bias into consideration. Through rhetoric, she reconstructs the text's socio-historical context to more adequately represent a marginalized historical perspective.

Fulkerson agrees with Schüssler Fiorenza's critique of historical and textual positivism, but argues that Schüssler Fiorenza's historical reconstruction commits the same modern fallacy. When Schüssler Fiorenza refers to her own reconstruction as a factual, more adequate representation of reality, she assumes that a pre-discursive reality exists and can be uncovered with the proper approach.

Fulkerson's critique is only valid for Schüssler Fiorenza's earlier work. In her later writing Schüssler Fiorenza is careful not to refer to her reconstructions as factual accounts of history. She does not propose historical accuracy or representation. Rather, she emphasizes the rhetorical nature of her own work much more explicitly. However, she is unwilling to dispense with her criteria of historical adequacy.[1] Even though one can never discover what really happened, there are enough literary and archeological clues that render some historical reconstructions more adequate than others. These clues can also declare certain reconstructions illegitimate. For instance, historical accounts that deny the genocide of the Beothuk Nation in Newfoundland or the extermination of Jewish, lesbian and gay, and mentally and physically disabled "undesirables" in the Holocaust must be discounted. By insisting on historical adequacy, Schüssler Fiorenza takes history seriously, especially in honour of those who have suffered. Her primary concern is reconstructing history from the perspective of the marginalized, and it is against these groups that she measures her historical adequacy. Postmodernists, she argues, are unable to take history seriously because they deem it inaccessible. She insists that biblical texts must not be locked away in ancient times by historical-critical scholars, nor removed from their historical contexts by poststructuralists and literary theorists, nor ahistorically adopted by literalists and postliberals.

Fulkerson is aware of the ahistorical tendency of her poststructural approach. To counteract this she acknowledges that it is possible to have an adequate historical interpretation discerned through construction. What makes it adequate is not its accurate representation of reality, but the location of its production in an historical community. Fulkerson underscores the importance of historical occasions that are formative for a particular community. It is of little significance whether or not these historical memories actually happened. What is crucial is the authoritative weight the community gives them. For the Presbyterian women, reformed doctrine and practices are crucial. For the Pentecostal women, holiness traditions and practices are paramount. Tanner's detailed account of medieval theological positions would have little, if any, effect upon both groups, as these traditions are not consciously part of either group's canonical systems. Thus, Fulkerson's primary concern is with historical doctrines, events and practices that are deemed formative and given meaning by particular faith communities. In this respect she acknowledges that Christianity must explore, reconceive, criticize, celebrate and be accountable to the past.[2]

Kwok builds upon both Schüssler Fiorenza and Fulkerson's approaches. She rhetorically reconstructs the histories of Asian Christians, with emphasis upon the women, using popular sources and eastern philosophy. Like Schüssler Fiorenza, she is primarily interested in those who have been shut out of the dominant Christian traditions. Like Fulkerson, she focuses upon historical aspects particular to certain groups. She recognizes the value of Schüssler Fiorenza's use of historical-critical tools. She also acknowledges the indebtedness of postcolonialism to postmodern theory. However, she questions the usefulness of both historical criticism and postmodern theory for marginalized communities. She notes that Asian and African-American Christian communities are less concerned with the historical reality of the Bible than with the application of the Bible's religious and moral insights in their contemporary lives. Kwok is more interested in the history of colonized peoples than in the history of Western faith communities. In her historical reconstruction, she focuses upon the interaction of Asian people within their own multicultural and multifaith traditions as they struggle against the multifaceted oppressions of colonization. She warns that the debate between modernists and postmodernists tends to be more interested in abstract concepts than in the concerns of colonized peoples. Historical reconstructions must therefore be judged not by particular methods, but by the communities themselves as to their adequacy.

In some measure of contrast to the other three, Tanner bases her measurement of historical adequacy primarily upon traditional Christian doctrines. She judges the accuracy and coherency of particular beliefs and practices by their adherence to fundamental Christian beliefs. Tanner acknowledges that certain Christian beliefs have proven oppressive, but she refuses a totalistic critique of all Christian beliefs. Even in her later work, when she challenges the fixed meanings of any theological statement, she admits that some beliefs that have been too closely associated with patriarchy should be suppressed and de-emphasised.[3] However, she is convinced that other traditional doctrines are liberative and she attempts to reclaim them for the benefit of those struggling against oppression. She wants to break the dualism between conservative Christian traditionalists and liberative Christian revisionists. If she can offer a convincing argument that the fundamentals of the Christian faith call for a radical, liberative response, she will remove the faith basis for the conservative protection of the status quo.

Although the other feminists do not emphasize the coherency of their methods with traditional Christian doctrine, they do draw upon particular Christian beliefs to support their emancipatory concerns. Schüssler Fiorenza refers to the *basileia* of God, Fulkerson refers to agapic ideals, and Kwok refers to the unity of the body of Christ. However, they clearly locate these Christian ideals within the relations of power of their communal construction.

These three feminists are wary of a postliberal approach that does not question oppressive power relations embedded in these accounts of history. Ecclesial pronouncements of heresy and right belief benefit dominant Christian groups at the expense of those shut out of power. Although Tanner explores contemporary and historical contextual readings of these statements that allow for widely diverse, sometimes contradictory interpretations, she does not question the statements themselves. Schüssler Fiorenza insists that all Christian doctrine be viewed suspiciously as patriarchal constructs. Only as they contribute to emancipation can they be reclaimed. Kwok agrees, adding that western Christian traditions are deeply embedded in a complex web of imperialist western cultures.

While Fulkerson is less willing to make such totalistic critiques of Christian traditions, she would be uncomfortable with Tanner's judgement of correct communal readings and faithful practice. What may be considered correct by one community may be considered heresy by another. To make external judgements of Christian communities is to commit the same fallacy of the "liberal economy:" one person is given the power to name correct belief or faithful practice for everyone else.[4] Since postliberals name those who judge correct belief as the saints, Fulkerson asks if they recognize any saints in the Pentecostal community.[5] As repeated church schisms prove, there is no doctrinal unity among the saints!

These criticisms may have influenced Tanner's move away from postliberalism towards postmodernism in her later work. She no longer refers to correct or proper interpretations, but the logical coherence of someone's position according to her or his own selection and organization of Christian materials. She still stresses the importance of traditional Christian beliefs and their persuasive influence in contemporary theological arguments. In fact, she urges feminist theologians to remain traditional by appealing to Christian materials. This would greatly enhance their political impact and credibility within Christian theology: "the more traditional the material with which it works, the greater the influence of feminist theology."[6]

In Tanner's later work she seems more concerned with the coherence of particular arrangements of Christian material than with their proper interpretation according to fundamental rules. Instead of appealing to historical continuity with *the* Christian tradition, she focuses on particular selections and arrangements of the diverse, multiple Christian traditions that will best support liberative practices.[7] Although she still bases her own theological positions upon traditional, overarching doctrines and canonical criticism, she is careful to base her critique of other positions upon their own selective use of Christian material.

In sum, each feminist recognizes the importance of historical traditions, cultures, events and faith practices. They also agree that they can only be accessed through rhetorical reconstruction. Where they differ is in the particular historical material considered, as it relates to their focus upon particular communities. Schüssler Fiorenza concentrates upon the material, both canonical and extra canonical, that best allows her to reconstruct silenced and marginalized voices from the early Christian communities. Fulkerson concentrates upon material which is most formative for particular, conservative Christian communities. Kwok concentrates upon material which is most formative for colonized Christian communities. Tanner's focus is much broader as she concentrates upon traditional doctrines that have been formative for different Christian communities throughout history. Her latest work concentrates on the manner in which different Protestant and Roman Catholic communities appropriate historical doctrines.

Scriptural and Doctrinal Agency

In this section I will discuss how each feminist enables scripture and doctrine to have agency within their particular communities of interest. Fulkerson's poststructural approach insists that biblical texts and Christian traditions do not have inherent patriarchal or liberative meanings. Rather, their meaning is constructed within the performance of the faith community. Thus, texts that are read as patriarchal in one community may be understood as liberative in another. Because Fulkerson resists granting any subject pre-discursive reality and agency, she views biblical texts and theological statements as unstable in themselves. They contain the potential for limitless meanings and are only stabilized within a particular community's performance of them. Stabilization occurs when a particular community's own ideal and resisting reading regimes grant biblical texts meaning and limit their number of possible interpretations. Thus, it is not Christian traditions or the biblical texts *per se* that have agency to limit and direct proper interpretations. Rather, it is through their appropriation and use by the community, as the community understands them in light of their own historical traditions, that scriptural and doctrinal texts gain agency to limit and adjudicate particular interpretations.

Particularly in her later work, Tanner agrees that the biblical texts and Christian doctrine are structurally indeterminate. They only become stabilized through communal use. In her later work she suggests that it is their relation to each other, as selected and organized in different patterns, that stabilizes their meaning. She also suggests that some doctrines, through established historical use, are more stabilized than others, but even these meanings can be shaken apart by future uses.[8] The community's assumed sense of scripture will also influence the reading and practice of other Christian materials. Essentially, Fulkerson and Tanner, in her later work, agree that scripture and doctrine gain meaning and critical force through their use within faith communities. As an example of the critical force of certain arrangements, Tanner suggests that if biblical texts are read in light of the gospel narratives, proper interpretation will support inclusive beliefs, attitudes and behaviours over conservative, exclusive practices. If Christian traditions are understood in light of God's transcendence and God's creative agency, liberative interpretations will be preferred to those supporting the status quo. Through their relationship with each other, biblical texts and doctrines provide a "general practical import" of guidelines which resist the oppressive status quo, but still allow a diversity of particular micro-level applications.

Schüssler Fiorenza grants agency to the biblical texts and limits their multiple meanings through grammatical and historical criticisms. Even though she has adopted many poststructural critiques in her later work, she still utilizes modern historical criticism to prevent an endless play of significations. However, although she suggests that historical criticism also allows the biblical texts the distance needed to challenge us,[9] she gives little attention to this. Instead, her primary interest is the emancipatory impact which scripture has within communities. In the interaction of the community with scripture, both have impact on each other.

Kwok is even less concerned than Schüssler Fiorenza with the need to limit scriptural readings. Rather, she focuses upon the need to multiply their possible interpretations in juxtaposition with Asian scriptures. Like Fulkerson and Schüssler Fiorenza, she is interested primarily in the meanings found in the performance of scripture. As with Schüssler Fiorenza, Kwok emphasizes the mutual impact that scripture and community have on each other. Her primary concern is the *enactment* of the biblical text within the practice of faith communities as they discern the living Gospel.

This concept of living Gospel has some affinities with Tanner's plain sense and her later reference to the Word of God. Kwok would be uncomfortable with my identification of the living Gospel with the Word of God. However, I believe that it is more a matter of disagreement over the meaning of the construct "Word of God" than with the association of the living Gospel with God's incarnated presence and ongoing revelation in the world. For Kwok and Tanner it is the connection of diverse faith communities with the living Gospel or Word of God that provides theological unity and correction to unjust practices and readings. The living Gospel or free Word of God, rather than the Bible, stands against us. Tanner uses the descriptive "free" in order to emphasize that our language and actions can only approximate and not contain the Word. In our judgements, we must always "remain open for new movements of faithfulness to a free Word."[10]

From this overview we can see affinities between Fulkerson and Tanner, and between Schüssler Fiorenza and Kwok. Fulkerson explores the formative influence of scripture and doctrine within the canonical systems of particular communities. Likewise, Tanner examines their critical force within particular patterns of use. Schüssler Fiorenza and Kwok are less concerned with doctrine than they are with scripture. Their interest in scripture is focused primarily on the liberative impact it has within marginalized communities. Thus, they locate scriptural agency in the interaction with community, in which scripture and community act upon each other. Tanner and Kwok also share a certain degree of affinity in their insistence that the living Gospel or Word of God is the ultimate source of critical agency.

Subjecthood and Community

Closely connected with scriptural and doctrinal agency is personal agency and subjecthood. In this section I will examine how each feminist retains political agency for discursively constructed subjects within particular communities.

In her later work, Schüssler Fiorenza affirms the poststructural notion of the discursively constructed subject. Identities such as woman or lesbian are not stable essences of identity, but the sites of conflicting discourses.[11] Her use of the term "wo/men" indicates that women do not constitute a unitary group, but are fragmented and fractured by multiple identities.[12] Schüssler Fiorenza is, however, unwilling to relinquish woman as subject or political unit. She takes issue with postmodern tendencies to erase the subjecthood of women and other marginalized groups. She notes that colonized others cannot afford to abandon the notion of subject nor the possibility of defining the world.[13]

Fulkerson defends postmodern theorists, including Foucault and Judith Butler, by explaining that they are only destabilizing, not destroying, the subject. Constitution of women or lesbian and gay people outside of discourse essentializes them. Fulkerson notes the horrendous historical consequences of gender or sexual orientation understood not as a social construction but as a natural essence. Although Schüssler Fiorenza recognizes the multiple identities of women, Fulkerson accuses her of still retaining a pre-discursive notion of woman underneath the social construction.[14]

Fulkerson does acknowledge the difficulty of the poststructural destabilization of the subject. Taken to its logical end, deconstruction renders communication impossible. If subjects can only exist within the context of each one's unique discursive context, there would be no basis for intercommunication across discourses or for social change. Similarity or identity associations, as well as common language construction, could not occur. In order to bridge this impasse, Fulkerson recommends rhetorical narrative. Stories about a God of justice within a particular situation and the occlusion of people from this situation will encourage connections and social change. A "narrative of conversion" enacted through religious and/or feminist rituals may allow an opening to the other and to threads of solidarity.[15]

It is at this point that Fulkerson concedes that she is "not finally a poststructuralist."[16] She finds poststructuralism to be the best method for breaking apart hegemonies, but agrees that it is insufficient for communication and social change.[17] For this reason, she also defends the need for new universals of structural sin. While she resists universalizing a subject or category, such as gender, she suggests that systemic violation based upon gender can be universalized. "Gendered fallibility" is based upon stories of the corruption of gender relations, and is therefore context dependent and discursively embedded. When taken together, these stories indicate sexuality to be a site where sinful response is a "likely possibility."[18] Thus, actions of discursively located subjects can be narrated to project likely future actions of subjects yet to be located. The fine line

Fulkerson draws between pre-discursive and socially constructed subjects has become precariously thin.

Kwok suggests that western debates between essentialists and poststructuralists focus on ontological rather than political identities.[19] She uses identity terminology, such as Asian and woman, only as a political description of position, and not as an ontological depiction of essence. She would resist any attempt to define subjecthood outside of multiple discourses. Along with Fulkerson, Kwok insists that even within discourses, identities remain unstable and fluid. Multiple subject positions produce multiple identities within multilevel discourses. It is not subjecthood that offers agency for change, but political affinities.

Tanner agrees that subjects are discursively constructed and offers a theological critique of essentialized subjecthood. Her conviction that all subjects are created by and are dependent upon God does not rule out social construction but qualifies it. As creatures of God, our identities are socially constructed within our relationships and contexts. However, the particularity and diversity of all created subjects transgresses human attempts to construct boundaries of social identity. Socially constructed categories of race, gender, and sexual orientation cannot contain this diversity and must not be identified as natural and divinely-created. Such identification essentializes particular identities and occludes diversity within these categories. In order to respect the diversity of all creation, Tanner emphasizes along with the other three feminists the shifting and multiple boundaries of identity. Similar to Kwok's preference of political identity over ontological, Tanner prefers to define identity relationally rather than ontologically in order to honour the multiple identities of the subject within the limitations and possibilities of relationships with God and one another.

All four feminists agree that subjects are socially constructed within community. Thus, discussions about subjecthood ultimately refer to community. Schüssler Fiorenza's fragmented and fractured identity of wo/men is stabilized through further identification of the multiple identities of subjects within particular contemporary and historical communities of oppressed peoples (the ekklēsia of wo/men). Fulkerson also stabilizes subjects through their construction within particular Christian communities and within rhetorical narration, although she warns that such stabilization is always temporary. Kwok is even more cautious about such stabilization, insisting that even within communities, identities remain unstable and fluid, as indicated by her focus upon political, rather than ontological identity. Tanner suggests that our relationship with God further relativizes and destabilizes our boundaries of social identity. Like Kwok, she prefers to define identity relationally with God and one another.

With these understandings of subjecthood and community in mind, let us return to the different types of communities upon which each feminist focuses. Let us recall from my earlier overview of their methods that their differing communal foci figure prominently in the distinction of their methods. The type of community chosen directly reflects the difference in the purpose of their methods, as I will now further elaborate.

Schüssler Fiorenza's purpose is to recognize the women and men who have been marginalized in historical and contemporary Christian communities. She therefore seeks to reconstruct the early Christian communities in order to reclaim the voices which have been obliterated or marginalized. Because Schüssler Fiorenza's vision of a democratic, liberative and inclusive faith community cannot be realized within institutional churches, she calls for alternate faith communities of people who have been marginalized in institutional churches and society, and who struggle against oppression. It is to these historical and contemporary faith communities, which she calls the ekklēsia of wo/men, that she is accountable.

In contrast to Schüssler Fiorenza, Fulkerson is not interested in the creation of new faith communities. Fulkerson's purpose is to recognize women whose faith traditions and commitments place them outside the realm of traditional feminist practice. She therefore examines the existing faith communities of these women in order to understand their compliance with and resistance to oppressive gender practices in their communities. Her analysis of the canonical system takes her into the past traditions and practices of these communities that remain formative in the social construction of the women and their biblical interpretations.

Kwok's purpose includes elements of both Schüssler Fiorenza's and Fulkerson's. Like Schüssler Fiorenza, Kwok is interested in people who have been marginalized within the dominant Christian traditions. Like Fulkerson, she is interested in the social construction of the identity and faith practices of a particular group of people. Therefore, she does not seek to establish new faith communities, but to conduct a postcolonial analysis of the faith communities of colonized peoples and their multicultural/multifaith contexts. She also extends her analysis beyond these particular faith communities into dialogue and solidarity with other faith communities around the globe.

Like Schüssler Fiorenza and Kwok, Tanner is interested in people who have been marginalized within Christian traditions. Like Fulkerson, she seeks to find liberative strands within Christian beliefs and practices that address this marginalization. However, unlike Fulkerson, she is not content to explain the resistance that is already present within faith communities. Rather, she seeks to further reconstruct liberative possibilities from particular selections and organizations of Christian materials. While Fulkerson concentrates upon certain faith communities, Tanner broadens her focus to a variety of different Christian traditions. Like Kwok, Tanner is interested in dialogue (or argument) amongst Christian communities as they seek to be united amidst diversity.

Revelation and Authority

The various purposes for each feminist's work have direct implications not only upon their communal foci, but also upon their choice of method and authoritative criteria. In turn, this has direct implications upon their understanding of revelation.

Throughout all of Tanner's work she has consistently underscored the universality of God's grace and the provisional nature of human judgements. She argues on the basis of God's transcendence that only God is absolute. All human perceptions and judgements must therefore be understood as partial. Any claims to absolute truth, "God-endorsed" decisions,[20] or empirically-proven facts that are placed beyond critique are idolatrous. Thus, human endeavours are limited and relativized in light of God's transcendence, and must be open to critique. Such recognition of our creaturehood and dependence upon God gives us a sense of humility.

Although none of the other feminists emphasizes the limitations and fallibility of human endeavours, no one would argue this point. Where they and many other theologians disagree is with Tanner's elaboration of God's transcendence in her earlier work. By positing fundamental and derivative rules to judge proper Christian interpretation, Tanner committed the same fallacies which she later critiqued within the work of postliberals.

Fulkerson joins Tanner in this later critique of postliberal use of grammatical rules to judge the appropriate use of Christian traditions. Fulkerson notes that, although postliberals agree that the rules originated within the context of Christian communities, they raise them to universals that retain a constant, inherent meaning outside of any signifying process. Their intratextual approach brings closure to biblical and historical texts by granting them their own self-contained meanings. When they are then used to measure other interpretations, the diversity of Christian traditions and the diversity of interpretations in different social locations is undermined. If each of these interpretations is judged by a meaning derived outside of their communities from a postliberal theologian's social location, the particular significations of each community will be lost. Different readings of a particular doctrinal rule will either be rendered invalid or will be dismissed as irrelevant to their overall adherence to this universal.[21]

Tanner acknowledges in *Theories of Culture* that the positing of rules or fundamentals is problematic and proposes style as an alternative. In order to discern Christian identity, she suggests looking at the style in which Christian materials are used. It is not the meaning of the materials, but the manner in which they are used that unifies diverse interpretations. Style is more general than the specificity of rules, and better honours the diversity of Christian interpretations. Interestingly enough, Tanner has not abandoned her rule of God's transcendence, nor presumably her rule for God's creative agency. What has changed is her use of these beliefs. Instead of positing them as fixed constants, she acknowledges that they may change in meaning as they are variously placed alongside different Christian materials. They can only offer general guidelines, at best. Her earlier work also emphasized their general practical import and she had cautioned against particularizing them outside of communal use. However, she is much more careful in her later work not to define theological statements beyond a general practical import.

As Tanner is beginning to identify more closely with postmodern than with postliberal methods, she is moving closer to Fulkerson's method. Their similarities include the insistence that the meanings of Christian materials are constructed by communal use. They also complement one another's method. Fulkerson's canonical system helps to explain how communities select and organize Christian materials. Tanner's use of style amplifies Fulkerson's canonical system by explaining how different Christian communities can communicate and be unified across their diverse contexts and interpretations. In addition, Tanner's understanding of plain sense as the community's traditional understanding of a biblical text can help inform Fulkerson's canonical system. In a recent article Fulkerson acknowledges the benefit of Tanner's understanding of plain sense as communal consensus.[22] This description explains the normative weight which communities give a particular biblical interpretation, regardless of their agreement with it.

Tanner's use of plain sense is helpful only to the extent that she dispenses with her additional, undefined concept of plain sense. Because of the confusion around the varying definitions of plain sense, and the related terms of literal sense and *sensus literalis*, I propose the construct "assumed senses" to convey the plurality of different community's traditional understandings of the biblical text. This construct emphasizes that the common sense, or community's sense of a text arises out of traditionally constructed assumptions.

Tanner's move towards postmodernism may lead her into the same apolitical dilemma of poststructuralism which Fulkerson experiences. As Tanner incorporates more postmodern critiques, she is less able to develop universal criteria with which to judge historical or doctrinal adequacy and ethical accountability. This political impasse of postmodernism has been extensively critiqued by Schüssler Fiorenza.

Schüssler Fiorenza notes that postmodernism abandons not only the agency of the subject, but also any metanarrative that can provide universal values of truth, justice, freedom and equality. Because of its relative pluralism and endless signifying, political change is inhibited and feminist standpoints are negated. There can be no epistemological privilege of the oppressed.[23] Although Kwok has difficulty with standpoint theory, she joins with Schüssler Fiorenza to insist that our critique cannot be limited to local and regional communities. Because we are part of both global and local communities and systems of oppression, we must critique global, systemic totalities and not privatize emancipatory struggles.[24]

In order to be constructive as well as deconstructive and offer a liberationist methodology, Fulkerson is turning increasingly to narrative Christian theology, and Tanner uses a political theory of culture to reformulate a postliberal emphasis upon Christian doctrine. Based upon a collection of socially located stories, Fulkerson offers potential universals of sin, gendered fallibility, grace, and agapic love. These provide general guidelines, to be particularized within community. Likewise, Tanner's doctrines of God's transcendence and creative agency offer general practical import that can be specified conditionally within particular contexts. This might result in the universalization of ethical norms borrowed from the wider society because of God's universal concerns. Hierarchical relations in the wider culture might also be dumped upside down because of our humility before God. Such characterizations are only possibilities, however, and not definitive. Reference to God relativizes all things, including characterizations.

While these guidelines move Tanner and Fulkerson out of the political impasse of postmodernism, their critical edge may still be too vague to be effective. In order to sharpen it, both turn to pragmatic norms. Fulkerson measures the degree to which women resist gender oppression within their own faith traditions. Tanner demonstrates that God's creative agency calls for a respect for the diversity of all creatures. This belief offers pragmatic guidelines that oppose intolerance and oppressive relations of dominance and exploitation: the least powerful deserve the greatest right to be heard; the concept of nonidolatrous esteem challenges the inflated self-esteem of oppressors and the lack of self-esteem of the oppressed; and communitarian goals should not sacrifice the individual but respect the diversity of the community.

Schüssler Fiorenza and Kwok also use a combination of various methods and pragmatic norms that allow both diversity and political action. Schüssler Fiorenza uses poststructuralism to explain the social construction of subjects and the historically contingent, constructed nature of truth.[25] Poststructuralism, combined with the rhetorical method, also helps to demonstrate the multiple, constructed meanings of the biblical texts. At the same time, she uses archaeology, historical criticism, literary theory, sociology, and political social theory to determine the limitations of multiple meanings and provide ethical criteria of accountability and historical adequacy. Recently, Schüssler Fiorenza has suggested that postcolonialism might be the best methodology to offer such an integration. As she explains, postcolonialism is the only "post" term which contrasts its method with an oppressive situation (colonialism) rather than with a philosophical approach (modernity, structuralism or liberalism). It is the only term which is explicitly emancipatory.[26]

Although Kwok is cautious about the use of postmodernism and other western methods for colonized peoples, she does acknowledge their value for Eastern scholars. She herself employs rhetorical criticism, poststructural theory, and on some occasions historical criticism, in her analysis of the biblical texts.[27] Similar to Schüssler Fiorenza, she calls for correlative thinking that will interweave historical criticism, postmodern and postcolonial theory, literary criticism, sociology and reader-response theory. For Kwok this reading strategy of parallel processing will incorporate eastern and western religious, cultural and philosophical traditions into a multifaith hermeneutic. In order to attend to the diversity of peoples throughout the globe, and give a systemic analysis of colonial systems of oppression, Kwok finds that such an integrative approach is necessary.

The risk of using multidisciplinary methods is the potential for contradiction and misconstrual of the methods. For example, Schüssler Fiorenza and Kwok continue to insist that certain scriptural texts are patriarchal, while at the same time emphasizing the rhetorical construction of their multiple meanings. Fulkerson points out the inconsistency of a poststructural emphasis on constructed meaning with such totalistic critiques of a text. In spite of the potential for contradictions, though, all four feminists agree that a multidisciplinary approach is necessary. They find the integration of various approaches key to a new emancipatory paradigm for theological method and would together reiterate Kwok's call to enter into another time-frame on the edges of modernity and postmodernity.

This new paradigm would insist that pragmatic, liberative criteria be located and discerned within local faith communities. Truth and revelation would be understood relationally, to be found within the interaction of the community and its traditions. To this end, Tanner and Kwok urge us to move beyond the particular communities, such as those emphasized by Fulkerson (conservative, Christian communities) and Schüssler Fiorenza (ekklēsia of wo/men), and call for dialogue amongst various Christian traditions, as well as various faith traditions. They both insist on a pragmatic approach to this dialogue that begins not on common points of belief, but on a common respect for differences and a concern for the welfare of the earth and its creatures.[28]

The impetus for this common vision comes, in part, from God's revelation variously expressed through the living Gospel, the Word of God, the *basileia* of G*d, and agapic love. Accompanying this openness to God's revelation is humility. Tanner believes that the limitations of our humanity require a humble acceptance of self-critique and openness to those with whom we disagree. She calls for a community of argument united in their common Christian tasks.[29] Kwok extends this understanding of humility to a multifaith context. Christians must humbly receive revelation and critique from other faith traditions.

Tanner and Kwok both stress the importance of unity amidst diversity and solidarity. Kwok emphasizes the unity and connectedness of the one body of Christ that is inclusive of diversity and conscious of inevitable conflict that accompanies diversity. In order to have a global consciousness, Kwok encourages diverse Christian communities to connect with the wider body of Christ. An interfaith process of dialogical imagination will enable conflicts to be faced within a deeper sense of solidarity or interconnection. It will also deepen the analysis of the intersection of race, class, gender, culture, and history. Without this analysis, Kwok warns that solidarity may be an excuse for indifference or the obliteration of diversity. "Such critical engagement is the beginning for solidarity."[30]

Conclusion

Each of the four feminists has developed a theological alternative to liberal, modern approaches in order to better attend to issues of diversity and marginalization within faith communities. Their methodologies share many similarities corresponding to their mutual concerns. Their divergence in methodology is related to their different purposes for their work.

While elements in each of their methods can be improved by the critiques from the others, as suggested in this chapter, each method is best suited to its particular purpose. For this reason, each one's purpose must be kept in mind during evaluation. Schüssler Fiorenza has not recognized the liberative attempts of women within conservative faith traditions to resist patriarchal oppression, but her primary focus is upon people marginalized by dominant Christian traditions. Fulkerson has not sufficiently developed global criteria of accountability, but her primary focus is upon liberative aspects of contemporary women who are marginalized not only by their own communities of faith but also by feminist communities. Kwok has dispensed with the concept of biblical canon, thereby discouraging the contribution of many faith communities which uphold the biblical canon (including ethnic minorities) to her dialogical imagination. However, her primary focus is upon Christian communities in Asia, which are multi-scriptural in orientation. Tanner has not incorporated reconstructed stories of the marginalized into her method, but her primary focus is upon the liberative aspects of dominant Christian traditions and the use of Christian materials by emancipatory Christian communities.

Gaps in each method may not necessarily be a weakness but may simply affirm a need for a variety of methodologies to work together and complement one another. Kwok urges us to enter into another time frame. She and Schüssler Fiorenza call for the integration of modern and postmodern approaches. Tanner humbly offers her methodology as a supplement to other approaches "in the service of greater justice."[31] Indeed, the political impact of revisionist theologies, such as Schüssler Fiorenza's, will be much greater if they are accompanied by an internal critique. The potential arising from Tanner's "politics of solidarity"[32] amongst methodologically diverse theologies is tremendous.

In the following section I will examine the usefulness of a braided combination of these four methods within a liberal, Protestant denomination that is struggling with issues of diversity and marginalization relating to sexuality.

Notes to Chapter 6

1. See in particular Elisabeth Schüssler Fiorenza, *But She Said: Feminist Practices of Biblical Interpretation* (Boston: Beacon Press, 1992), 90.

2. Mary McClintock Fulkerson, *Changing the Subject: Women's Discourses and Feminist Theology* (Minneapolis: Fortress Press, 1994), 128, ftnt. 20.

3. Kathryn E. Tanner, "Social Theory Concerning the 'New Social Movements' and the Practice of Feminist Theology," in *Horizons in Feminist Theology: Identity, Tradition, and Norms*, ed. Rebecca S. Chopp and Sheila Greeve Davaney (Minneapolis: Fortress Press, 1997), 189.

4. Fulkerson, *Changing the Subject*, 162.

5. Fulkerson, *Changing the Subject*, 162, 364.

6. Tanner, "Social Theory Concerning the 'New Social Movements,' " 192.

7. Tanner, "Social Theory Concerning the 'New Social Movements,' " 188.

8. Kathryn E. Tanner, *Theories of Culture: A New Agenda for Theology*, Guides to Theological Inquiry (Minneapolis: Fortress Press, 1997), 78.

9. Elisabeth Schüssler Fiorenza, "The Ethos of Interpretation: Biblical Studies in a Postmodern and Postcolonial Context," Presentation, The Association of Korean Theologians at Usong, The Republic of Korea, October 26, 1996, 17.

10. Tanner, *Theories of Culture*, 155.

11. Schüssler Fiorenza, *But She Said*, 108.

12. Elisabeth Schüssler Fiorenza, *Jesus: Miriam's Child, Sophia's Prophet: Critical Issues in Feminist Christology* (New York: Continuum, 1994), 24.

13. Elisabeth Schüssler Fiorenza, *Discipleship of Equals: A Critical Feminist Ekklesia-Logy of Liberation* (New York: Crossroad, 1993), 284.

14. Mary McClintock Fulkerson, "Contesting Feminist Canons: Discourse and the Problem of Sexist Texts," *Journal of Feminist Studies in Religion* 7, no. 2 (Fall 1991): 66.

15. Fulkerson, "Feminist Exploration," 216–219.

16. Mary McClintock Fulkerson, "Contesting the Gendered Subject: A Feminist Account of the *Imago Dei*," in *Horizons in Feminist Theology: Identity, Tradition, and Norms*, ed. Rebecca S. Chopp and Sheila Greeve Davaney (Minneapolis: Fortress Press, 1997), 245, ftnt. 8.

17. Fulkerson, "Contesting the Gendered Subject," 113.

18. Mary McClintock Fulkerson, "Sexism as Original Sin: Developing a Theacentric Discourse," *Journal of the American Academy of Religion* 59, no. 4 (Winter 1991): 671–73.

19. See Kwok Pui-lan, *Discovering the Bible in the Non-Biblical World*, The Bible and Liberation Series (Maryknoll: Orbis Books, 1995), 24–26.

20. This term was used in reference to capital punishment in a Letter to the Editor of a local newspaper. See James Knox, "God's Power is Life-Transforming," *The Toronto Star*, February 18 1998, A19.

21. Fulkerson, *Changing the Subject*, 130, 148, 156–64.

22. Mary McClintock Fulkerson, " 'Is There a (Non-Sexist) Bible in this Church?' A Feminist Case for the Priority of Interpretive Communities," *Modern Theology* 14, no. 2 (April, 1998): 225–42.

23. Elisabeth Schüssler Fiorenza, "Text and Reality—Reality as Text: The Problem of a Feminist Historical and Social Reconstruction Based on Texts," *Studia Theologica* 43 (1989): 24–27; Elisabeth Schüssler Fiorenza, "The Politics of Otherness: Biblical Interpretation as a Critical Praxis for Liberation," in *The Future of Liberation Theology: Essays in Honor of Gustavo Gutiérrez*, ed. Marc Ellis and Otto Maduro (New York: Orbis

Books, 1989), 316, 322; Schüssler Fiorenza, *Discipleship of Equals*, 370.

24. Schüssler Fiorenza, *Jesus*, 10–13.

25. Schüssler Fiorenza, *But She Said*, 108; Schüssler Fiorenza, "Text and Reality," 24.

26. Schüssler Fiorenza, "Biblical Studies in a Postmodern and Postcolonial Context," 1–5, 13, 15.

27. One example is her study of the Syrophoenician woman in which she refers to form criticism. See Kwok, *Discovering the Bible*, 76.

28. See in particular Kathryn E. Tanner, "Respect for Other Religions: A Christian Antidote to Colonialist Discourse," *Modern Theology* 9 (January 1993): 1–18; Kwok Pui-lan, "Ecology and the Recycling of Christianity," in *Ecotheology: Voices from South and North*, ed. David G. Hallman (Geneva: World Council of Churches, 1994), 107–11.

29. Tanner, *Theories of Culture*, 123–25, 152–54, 174–75.

30. Kwok Pui-lan, "The Sources and Resources of Feminist Theologies: A Post-Colonial Perspective," in *Sources and Resources of Feminist Theologies*, ed. Elisabeth Hartlieb and Charlotte Methuen, Yearbook of the European Society of Women in Theological Research, vol. 5 (Kampen: Kok Pharos Publishing House, 1997), 13.

31. Kathryn E. Tanner, *The Politics of God: Christian Theologies and Social Justice* (Minneapolis: Fortress Press, 1992), 257.

32. Tanner, *The Politics of God*, 257.

Part Two

Diversity
&
Community

within

Protestant
Denominations

Chapter 7

Theological Methods within Sexuality Documents of The United Church of Canada

Since its formation in 1925, The United Church of Canada has established itself as a faith community strongly committed to social justice issues.[1] Its official policies have reflected this concern about the welfare of the marginalized and oppressed in society, according to its understanding of the gospel of Christ. It has also established itself as a liberal church, open to and inclusive of a diversity of theological positions and political beliefs.

As defined in the first part of Chapter One, the term "liberal" refers to an emphasis upon human rights, equality, individual freedom, and democracy. By extension, within the United Church I am using the term "liberal" to refer to its emphasis upon the inclusion and equality of all voices with their diverse identities and theological perspectives. Its unwritten motto is "united amidst diversity" which is reflective of its liberal identity.

Although theologically conservative groups have been marginalized within the United Church, I will be using the word "marginalize" in reference to societal status. Western society attributes power and privilege to those who are white, heterosexual, and male. Those who differ from this dominant identity experience certain degrees of marginalization proportional to the degree of their divergence from the dominant identity. For instance, a First Nations lesbian would experience multiplicative forms of marginalization. Within this chapter I will be focusing upon the tension between conservative groups who uphold the status quo privileging heterosexual males, and those marginalized in society by gender and/or sexual orientation.

As a mix of conservative, liberal, and marginalized views, the United Church has found itself caught in this tension time and time again, torn between upholding a balance of diverse theological opinions, and siding with those marginalized by dominant identities within Canadian society. When the United Church has addressed issues of marginalization and confronted the oppressive aspects of the status quo, it has alienated some of its own members. In turn, their requests for equal consideration and inclusion have pressured the United Church to soften its political stands.

This conflict between its liberal and liberation agendas is particularly evident in its struggles around sexuality.[2] In what has proven to be one of the most divisive issues in its history, the United Church has tried to be inclusive of diverse opinions while still taking political action on behalf of lesbian and gay people. It has tried to be united amidst diversity while following through on commitments to social justice.

One of the ways in which the United Church deals with controversial issues is to develop documents that explore the theological and ethical components of these issues. In this section I will be examining sexuality documents from the 1960s and 1980s that have proven to be central in the debate over sexual orientation. After giving a brief introduction to each document, I will identify the theological methods employed in these documents, with particular attention given to authoritative sources and biblical interpretation.[3] I will then identify the liberal and modern aspects of these theological methods and examine the implications of these methods for women, as well as for lesbian and gay people. Although I will be making some reference to bisexual people in this chapter, these documents made little, if any reference to bisexuality, and none to transgendered people. Therefore, with reference to homosexuality, my comments will be limited primarily to lesbian and gay people. Because the term "homosexual" is usually used *about* us rather than *by* us, I will use it only in reference to the documents' own wording.

Before continuing, I must emphasize that my analysis and critiques of these sexuality documents use methods not yet established at the time most of these documents were written. Therefore my intent is not to criticize the documents for their failure to attend to particular concerns. On the contrary, most of these documents were as attentive as possible to the new insights and critical theories of their time. Rather, my intent is to expose problematic implications of modern and liberal approaches for the benefit of future work within Protestant contexts.

Overview of Sexuality Documents (1960–1988)

The United Church has produced numerous documents dealing with issues of sexuality, of which the most contentious have included discussion of sexual orientation. The most explosive and divisive debate took place in 1988 around the ordination and commissioning of lesbian and gay candidates, and centred around one of these documents. In addition to this document, three others have been central to these debates. One was published in 1960 while the others were published in the 1980s. Although the 1980 documents were the most controversial, I have included the 1960 document for two reasons. The first is that groups opposing the 1980 documents would often cite this 1960 document in support of their opposition. The second reason is that the parallels between the debates over gender in the 1960s and the debates over sexual orientation in the 1980s illuminate my arguments. I will begin with this 1960 document. Similar to Kathryn Tanner's method, I will use the same Christian materials as those who oppose homosexuality use in order to demonstrate the coherence of these materials with a liberation approach, rather than a conservative preservation of an anti-gay status quo.

Toward a Christian Understanding of Sex, Love, Marriage (1960)

In September 1956, the 17th General Council[4] initiated a "re-studying of the whole matter of Christian Marriage and Divorce," in part to provide a means for including humble repentance in church policy regarding the remarriage of divorced people.[5] This resulted in the first part of a report from the Commission on Christian Marriage and Divorce, as titled above, which was approved by the 19th General Council in 1960.

Sources for its theological method included scripture, Christian doctrines, previous United Church documents, special studies requested from social scientists and counsellors, recent studies of other denominations, media articles, and submissions from individuals, youth groups, married couples, United Church courts, and social agencies.[6] In this section I will look at the manner in which these sources were used and their implications for women, and for lesbian and gay people.

Care was taken not to base the report on isolated passages of scripture, "especially if they support a literalism and legalism which Jesus denounced." Instead, scriptural interpretation was to be based upon "the spirit of Christ as revealed in the whole of the New Testament."[7] The general purpose and order of the Kingdom of God was deemed more important than specific laws or social precepts.[8] The love of God and neighbour established the underlying purpose of life, while monogamous marriage contributed to the basic order.[9] This emphasis upon the social order had particular impact upon their view of marriage, gender roles and homosexuality, as I will now summarize.

Sexual expression was restricted to monogamous marriage, God's preordained institution which would allow men and women to complement and therefore complete each other, to procreate and raise their offspring, and to protect the stability of society.[10] Birth control was advocated for family planning, thereby indicating approval of sexual intercourse purely for the fulfilment of relationship. However, procreation and parental responsibility were still considered part of the primary purpose for marriage, and those who could not conceive were expected to adopt. Couples who chose not to raise children were therefore considered to be as "sinful" as those who bore children without regard to their care.[11]

This report exhibited ambivalence on women's emancipation. It supported the changing roles of women, which it attributed primarily to birth control. It also supported the corresponding change in men's roles.[12] The authors of the report wrote that women were spending more time outside of the home with social activities, and with work that was both volunteer and paid, while men were spending more time in the home, jointly sharing parental and housekeeping duties.[13] The authors stated this as a fact, although I assume that this was more a reflection of their hopes rather than statistical data. However, some literature from that time did indicate that men were beginning to participate in domestic duties both at home and at church socials.[14] The report noted that stereotypes of masculine and feminine roles were said to be giving way to a new "wholesomeness" and "full appreciation of human potential" which would no longer force partners into "performing puppet characterizations of husband, wife, parent."[15] One of the dangers of a rigid sex limitation of roles was social convention misconstruing a man's desire to paint or dance as homosexual tendencies. Because of societal misconstrual, the report feared that men might become homosexual.[16] Remarkably, therefore, gender stereotypes were discouraged as they were considered to threaten the institution of marriage. However, the same document stated that the stability of society could only be maintained by women and men accepting their traditional feminine and masculine roles. Clearly, the new "wholesomeness" was not without its ambiguity.

Acknowledgement was made of a small minority of people with a "learned" homosexual or bisexual orientation. Popular misconceptions that homosexual people were more criminally inclined were refuted. It encouraged fair, unprejudiced, and charitable attitudes towards homosexuals. However, it upheld the common societal view which considered homosexual acts as unnatural and indecent because of their inability to accomplish reproduction, one of the fundamental purposes given for the "sexual instinct."[17]

Four reasons were given for their view of homosexual conduct as immoral: 1) it was a sin against God (or nature)[18] because it violated God's will for "proper" sexual expression within monogamous marriage; 2) it was a sin against the self because of its "misuse of natural functions;" 3) it was a sin against other people because it involved sexual partners and was therefore "unedifying and destructive of neighbour love;" and 4) it was a sin against society because it tended "to undermine the foundations of a stable society based upon heterosexual marriage and family responsibility."[19]

Sin referred to sexual expression, both within and outside of marriage, which destroyed, degraded or fragmented life. It also referred to any sexual relations which contradicted the divine order, including common-law, extra-marital, pre-marital, and homosexual. With an understanding of redemption that included forgiveness and reconciliation, the documents urged the church to provide counselling for those experiencing marital problems, and to recognize that temporary or final separation may be eventually necessary.

The Commission was committed to a serious study of traditional Christian attitudes towards marriage and sexuality in light of modern advancements in medicine. United Church members were therefore urged to love God with their minds by considering these findings.[20] As an example they were encouraged to exercise responsible parenthood through the use of contraception. Under certain situations, voluntary sterilization and artificial insemination by the husband were also deemed acceptable.

Specific studies and statistics in the social sciences were also requested by the Commission on the role of women. The report referred to a survey distributed to Hamilton Conference youth in which a large majority believed that wives could "work after marriage for financial reasons."[21] In addition, most articles and letters published in the *United Church Observer* supported married women in the work force.[22] All of this led the Commission to consider in a positive light the changing roles of women and men, in spite of great reticence amongst church leaders.[23] The Commission gave more weight to these studies and the views of youth than they did to more conservative submissions supporting traditional gender roles.[24]

Normative value appears to have been given to scripture, traditional Christian doctrine, findings from the medical field and the social sciences, and the views of individuals and youth organizations. Scientific findings were particularly persuasive. The report carefully balanced each of these sources against the other to reach its conclusions. When in conflict, it favoured the more progressive views and interpretations of scripture that supported the emancipation of women and the challenge of patriarchal societal structures.

In God's Image ... Male and Female:
A Study on Human Sexuality (1980)

After a lengthy and strenuous debate, the 28th General Council approved *In God's Image* in 1980 not as church policy, but as a study document.[25] They also heeded mounting criticism to it and called for an accompanying document which would better reflect "the range of theological and ethical opinion in this area."[26]

As with previous documents, the sources for *In God's Image* were diverse. Social scientific research on sexuality and theologians who drew upon these findings, such as Paul Jewett, James Nelson, Tom Harpur, Tom Driver, and Virginia Ramey Mollenkott figured prominently in this report. It also referred to the Kinsey sexuality studies and to the removal of homosexuality from the list of mental disorders within the American Psychiatric Association and American Psychological Association.

Reference was made to federal, provincial, and municipal laws decriminalizing homosexual activity and protecting the rights of homosexual citizens. These included the 1969 amendment to the Criminal Code[27] legalizing sexual activity between two consenting adults in private, Québec adding sexual orientation to its Human Rights Code in 1977, and several major Canadian municipalities protecting the rights of homosexual people. These changes in Canadian law reflected the shift in societal attitudes towards sexual boundaries, and homosexuality in particular.

The report noted that the United Church had submitted briefs in 1976 and 1977 requesting that sexual orientation be added to the prohibited grounds of discrimination in the Ontario Human Rights Code and the Canadian Human Rights Act. Previous United Church documents and statements on sexuality and gender issues were also studied. Church tradition was mentioned as a source of authority[28] but, apart from mention of Martin Luther's Christological key to the interpretation of scripture,[29] minimal or negative reference[30] was given to traditional church practices and beliefs about sexuality.

These various sources, together with scripture, personal experience, and studies from other denominations, were assumed to belong to one of two categories: Christian heritage or contemporary knowledge. Both were considered essential sources of revelation that should be brought together in dialogue because "scientific research ... may speak the truth more faithfully about our world, and ourselves ... [and] may be a deeper and more authentic theology."[31]

The approach to biblical interpretation included the following principles:

1. All consciousness and understanding is historically conditioned. Biblical characters lived in their own language worlds.
2. Biblical texts must be given the distance needed to have their own integrity and be authentically themselves.
3. Scripture is a record of an ongoing hermeneutical process which builds upon, reinterprets and corrects itself. Jesus often appealed "beyond Scripture to Scripture," when he negated a particular biblical law in order to uphold a broader biblical principle.
4. Scripture must be set free to make contact with our lives and illumine the

present. This is accomplished through remembrance of our common
humanity.

5. The goal of biblical interpretation is not to critique or master the text, but to
    be critiqued and mastered by it. One must never assume complete knowledge
    of the meaning of a passage nor use the text to confirm prior values.

6. The Bible as a whole reveals Jesus Christ, who is the central norm by which
    scripture is judged.[32]

The Christological key was often observed throughout this document,
according to the following assumptions about Jesus' ministry. Jesus was
depicted as a "radical feminist" who resisted the patriarchal bias of
scripture.[33] Jesus also treated people holistically, honouring the body as
much as the spirit. Therefore he seemed to be comfortable with the
sexuality of himself and others, especially those considered sexually
unclean and sinful. Accordingly, he was more concerned with people than
with legalisms, and did not call for puritanical asceticism. These
characteristics were given as the Christ-like standard by which to judge all
scriptural passages and contemporary experience relating to sexuality. On
the basis of "the Movement and the Man," the following basic guidelines
regarding sexual behaviour were reached:

Is it creative and liberating? *In God's Image* continued to assume male
and female complementarity with one notable difference from the 1960
documents. No longer did women and men need each other to be complete.
Rather, masculine and feminine characteristics were to be recognized and
developed within each person.[34] The holistic goal was to become
androgynous, as Jesus was assumed to have been.[35]

Is it mutually supportive? The quality of relationship was deemed more
important than the form. Sexual relationships outside of marriage, including
non-permanent, extra-marital, and homosexual relationships, were
considered appropriate if they were faithful and mutually supportive. The
report suggested that "intention to faithfulness" be the basis of primary
relationships. However, exclusivity and permanence were understood as
mutually incompatible for many Christian couples. Therefore, permanence
and primacy of the marriage in honesty, openness and trust were valued at
the possible expense of sexual exclusivity.[36] Sexuality was considered

distorted when it was debased, trivialized, mechanized, exploitive, commercialized and manipulative.[37] When sexuality was "reduced to sex and used for ends other than the wholeness of persons" it was considered to be demonic.[38]

Is it socially responsible? No longer was procreation or the upholding of the social order mentioned as part of the purpose of sexuality. In fact, many oppressive aspects of the social order, such as double standards and institutionalized sexism in language, social and economic structures, attitudes, and social conventions were condemned.[39] Social responsibility no longer entailed a preservation of the social order, but a critical resistance to exploitation.[40]

Is it joyous? Sexuality, as a gift from God, was meant to enrich the individual and society in relationship with the self, with others, and with God.[41]

Gift, Dilemma and Promise:
A Report and Affirmations on Human Sexuality (1984)

In God's Image was circulated as a study document with other materials and over seventy facilitators were trained across Canada to assist in this study.[42] Four years later, in 1984, *Gift, Dilemma and Promise* was approved by the 30th General Council as a concluding report. This document made much less reference to external sources than *In God's Image*, but this could be due to its purpose of following up, with study and response, to *In God's Image*, rather than presenting new material. The negative reactions from the majority of the responses to *In God's Image*, together with negative reaction from the media and from at least one petition approved at the General Council in 1982,[43] may well have influenced the writing team's cautious approach and conclusions.

In order to indicate (and possibly defend) its faithfulness to United Church practice, the report claimed that it followed the way in which theology is developed in the United Church (assuming a common United Church theological method). It stated that the United Church does not form its theological positions on the basis of majority opinion, sharing of experiences or consensus. Rather, the report stressed that the United

Church carefully seeks God's will through consultation with the Bible, the great traditions, modern voices, and contemporary experience.

These four sources were categorized into church tradition and contemporary experience. The report suggested that church tradition, defined as "the Bible and the history of Christian thinking," is critical for the development of theology. In order to attend to the Bible and historical Christian thought, "experts in these must be consulted."[44] The work of the Spirit in the contemporary experiences of Christians constituted the other critical theological source, and could be accessed primarily through personal stories and scientific research. Church tradition and current Christian experience were given as the two criteria that "must constantly be tested against each other."[45] Elsewhere in the report the Spirit of Christ was named as an authoritative source which should guide scriptural interpretation.[46] The conclusions from this mutual testing of tradition and Christian experience were then to be debated within the Church courts with the recognition of the potential fallibility of their decisions. The report suggested that the church gains life, energy and God-granted insight from these debates "even while it is ready for divine correction and redirection."[47]

The particular approach followed throughout the report attempted to reflect this theological method. Each chapter set forth a description of the particular topic, illustrated these descriptions with different life stories (assumed to be fictional), explored related biblical passages, presented questions for study, and concluded with acknowledgements of "descriptions of ... social and personal reality" and affirmations of guidelines for use in the United Church.[48] Missing from its method, however, was attention to the "great traditions" of the church. It drew upon sociological research, life experiences (although not directly attributed to the experience of the Holy Spirit) and biblical passages, but made only passing reference to previous United Church statements and studies.[49]

As mentioned earlier, this report was more cautious than its 1980 predecessor, perhaps because of the adverse reaction to *In God's Image*. In particular, it recommended sexual exclusivity in marriage and was ambiguous in its affirmation of homosexual relationships. It affirmed that homosexual people can be full members of the church and referred to previous church resolutions that call for the inclusion of sexual orientation in the Canadian Human Rights Act. It also noted that some Christians understand the Spirit of Christ to override specific biblical verses which appear to condemn homosexuality.[50] At the same time it tried to include a balanced version of various perspectives by allowing room for negative response and including as an appendix a study of the Bible and homosexuality which condemns homosexuality.

The report's chapter on sexism, society, and the self was the most clearly advocatory chapter of the book.[51] It did not leave openings for those who might disagree, but clearly called the church to work towards the elimination of sexist structures within the church and society. It was also the only place in the document which suggested a hermeneutics of suspicion regarding sexism found in scripture. It acknowledged that scripture contains the Word of God, but is not to be equated with it. The biblical texts are to be wrestled with "until they become guidelines for life."[52]

The affirmations that concluded each chapter were adopted as general guidelines for the United Church in order to: 1) call Christians into "responsible freedom in which we must ponder and respond to God's gift and dilemma of sexuality;" 2) call for programs of advocacy "to defend the powerless," pastoral support "to guide the confused," and education "to help us grow into maturity in Christ;" and 3) call for political action to develop "policies for women's rights, for strengthening marriage and family, for divorced persons, for the single, the elderly, the disabled and many more."[53] It should be noted that no specific reference is made to lesbian and gay people in this summary list, even though political action for the civil and human rights of homosexuals was previously affirmed. This subsumption of lesbian and gay people into the unnamed category of leftovers could well have been another safe strategy of the authors, in light of the negative reaction to the 1980 report.

**Toward a Christian Understanding
of Sexual Orientations, Lifestyles and Ministry (1988)**

In 1984 the 30th General Council mandated the church

to develop an educational programme with thorough and well developed biblical, ethical and theological components reflecting in a balanced way, the theological diversity of The United Church of Canada ... to understand homosexual orientation and practice as well as a theological understanding of marriage and creation ... with a comprehensive statement concerning ... fitness for ordination/commissioning.[54]

The National Coordinating Group was established, and they developed two kits of study material that included response forms. As with *Gift, Dilemma and Promise,* the responses were carefully collated and included in a summary statement in an appendix to the report. The 1988 report (referred to as SOLM hereafter) also gave similar reasons as *Gift, Dilemma and Promise* for the difficulty of shaping a report on the basis of voluntary responses which "may be biased, or they may not."[55]

SOLM explained how different approaches to truth, understood as transcendent and eternal, affect our biblical interpretation and views of biblical authority. The absolutist approach suggests that truth "makes itself known and is self-revealing" through rational arguments. The relativist approach suggests that humans can only know a culturally and personally conditioned view of transcendent truth. Because it "arises" in particular contexts, it is only true for that particular context. Thus, truth is contextual and no overall criteria can be found to judge competing claims to truth. The third approach is the pluralist, in which all humans have provisional and contextual understandings of transcendent truth, as with the relativists. However, the pluralist believes that through dialogue with other people we can arrive at better understandings of truth and discover transcendent truth that is basic to all cultures.[56] SOLM concluded that our provisional and contextual understanding of truth must be tested, validated, and enacted within the faith community. The more diverse and inclusive the community, the more reliable the testing.

In order to relativize our interpretation of the Bible, SOLM noted our contextually limited interpretations of scripture. It did not celebrate these differences between contextually shaped interpretations, however, but warned that they will "distort the original meaning and intention" of scripture if we are not aware of the differences between our context and the Bible's original context. Historical criticism and humble dialogue with people from different cultural and faith traditions were therefore considered crucial in the discovery of truth.[57]

SOLM also suggested that the Bible itself has been humanly shaped and therefore culturally and historically conditioned. Thus, not everything in the Bible should be considered equally authoritative. Rather, the authority of Bible is found in its overall witness and inspiration for new ways in which to find healing, empowerment, and liberation. It suggested that the Bible's relation to insight and imagination is more important than an "exact recording of objective facts." Therefore, if one uses the Bible as an infallible guide, one misuses it.[58] Instead of following the letter of the law, the church should be guided by the spirit and mind of Christ.[59]

Of the four sexuality documents, SOLM was the only one which drew upon United Church tradition to any extent. It referred to previous United Church faith statements and "mainstream" Reformed understandings about the authority of the Bible to support its position, although it does not elaborate what these mainstream Reformed understandings are. However, it does quote United Church faith statements from the 1925 Basis of Union, and the 1977 Lordship of Jesus study.[60] It noted that United Church tradition believes the Bible, as interpreted by tradition, reason and experience, demands Christian loyalty and is a trustworthy guide to action. Thus, historical criticism and dialogue were viewed together with tradition, reason (in addition to historical criticism) and experience as important tools to understand the meaning of a text and test its appropriateness and application for our lives.[61]

By extending these theological and biblical principles to sexuality it stated that United Church practice has usually begun with biblical themes, such as grace, redemption, and justice, rather than specific texts, to guide our actions. The biblical theme which SOLM recommended was the covenant relationship of God with Israel and the people of Christ. As this covenant relationship is characterized by faithfulness, justice, and compassion, SOLM suggested that these characteristics should guide our understanding of sexuality and our sexual behaviour. Accordingly, sexual behaviour for heterosexual, as well as gay and lesbian people is morally responsible when it is "faithful to God's call to be just, loving, health-giving, healing, and sustaining of community."[62] It should also be engaged within committed relationships that have an intention of permanence. Because of human tendencies toward deception, this judgement of sexual behaviour should occur within the community of faith. SOLM also recommended that sexual orientation not be a barrier to ministry within the United Church, including the order of ministry.[63]

The writing team of SOLM struggled between concern for a liberal balance and concern for emancipatory decisions that would, by definition, exclude those who disagreed. The team included lesbian and gay members of Affirm, the support and advocacy group for lesbian, gay and bisexual people within the United Church,[64] as well as two theologically conservative people, one of whom was ex-gay. Rather than take a more cautious, inclusive, and consensual approach indicative of *Gift, Dilemma and Promise*, the writing team chose to retain clear justice statements for the support of lesbian and gay relationships and ordered ministers. One consequence of this choice was the alienation of the two conservative members of the writing team, who attached dissenting statements to the report's appendix. Another consequence was General Council's rejection of this report because it was considered too one-sided. In its place General Council accepted another statement entitled *Membership, Ministry and Human Sexuality* (MMHS), written by a committee at General Council operating on a consensus model and representing anti-gay, liberal, and pro-gay views. This statement declared that anyone, regardless of their sexual orientation, was eligible to be considered for ordered ministry. Church courts responsible for these decisions were to work out the implications of this "in light of Holy Scripture" and the call of all Christians "to a lifestyle patterned on obedience to Jesus Christ."[65] General Council's emphasis on consensus stressed the liberal inclusion of all voices. Ironically, after General Council was over at least one of the members of the committee withdrew support for MMHS, suggesting that the consensus model had forced an uncomfortable agreement.[66]

Authority, Gender and Sexual Orientation

Although each of these documents presents contrasting theological arguments and conclusions, they share similar theological methods that contain modern and liberal assumptions. After briefly identifying these assumptions, I will compare the impact of the 1960 document upon women with the impact of the 1980 documents upon lesbian and gay people.

Although the conclusions of the 1960 document are significantly different from those in the 1980s, their theological methods are similar.

They all took a non-literal approach to scripture, followed a Christological norm, used a variety of theological sources including historical criticism and scientific research, and attempted to include all voices while challenging injustice directed at specific marginalized groups. As the scientific data changed along with the opinions of biblical and theological scholars, so did the conclusions.

Each document assumed a singular meaning of the biblical text that could best be discovered with the use of historical-critical tools. The opinion of biblical scholars was sought in order to gain insight from the latest historical-critical findings. Expert opinion was also sought from the social sciences in order to make a credible theological correlation between the biblical and contemporary worlds. Another reason for their emphasis upon scholarly work was to provide as "objective" a document as possible. This tended to devalue the opinions of those most affected by the documents because of their political interests in the conclusions. It also tended to devalue the studies and responses from faith communities. When input from individuals and communities was encouraged, attempts were made to balance the voices so as to include everyone.

The modern and liberal aspects of the theological methods employed in the United Church sexuality documents have significant implications for biblical interpretation. When the original meaning of the biblical text is sought, there is an underlying assumption that a singular, correct meaning exists within the text and can be found with the appropriate historical-critical tools. However, this assumption has proven problematic in United Church documents dealing with gender and sexual orientation, and particularly so when the different documents use the same passage of scripture. As I will show below, the meaning of the same scripture passage changed from document to document.

Poststructural theorists expect this change in meaning according to the changing contexts, theological sources, scientific findings, and writers for each document. However, due to the modern perspective taken in the documents, this change in meaning indicated that some interpretations must be "in error." In order to grant authority to their particular interpretation, each document sought expert authority to prove that their interpretation was correct. If an interpretation contradicted that given in previous documents, it assumed the advantage of more recent, and therefore more trustworthy, biblical scholarship. This became even more problematic if the writing team itself was divided over the correct interpretation. In the case of the sexuality documents, it was usually the more socially progressive interpretations which were favoured. When the writing teams could not agree on the correct interpretation, those interpretations that preserved the patriarchal status quo, if included at all, were moved to the back of the document as an appendix. The inclusion of these appendices indicates the church's attempt to honour the diversity of all opinions, but their placement at the back of the documents indicates the church's attempt to emphasize the liberative perspectives. The result is a contradictory mix of competing claims to the correct, and therefore authoritative, scriptural interpretation.

As an example we will look at the doctrine of creation, based upon the Genesis stories. The 1960 document used the Genesis creation stories to support women's increasing social and economic independence while still insisting upon their acceptance of traditional family roles.[67] The changing roles of women could be accepted as long as they continued to be the primary caregivers for their children and husband. Women could gain a certain degree of independence as long as they accepted the theory of complementarity: women and men are not complete without the other. The stability of society depends upon women and men accepting their traditional feminine and masculine roles. These were the three purposes given for marriage: the complementarity and therefore completion of women and men in a mutually fulfilling partnership; procreation; and the stability of society.[68] Because homosexuality refutes all three purposes, it was considered immoral.[69]

The Genesis stories in the 1980 document served a dual purpose. One was to illustrate the origins of the patriarchal "orders of creation" as elaborated by Thomas Aquinas.[70] That Genesis had been used to justify male supremacy was proof of the need for biblical reinterpretation. The historical context and original meaning of the biblical text in light of modern sciences and God's revelation in Christ therefore needed to be examined.[71] The second reason for using the Genesis stories was to support the 1980 document's following androgynous theory. Genesis 1:27 indicates that God has created each of us to be male and female, and therefore complete, in ourselves. We are then to share this maleness and femaleness with each other.[72] Based upon this androgynous goal, the 1980 document negated the need to uphold traditional gender roles and supported the possibility of healthy homosexual relationships.

The 1984 document referred to the Genesis stories to suggest that sexuality and gender reflected the divine image, that the full equality of all persons was to be affirmed, and that God intended human beings to live in covenanted relationship.[73] Genesis 2 was taken to support a mutually enhancing, genitally exclusive, life-long marriage relationship between a husband and wife.[74] Genesis 1:27 was used to indicate that everyone, regardless of their sexual orientation, is created in God's image.[75] Although this document gave tentative support for homosexual people (not necessarily relationships), an appendix cited Genesis to condemn homosexuality. Like the 1960 document, the appendix believed that Genesis confirms God's intention for women and men to complement each other and to procreate in marriage. Homosexuality was therefore not part of God's purpose for humanity.[76]

These examples demonstrate the wide divergence of opinion on the meaning of a particular biblical text. Each view established its own singular meaning which was then posited as scriptural authority for its opinion on gender and sexual orientation issues. However, no position acknowledged the diverse factors that informed its derivation of meaning. There was only occasional recognition of the disagreement amongst scholarly sources,[77] and there was little awareness of the impact of the writers' own cultural, political, and personal biases and interests.[78] Scriptural authority, and therefore truth and revelation, were based upon the opinions of biblical experts (seldom Canadian) who were removed from the United Church context.

Similar authority was given to scientific experts. All sexuality documents cited medical, sociological, and psychological studies as uncontested authority for issues of gender and sexual orientation. The 1980 document explicitly named empirical scientific research as a source of truth equal in authority to that of scripture.[79] However, in effect all documents gave much more weight to scientific findings than to any other authoritative source. If scientific findings should contradict traditional biblical interpretations, science was welcomed as an undisputed correction.

As a consequence of this reliance upon expert knowledge and "objectivity," the United Church documents tended to devalue and mistrust three sources of authority that they mentioned as also important: tradition, the response of faith communities, and the response of those, such as women, and lesbian and gay people, who were the object of study.

The first source of devalued and mistrusted authority was tradition. Apart from the 1960 document, reference to any tradition was scant. When positive reference to tradition was made, particularly in the 1988 document, it was in regard to earlier United Church statements concerning Christological norms that guided nonliteral biblical interpretation.[80] Occasional reference to reformed tradition was made, but only in passing remarks. Apart from this positive reference, tradition, when mentioned at all, was usually viewed with suspicion.[81] Documents of the 1980s echoed Schüssler Fiorenza's and Kwok's concerns by asking whose heritage and whose tradition is being considered. They were particularly attentive to the silencing of women in these traditions. While these concerns are crucially important, there may be another reason for the questioning of tradition in these documents.

In my experience, Protestants have typically viewed church traditions emerging after the formation of the biblical canon and prior to the Reformation as Roman Catholic distortions of the gospel. This bias can be found in the United Church documents. To note the misogynist theology of Thomas Aquinas in order to justify the superiority of empirical science[82] serves to reinforce the anti-Roman Catholic and modern biases of United Church members. While most references to tradition in the documents were not this blatantly negative, they still singled out tradition as the most suspect source of authority.

Although Christian traditions should be examined critically as potentially oppressive, they should also be examined as potentially liberative. By ignoring the liberative aspects of United Church tradition, the sexuality documents reinforced conservative accusations that the documents of the 1980s were based upon secular knowledge and were void of its faith heritage. It is usually those opposed to issues of inclusive language or the ordination and commissioning of lesbian and gay candidates who refer positively to tradition. They have accused the United Church of forsaking its tradition regarding moral standards, biblical interpretation, and theological foundation.[83] Only a few have insisted that the United Church's response to homosexuality has been consistent with its traditional roots.[84]

The second devalued and mistrusted source of authority was the response from faith communities. Although most documents demonstrated serious consideration of congregational studies, biblical interpretations arising out of faith communities, both marginalized and mainstream, were not accorded much weight. Authority was given primarily to the opinions of biblical and scientific experts, and inadvertently to the interests and biases of the writers' own experiences.

With the exception of the 1988 report, the third devalued and mistrusted source was those who were the subject of study. As a result, United Church treatment of women, and gay, lesbian and bisexual people has been directed by the vacillations of scholarly opinion. Expert advice was privileged over the experiences of "the other" in order to form "objective" and "unbiased" judgements about their sexuality and their fitness for ministry. Fears expressed in the 1960s about women were similar to those expressed in the 1980s about gay men.[85] Both were thought to have uncontrollable sexuality. Up until the early 1960s the United Church debated whether or not the approval of contraception would encourage women to become promiscuous.[86] Likewise, the United Church expressed concern in the early 1980s over the possibility of promiscuity and pederasty if homosexuality was accepted.[87] In addition, independent women in the 1960s, and gay men in the 1980s were seen as threats to the stability of the family and society. In 1962 the United Church General Council voted to restrict the ordination of women to those who were unmarried or widowed, unless it could be demonstrated that ordination would not interfere with women's positions as mothers and/or wives. After heated debate, this decision was referred to a committee for further study, and at the next General Council two years later, all restrictions on the ordination of married women were removed.[88] The 1984 and 1988 documents went to great lengths to reiterate their support for marriage. This was in response to concerns that the acceptance of lesbian and gay relationships would destroy marriage and the family.

These fears led to a suspicion of biblical interpretation and to critiques from women, and from lesbian, gay and bisexual faith communities. Unlike the scholars' data, these views were considered biased. Information *about* the other was more reliable than information *from* the other. If their views were to be considered, they must be balanced by the other side (i.e. those opposing the ordination of married women in the 1960s and of lesbian and gay candidates in the 1980s). This is particularly evident in the 1960 report's ambivalence over the emancipation of women, and in the 1984 report's inclusion of opposing viewpoints and biblical interpretations regarding homosexual relationships.[89]

All of these sexuality documents indicate a struggle between a liberal balance that respects the equality and importance of every opinion, and a liberation approach that privileges the voices of the marginalized and silenced within society. The 1988 report recognized that full inclusion of all voices means including those who exclude others. They were clearly uncomfortable with including voices of condemnation, leading them to qualify the liberal goal of inclusivity with a clear support for society's marginalized. However, General Council's rejection of the 1988 report and substitution of a weaker statement indicated a preference for a liberal balance of viewpoints. The results of this decision varied across the country. Some Conferences decided to reject openly lesbian or gay candidates. Most did not, although it is still difficult to settle (place in a pastoral charge) openly lesbian or gay candidates, a condition of ordination or commissioning.

Although all of these documents attempted to be both inclusive and just, people who supported traditional sexual norms often felt ignored and people who were marginalized within society, such as women, and those who were lesbian, gay, and bisexual, often felt patronized and silenced. Just before the release of the 1980 document, a United Church gay support group questioned how the church could make authentic decisions regarding homosexuality without open dialogue, forums, and discussions with homosexual men and women.[90] Particularly in the earlier documents, few questions were asked about relations of power and the danger that open dialogue between opposing sides creates for those whose very identities are at stake. The 1984 report called for reconciliation between homosexual and heterosexual Christians, and the need for both to hear and understand the other.[91] This type of call appears to value both sides equally, assuming a balance of power that would enable reconciliation. It also assumes the controversy was a matter of disagreement that could be resolved between homosexual and heterosexual people. Rather, the controversy was over a conservative group challenging lesbian and gay people's right to existence within the life and ministry of the church. Lesbian and gay people who dared to come out of the closet in order to contribute to the dialogue risked losing their jobs, and in some instances risked physical safety. Many of us who were somewhat closeted found ourselves ministering in congregations rife with fear and hate. At times we felt forced to choose between our sense of integrity and our call, our careers and our safety. With no protective policies or creative means of dialogue that could offer some degree of confidentiality and safety, dialogue between unequal partners is not possible.

The 1988 report recognized the vulnerability of lesbian and gay people and that the 1984 report's call to dialogue had created an imbalance of power that led to further silencing, not dialogue.[92] Because the United Church did not provide equal opportunity for all to participate, its values of diversity and inclusivity led to the valuing of some and further marginalization of others.[93]

These conflicts, which were heightened in 1988, have made the United Church question the possibility of remaining united amidst diversity. Offering a liberal inclusion of all voices without questioning oppressive power structures has retained the patriarchal status quo and further silenced the marginalized. Conversely, 25,000 United Church members, or 3.5% of its membership, are estimated to have left the United Church because of its decisions over sexual orientation.[94] Supporting the marginalized of society has proven costly to community and diversity, although there are no figures that estimate the number of people who have joined or returned to the United Church in the wake of these decisions.

In the following chapter I will further analyze the problems of these modern and liberal aspects through the earlier critiques of the four feminists. I will then explore their alternative theological methods and identify aspects from each one that might be helpful for the United Church and other liberal, Protestant denominations in their struggle to support the marginalized while remaining united amidst diversity.

Notes to Chapter 7

1. In 1925 the Methodist Church of Canada, the Congregational Union of Canada, and about 62 percent of the members of the Presbyterian Church in Canada joined together to form The United Church of Canada. Over 40 years later, the Evangelical United Brethren joined this union in 1968. The United Church is the largest Protestant denomination in Canada. See Steven Chambers, *This Is Your Church: A Guide to the Beliefs, Policies and Positions of The United Church of Canada*, 2nd edition (Toronto: canec, 1986), 36–37, 132.

2. Clark Saunders has identified the United Church positions as liberal and radical, in contrast to the conservative position of some of its members. See "Conservative, Liberal, Radical: Three Ways of Understanding Gay Issues in Church and Society," *Torquere*, 2 (2000): 58–79.

3. For further analysis of United Church sexuality documents see Tracy Trothen, "A Feminist Critical Analysis of The United Church of Canada's Evolving Understanding of Violence Against Women," dissertation (Toronto: Victoria University and University of Toronto, 1996).

4. General Council is the highest court of The United Church of Canada and meets once every two or three years. Among other things, General Council legislates on matters respecting the doctrine, worship, membership, government, and property of the United Church. Decisions are made by approximately 200 lay and 200 ordered ministry Commissioners, who are elected for each General Council by the 13 Conferences across Canada. See The United Church of Canada, *The Manual* (Toronto: The United Church Publishing House, 1995), The Basis of Union 8.6.2 and Section 505.

5. The United Church of Canada, "Evangelism and Social Service Report No. 2," *Record of Proceedings of the 17th General Council* (1956): 90.

6. These are all mentioned in the report with the exception of media articles. The Commission's interest in the media was indicated by a file of clippings from Toronto newspapers, and Canadian and British magazines. See The United Church of Canada, Commission on Marriage and Divorce, "Clippings" (United Church Archives 82.084C 4–41).

7. The Board of Christian Education of The United Church of Canada, *Toward a Christian Understanding of Sex, Love, Marriage* (Toronto: The United Church, 1960), 5.

8. *Sex, Love, Marriage*, 7.

9. *Sex, Love, Marriage*, 7.

10. This was based primarily upon Mark 10:7–8, Genesis 1:28, and I Corinthians 6:16. See *Sex, Love, Marriage*, 1–11.

11. *Sex, Love, Marriage*, 2.

12. The authors referred to an essay that had been recently published on the Welfare State by Professor Titmus of the London School of Economics. He suggested that planned parenthood had a much greater influence on women's freedom than political emancipation (*Sex, Love, Marriage*, 25).

13. *Sex, Love, Marriage*, 27.

14. Dorothy Vipond, "Out of the West," *Observer* (January 15, 1962): 21; "Divorce Isn't That Bad," *Observer* (March 1, 1962): 10.

15. *Sex, Love, Marriage*, 27.

16. *Sex, Love, Marriage*, 26.

17. *Sex, Love, Marriage*, 14–16.

18. In a letter dated Sept. 22, 1959 to Frank Fidler, Secretary for the Commission on Christian Marriage and Divorce, from J. Arthur Boorman, professor in the Faculty of Divinity at McGill, homosexuality was considered to be a moral problem because it was against nature, the self, other people, and society. See The United Church of Canada, Commission on Marriage and Divorce (United Church Archives 82.084C 2–22). Concern was expressed about a paper written for this Commission by Dr. W. E. Boothroyd. Issue was taken with his analogy of homosexuality with left-handedness. See The United Church of Canada, Commission on Marriage and Divorce "General Council Specific Subjects: Homosexuality" (United Church Archives 82.001C 140–4).

19. *Sex, Love, Marriage*, 15.

20. *Sex, Love, Marriage*, 16.

21. *Sex, Love, Marriage*, 43.

22. Articles and responses in the *United Church Observer* in the late 1950s and early 1960s indicated a general support for women to work outside the home and take church leadership roles. See Jean Shilton, "Prudence in the Parsonage," *Observer* (March 15, 1957): 17, 21; (May 1, 1957): 17; (August, 1957): 17; (February 1, 1958): 15; (March 15, 1959): 16. See also "The Question Box," *Observer* (February 15, 1958), and (December 1, 1961); Marjorie Macdonald, "Putting Women in Their Place," *Observer* (September 15, 1958): 12–13, 24; and an editorial entitled "Feminism," *Observer* (January 15, 1962): 11, 22, 24.

General support was also expressed in the *Observer* for the ordination of married women. See Ralph Barker, "Is Ordination for Unmarried Women Only?" *Observer* (October 1, 1957): 13, 14; an editorial "Women Ministers—A Good Record." *Observer* (October 15, 1960): 6; and A.C. Forrest, "Little Girl Minister," *Observer* (July 1961): 8–10, 20. It was only an article by R.B. Craig, speaking against married women in the ordained ministry in 1957, which elicited letters to the editor. See "A Married Woman's Place is in the Home," *Observer* (November 1, 1957): 13, 30. One letter from Nova Scotia commended Craig's views, suggesting that his argument could support a celibate ministry (J.T.N. Atkinson, December 1, 1957: 2). The following edition contained two letters, one from Pickering and the other from Toronto, protesting Craig's article (Honor Buttars and Mr. & Mrs. E.B. Swinton, December 15, 1957: 2).

23. This was evident in the heated debate around the ordination of married women at London Conference in 1957. Although they decided to ordain Eleanor Leard, who was the first married woman with young children to be ordained in the United Church, they requested guidance from General Council. See News article "Marriage no Obstacle," *Observer* (December 15, 1963): 7; "Settling Married Women," *Observer* (August, 1964): 4; and Barbara Bagnell, "Women Ministers: Are They Really Worth Stalling Church Union For?" *Observer* (March 1, 1968): 12–15, 40. At the same General Council in 1960 which approved this sexuality report, an Interim Report of Commission on Ordination mentioned the "problem of the ordained woman who subsequently marries and becomes a mother." See The United Church of Canada, *Record of Proceedings of the 19th General Council* (1960): 241.

24. "It is extremely important to discover what young people are thinking, even though they may say things that irritate and annoy, and even though we may not accept their statements as ours." See The United Church of Canada, Commission on Marriage and

Divorce, "Minutes 1957–1958" (United Church Archives 82.084C 1–1): Minutes November 26, 1957. The conclusions of this report indicate that they did, indeed, tend to agree with the statements of the youth, rather than statements supporting traditional gender roles. An example of the latter is a submission from Earl Lautenschlager, the Principal of Emmanuel College 1963–71, whose opinion against married women working outside of the home was later published in the *Observer*. See "The Marriage Partnership: Part I," *Observer* (April 15, 1962): 25–27 and "The Marriage Partnership: Part II," *Observer* (May 1, 1962): 25–27.

25. The Division of Mission in Canada of The United Church of Canada, *Gift, Dilemma and Promise: A Report and Affirmations on Human Sexuality* (Toronto: The United Church of Canada, 1984), 4.

26. Division of Mission in Canada of The United Church of Canada and the Committee on Theology and Faith, *Faith & Sexuality: A Spectrum of Theological Views in The United Church of Canada for The General Council* (Toronto: The United Church of Canada, 1981).

27. It was noted that the 1969 revision of the Criminal Code still discriminated against homosexual people by allowing a younger age of consent for heterosexual relations. See The Division of Mission in Canada of The United Church of Canada, *In God's Image ... Male and Female: A Study on Human Sexuality* (Toronto, The United Church of Canada, 1980), 97.

28. *In God's Image*, 10.

29. *In God's Image*, 81.

30. *In God's Image*, 11.

31. *In God's Image*, 11.

32. *In God's Image*, 14–18.

33. *In God's Image*, 81–82.

34. *In God's Image*, 2, 41, 57.

35. *In God's Image*, 83.

36. *In God's Image*, 66–68.

37. Examples of sexual exploitation were rape, incest, sexual assault, prostitution, sado-masochism, sexual favours for job promotion or security, deceptive misuse of birth control, neglect, and teenage peer pressure of sexual performance (*In God's Image*, 45).

38. *In God's Image*, 1–2.

39. *In God's Image*, 71–72, 84–85.

40. *In God's Image*, 69–73.

41. *In God's Image*, 1–7.

42. Over 10,000 copies of *In God's Image* were sold and distributed together with a response form, study suggestions, and *The Permanence of Christian Marriage*, the 1975 statement of the Committee on Christian Faith. See *Gift, Dilemma and Promise*, 4.

43. Approximately 1,000 responses were received, 833 of which were collated and included in an appendix of *Gift, Dilemma and Promise*. Because they were not a "scientific sampling" of the church, because "many of them were written out of strong conviction ... and some quite emotionally" and because the United Church does not develop its theological positions through majority vote, through the "mere sharing of experiences" or through consensus, they did not figure significantly in the report's conclusions. However, the report still tried to honour and reflect the insights, feelings and experiences of the respondents. See *Gift, Dilemma and Promise*, 4–5, 83–90. For media response and the 1982 General Council petition see *Gift, Dilemma and Promise*, 3, 40–41.

44. *Gift, Dilemma and Promise*, 5.
45. *Gift, Dilemma and Promise*, 5.
46. *Gift, Dilemma and Promise*, 78.
47. *Gift, Dilemma and Promise*, 5.
48. *Gift, Dilemma and Promise*, 7.
49. *Gift, Dilemma and Promise*, 50, 80.
50. *Gift, Dilemma and Promise*, 78.
51. It gives extensive reference to demographic surveys of societal violence against women, and women's leadership roles within the United Church.
52. *Gift, Dilemma and Promise*, 64.
53. *Gift, Dilemma and Promise*, 81.
54. See The Division of Ministry Personnel and Education & The Division of Mission in Canada of The United Church of Canada, *Toward a Christian Understanding of Sexual Orientations, Lifestyles and Ministry* (Toronto: The United Church of Canada, 1988), i.
55. In fact, they note that the multiple problems associated with this invitational approach "raises significant questions about what consultation means in our councilliar (sic) church system and how subsequent policy decisions are made." See *Sexual Orientations, Lifestyles and Ministry*, 22.
56. *Sexual Orientations, Lifestyles and Ministry*, 29, 30.
57. *Sexual Orientations, Lifestyles and Ministry*, 30, 31.
58. *Sexual Orientations, Lifestyles and Ministry*, 32.
59. *Sexual Orientations, Lifestyles and Ministry*, 3.
60. *Sexual Orientations, Lifestyles and Ministry*, 31–33.
61. *Sexual Orientations, Lifestyles and Ministry*, 33, 34.
62. *Sexual Orientations, Lifestyles and Ministry*, 3.
63. *Sexual Orientations, Lifestyles and Ministry*, 3–4.
64. Affirm (lesbian, gay and bisexual people in the United Church) has since amalgamated with Friends of Affirm (supporters of lesbian, gay and bisexual people) to become Affirm United. In 2001 Affirm United added "transgendered" to its mandate.
65. The United Church of Canada, *Membership, Ministry and Human Sexuality: A New Statement of The United Church of Canada by the 32nd General Council* (Toronto: The United Church of Canada, 1988).
66. It should be noted that the committee members also faced difficult opposition to their decision upon returning to their home communities.
67. *Sex, Love, Marriage*, 11.
68. *Sex, Love, Marriage*, 8.
69. *Sex, Love, Marriage*, 13, 14.
70. *In God's Image*, 11.
71. *In God's Image*, 12–18.
72. *In God's Image*, 40–41.
73. *Gift, Dilemma and Promise*, 17, 64.
74. *Gift, Dilemma and Promise*, 26.
75. *Gift, Dilemma and Promise*, 79.
76. *Gift, Dilemma and Promise*, 93.
77. Although the 1960 document recognizes disagreement amongst biblical scholars regarding the gospel teachings about divorce, it does not recognize disagreement regarding the Genesis passage. See *Sex, Love, Marriage*, 5–10.

78. The 1988 document does acknowledge the impact of the reader's biases and cultural context, but assumes this to be a problem that can be set aside if acknowledged. See *Sexual Orientations, Lifestyles and Ministry*, 30.

79. *In God's Image*, 10–13.

80. *Sexual Orientations, Lifestyles and Ministry*, 32–36. Although all documents followed this pattern of biblical interpretation, only the 1988 document supported this with reference to earlier United Church statements.

81. *In God's Image*, 11; *Sexual Orientations, Lifestyles and Ministry*, 15–16.

82. *In God's Image*, 11.

83. Terrence Anderson, "Further Reflections on the General Council Statement," *Touchstone* 7, no. 2 (May 1989): 17–24; Donald Faris, *Trojan Horse: The Homosexual Ideology and the Christian Church* (Burlington, ON: Welch Publishing Company Inc., 1989); Victor Shepherd, "The United Church and Ordination of Active Homosexuals: A Critique," in *A Crisis of Understanding: Homosexuality and the Canadian Church*, ed. Denyse O'Leary (Burlington, ON: Welch Publishing Co. Inc., 1988), 35–50; Vernon R. Wishart, "The Making of the United Church Mind—No. 1," *Touchstone* 18, no. 1 (January 1990): 6–16.

84. Roger O'Toole, Douglas F. Campbell, John A. Hannigan, Peter Beyer, and John H. Simpson, "The United Church in Crisis: A Sociological Perspective on the Dilemmas of a Mainstream Denomination," *Studies in Religion* 20, no. 2 (Spring 1991): 151-63; Harold Wells, "The Making of the United Church Mind—No. 2," *Touchstone* 18, no. 1 (January 1990): 17–29.

85. Pamela Dickey Young has given an excellent analysis of the parallels of resistance to women, and to lesbian and gay candidates for ordered ministry in the United Church. See Pamela Dickey Young, "Homosexuality and Ministry: Some Feminist Reflections," in *Theological Reflections on Ministry and Sexual Orientation*, ed. Pamela Dickey Young (Burlington, ON: Trinity Press, 1990).

86. The United Church of Canada, "Record of Proceedings of the 20th General Council" (Toronto: The United Church of Canada, 1962), 87, 105–06; The United Church of Canada, "Record of Proceedings of the 12th General Council" (Toronto: The United Church of Canada, 1946), 112–13.

87. *Gift, Dilemma and Promise*, 68–69.

88. The United Church of Canada, "1962 ROP," 59, 76, 80–81.

89. *Gift, Dilemma and Promise*, 78, 68, 91–93.

90. T.O.U.C.H. (Toronto Organization of United Church Homosexuals), "Letter to the Editor," *The United Church Observer*, May 1980, 4.

91. *Gift, Dilemma and Promise*, 70.

92. *Sexual Orientations, Lifestyles and Ministry*, 15.

93. *Sexual Orientations, Lifestyles and Ministry*, 12.

94. Thomas G. Bandy, "The United Church of Canada: Crisis and Creativity," in *The Sexuality Debate in the North American Churches*, ed. John Carey (Lewiston, N.Y.: Edwin Mellen Press, 1995); Ann Naylor, "Reflections on Sexual Orientation Issues in The United Church of Canada" (Toronto: October 29, 1993).

Chapter 8

Assessment of United Church Theological Methods

In the first section of this chapter I will engage the analyses from the four feminist methods considered earlier to further the critique of the modern and liberal approaches used within the United Church sexuality documents. In the second section I will explore alternative approaches to the use of scripture and Christian tradition, with particular emphasis upon Fulkerson's canonical system. After I have noted the advantages of attending to the faith traditions of particular communities, I will draw upon the works of Tanner and Schüssler Fiorenza to suggest ways in which connections with the diversity of traditions within the wider body of Christ might be made. In light of these diversities, the final section will refer to Kwok and Tanner to suggest sources of criteria that can offer universal guidelines which support the marginalized and respect diversity.

Critique of Modern, Liberal Approaches

As noted in the previous chapter, the sexuality documents assumed that we can better understand scripture if we know the original context, the authorial intent, the intended audiences and the evolution of particular manuscripts. These aspects of the biblical texts, discovered through historical criticism, shed light on their original meaning which can then be assessed against the gospel as to its authoritative claims for contemporary Christians.

There are a number of problems with such reliance on historical criticism. First, the sexuality documents relayed particular historical-critical analyses as factual representations of reality. They understood these analyses as windows into the original context, meaning of terms and authorial intent of biblical passages deemed relevant to sexuality. All four feminists dispute the assumption that, with the proper tools, one can unearth reality. Nor do they believe that historical texts of any kind represent reality. Schüssler Fiorenza warns against such historical positivism, suggesting that these assumptions ignore the rhetorical nature of the texts. She would ask the following questions: How would a particular biblical story be reenacted by women at that time? How would the texts' patriarchal bias affect their marginalization of women and condemnation of homosexual acts?

Fulkerson challenges the concept of scriptural representations of reality by honouring the validity of opposing interpretations. She would affirm the liberative interpretations that certain communities make of texts which historical critics consider oppressive to women or homosexuals. For instance, some lesbian and gay people have read Romans 1:26–27 in a manner that is supportive, rather than condemning. They would argue that this passage merely condemns unnatural sexual expressions of any type. Because people with homosexual orientations are naturally attracted to their same gender, it would be unnatural for them to have heterosexual relations. For them, heterosexual relations would therefore be condemned by this passage. Even when historical criticism is used in the sexuality documents, Fulkerson would encourage it to be understood as rhetorical constructions of the biblical text that present likely possibilities, not facts. An emphasis upon the multiple meanings of scripture will challenge competing claims to its singular meaning and accurate representation of reality.

A second problem with the reliance upon modern, historical-critical methods is the devaluing of faith-based performances of scripture within community. When objective study of the biblical texts is preferred over the performance of the biblical texts as scripture, there are a number of consequences. Kwok notes that the first approach, indicative of western, linear, abstract thought, strives for logical, sophisticated, and internally coherent results. The second approach, indicative of eastern holistic and embodied thought, values intuition, imagination, and free association of ideas. When historical-critical methods are used to prove the logical, definitive, and correct meanings of scripture, factually based, objective interpretations are preferred over faith based, subjective interpretations. In this sense, faith becomes a liability, not an asset, in biblical interpretation. The role of communities with their diverse and disordered readings of scripture are thereby negated.

Ironically, it is in this neglected hodgepodge of communal performances that I have often found the sacred mystery of an encounter with God to be the most powerful. The performance of scripture through liturgy, song, drama, and sermon reveals an embodied, communal sense of the divine and engages participants with the transformative, liberating Word. Worship has always been a central aspect of Affirm United, enabling new, transformative interpretations of scripture and grace-filled encounters with the divine. Affirm United has found the liberating Word of God to be radically engaged and revealed when lesbian, gay and bisexual Christians finally find a safe, affirming family of faith. These performances of scripture have been ignored or downplayed in the sexuality documents for fear of emotionally-based, biased interpretations of scripture. Only the 1984 document refers to the worship experiences of Affirm, and then not by name. It mentions "a recent gathering of homosexual Christians in Montreal" at which "those attending testified to being suddenly aware of the Holy Spirit among them."[1] This was actually the founding meeting of Affirm. Likewise, the scriptural performances of conservative renewal groups and congregational study groups have been given little consideration. Although most documents elicited and collated numerous responses, the responses made little impact on the conclusions or theological methods employed in the documents.

This leads to a third problem with the privileging of historical criticism which Fulkerson calls the professionalization of knowledge. Control of knowledge is retained by biblical experts who set universal standards on the basis of their historical findings and challenge any interpretations that differ from their own. Because of ongoing archaeological discoveries and the modern belief in the progression of human reason, the most recent scholarly opinion is often taken to be the most reliable.

Within the sexuality documents the contradictory interpretations of the creation stories evolved only as they were factually supported by historical-critical analyses. As church communities read these documents, some were left confused, intimidated and silenced. If the conclusions and interpretations were not in accord with their own beliefs and they were not trained in historical criticism, they could not contest the conclusions. Just as they must trust the expertise of professionals in other areas, they must trust the expertise of biblical scholars. This leads to a broader question of the use of the Bible within congregations. How can people engage the Bible if they do not have access to historical-critical tools? In the United Church I have heard many laity say that they are not knowledgeable enough to read or study the Bible. When a few brave souls do gather together for Bible Study, they expect me to teach them out of my expertise, and they resist suggestions to read from our own places. Reading the Bible has become an intimidating enterprise.

The fourth problem with the reliance upon modern, historical-critical biblical scholarship is its emphasis upon objective impartiality. The writers of the sexuality documents gave the opinions of biblical and scientific experts more weight than the opinions of congregational members because the experts were assumed to be governed by empirical, scientific methods rather than interest. All four feminists note that this assumption occludes the biases and interests of the experts. As Schüssler Fiorenza points out, historical-critical analyses of scripture tend to produce interpretations reflective of the identities and interests of the biblical scholars. The preference of expert opinion also values those removed from the context over those most affected by the issue at hand. For instance, some of the documents relied heavily on American sources. When American experts are used, the typical Canadian deference to American expertise enforces the devaluing of Canadian opinion. Kwok recognizes this same deference of Asian theologians to Euro-American biblical scholarship. In addition, the input of lesbian and gay groups into the sexuality documents was curtailed, as I have already suggested, because they could not be trusted to give impartial views. Instead of following an epistemological privilege of the oppressed, the documents supported an epistemological privilege of the impartial expert.

Another consequence of assumed impartiality was that the writing teams did not indicate any awareness of their own impact upon the documents. They didn't recognize that marginalized people were invited into the documents' discussions and conclusions on terms set by and beneficial to the writing teams, which consisted primarily, if not entirely, of the dominant identity. For example, when the right of women to economic and social independence was debated in the context of married women's right to ordered ministry, the writing team of the 1960 document was primarily male. Similarly, when the right of lesbian and gay people to membership and ministry within the church was debated in the documents of the 1980s, the writing teams had better gender balance, but were all primarily if not entirely heterosexual. Only the 1988 document identified two members of its writing team as lesbian and gay, but an ex-gay was later added to the team to keep the balance.

The conclusions of the earlier reports, and to a lesser extent the 1988 report, therefore reflected attempts to attend to the marginalized on the terms and conditions preferred by the dominant group. For instance, in the early 1960s married women were encouraged to work outside the home only if they continued in their role as primary homemaker and caregiver for their husbands and children. Thus, the United Church documents reached conclusions reflective of the dominant male identities of the writing teams. The documents also reflected the dominant middle-class identities of the writing team, as they assumed that married women had enough income to afford the option of not working outside of the home.[2] Similar dominant, heterosexual interests were reflected in the earlier 1980 documents when lesbian and gay relationships were accepted only if they conformed to heterosexual norms.

Bisexuality was more difficult to assimilate and is only beginning to be given serious consideration. Members of Affirm urged the writing team for a 1995 document to consider bisexuality. After much resistance, the team decided to mention bisexuality, albeit only briefly. The team also insisted that its suggested covenanting services for lesbian and gay couples be patterned after United Church heterosexual marriage services, once again following a liberal model of inclusion into structures that remained unquestioned. Some consideration was given to the oppressive effects of heterosexism, and the report acknowledged the problem of assimilation into the dominant heterosexual identity. However, it concluded that the church is not yet ready to accept lesbian and gay people on their terms, and posited heterosexual norms for homosexual relationships.[3]

Schüssler Fiorenza describes this dominant bias through the logic of identity where the identity of the other is subsumed into the identity of the dominant. The logic of identity is particularly evident with the readings of Genesis which understand it to prescribe God-ordained complementary, heterosexual gender relations and roles. Tanner notes that whenever any social order such as patriarchal gender relations or compulsory heterosexuality is identified as natural, it is assumed to be divinely created. *De facto* norms, situationally dependent, are identified with *de jure* norms, absolute ontological descriptions that are beyond critique. Thus norms that are created on the basis of a certain social order are assumed to be universally applicable and divinely prescribed for all people at all times.

This assumption informs those readings of Genesis which understand it to prescribe God-ordained complementary, heterosexual gender relations and roles. Corresponding absolute norms are established which reify these dominant-submissive relations. These standards of behaviour and relationship reflect the identity of the dominant group (heterosexual, white, middle-class males) and benefit them by protecting the status quo. Anything deemed characteristic of gay men, people of colour or women are considered peripheral and dispensable to the essence of humanity. Only the dominant group's identity corresponds exactly to humanity's essence. Norms established to protect humanity's essence therefore protect the dominant group and pressure others to deny their otherness. Thus, in the 1960 document women could have independent rights as long as the interests of their husbands were prioritized. In the 1980s up until the present, lesbian and gay relationships can be recognized as long as they are controlled by heterosexual norms and the heterosexual institution of marriage is uplifted.

This identity logic leads to Tanner's "peculiar dialectic of identity and difference." The difference between the dominant and marginalized is absolutized while the differences amongst the marginalized are ignored. This is similar to Kwok's "ideological construction of sameness and difference." An artificial polarity between women and men, straight and gay, western powers and the Third World is produced. At the same time the differences within each marginalized group are flattened. For instance, no attention is given in the 1980 documents to the differing interests and needs of lesbian women and gay men, of working class and middle-class lesbians, or of white and First Nations gay men.

Kwok also points out the fallacy of the liberal notion that all humans are equal and the same. In fact, all humans are not equal according to the distribution of power and wealth. This notion of equality is assumed when one calls for a balance of voices on all sides of the issue so that everyone's views can be given equal consideration. Yet, with no account of power differentials amongst the people called into dialogue, everyone's views cannot be given equal consideration. As my partner has observed, "There is nothing more unequal than the equal treatment of unequals."[4] A liberal focus upon the inclusion of marginalized people into the existing structures of church and society also ignores questions about the oppressive nature of the structures themselves, which may have contributed to the exclusion of marginalized people in the first place.

The dominant heterosexual bias on the writing teams made it difficult for them to anticipate the dangerous situation these reports would create for closeted lesbian and gay ministers. It also hindered the team from realizing the complex range of issues and power dynamics involved in a call to dialogue. The issue of sexual orientation sparked strong *emotional* reactions, and an educational program designed to inform and persuade was geared towards an *intellectual* response. It was assumed that if people could put a face to homosexuality and hear the stories of lesbian and gay people, they would become supportive. While this had varying degrees of success, it also resulted in the abuse of lesbian and gay people. Some who risked being "out" were invited to congregational educational sessions only to be castigated publically. Witch hunts began, targeting anyone who was not married or who exhibited behaviour that challenged gender stereotypes. It was only later that employment policies within the United Church prohibiting discrimination on the basis of sexual orientation were put into place and began to be enforced.[5] Protective measures are necessary to ensure some degree of safety before dialogue is possible.

African Americans tell those of us with white-skinned privilege to do our own anti-racism work. They do not need to be subjected to our racist comments and attitudes, which inevitably come out as we work on our own racism. Only after we have spent considerable effort on becoming "recovering racists" are we ready for dialogue with them. Similarly, the church needs to take great care not to further marginalize other minorities when it is struggling to be more inclusive of them. Just as lesbian and gay people were further victimized when the church was dealing with sexual orientation, Aboriginal people are now being further victimized as the church is dealing with its contribution to the cultural, physical, and sexual abuse that occurred at residential schools. Perhaps the church can learn from these experiences and refuse to do its own anti-oppression work on the backs of those already oppressed. Structural changes must first happen to lay the groundwork for dialogue and reconciliation. Simple inclusion of marginalized people into dialogue with the rest of the church ignores safety issues, power imbalances, and structural systems of oppression.

Fulkerson suggests that simple inclusion of the marginalized erases not only structures of domination, but also multiple identities and social locations. As an alternative, she and Kwok both argue for the poststructural insistence on the instability of identity. Kwok notes that multiple subject positions produce multiple identities within multilevel discourses. Fulkerson agrees that multiple identities are socially constructed, and not based upon a natural essence of that identity. Women do not share a natural essence that defines their gender, nor do lesbian and gay people share an essence of sexual orientation. Thus, women in general, as well as lesbian, gay and bisexual people, should not be essentialized into one category that can be excluded or included. Fulkerson suggests that this will create a binary gender system that will produce patriarchal, heterosexual norms against which women or lesbian and gay people will be measured. Such is the case for all of the sexuality documents, including the 1980 document which suggests an androgynous ideal for women and men, patterned after an androgynous image of God. Rosemary Radford Ruether points out that androgynous images of God perpetuate the male-female split in which the subordination of female roles and characteristics can be maintained.[6] The 1980 document also asks the readers to speculate on the possibility of Jesus' sexual arousal and attraction to women. It suggests that Jesus could have been married. By considering the possibility of Jesus' sexuality only within a traditional, heterosexual marriage, divine incarnation is further entrenched in a patriarchal institution that primarily benefits heterosexual males and has proven abusive to many women, as well as to lesbian, gay and bisexual people.

Awareness of the above problems arising out of modern and liberal assumptions leads to a consideration of alternative theological methods that better attend to issues of diversity and marginalization within Protestant churches. I will now explore the adequacy of the theological methods proposed by the four feminists for use within the United Church.

Scripture and Tradition

As all four feminists repeatedly insist, any approach to theology and biblical interpretation is informed by one's social location. It is therefore essential to identify our social location and be consciously aware of the multiple discourses which shape our multiple, shifting identities, out of which our theology is formed.

One formative influence on our theology and interpretation of scripture is our faith tradition. The assumed sense of biblical texts (which Tanner calls the plain sense), faith practices, communal norms, historical doctrines and beliefs all contribute to a community's canonical system and shape the present understanding of these texts. The historical doctrines that contributed to the formation of the United Church include the centrality of Jesus the Christ, the primacy of scripture, the teaching of the ancient creeds, and the evangelical doctrines of the Reformation as adopted by the Presbyterian, Methodist and Congregational Churches in Canada.[7] The liturgical practices of these founding denominations also contribute to the United Church's canonical system.[8] These founding traditions incorporate the Reformed principles of *sola scriptura* and of the church reformed and always reforming. The United Church's canonical system also includes United Church statements of faith and the social gospel movement as it has impacted our Canadian context. Regional differences across Canada have contributed to the United Church's diverse ethos, including the cooperative movement and the Union Churches on the prairies, and the cultural isolation of Newfoundland's Methodist communities.[9] Protest movements speaking out against the injustices perpetrated against the First Nations, Japanese Canadians, women, the poor, lesbians and gays, and the environment have all contributed to the United Church's identity. First Nations and ethnic minority congregations bring multifaith and multicultural traditions. This is only a brief summary, not an exhaustive list, of some of the primary components of the United Church's canonical system.

A community's canonical system helps to construct and therefore stabilize the meaning of biblical texts. Within this system, Fulkerson suggests that there are ideal and resisting reading regimes which alternately restrict and widen the possibilities of meaning of these texts. The distinction between ideal and resisting regimes is not obvious within the

United Church. Particularly on the prairies, the United Church was born out of protest against injustice.[10] This protest has been directed both externally and internally. Resistance against societal injustice has repeatedly led to protest against our own church's unjust practices. Calls for the right of married women to work outside the home were accompanied by calls for the right of married women to be ordained. Calls for the right of lesbian and gay people to employment and housing were accompanied by calls for the right of lesbian and gay people to be in ordered ministry. Hence it is difficult to separate ideal from resisting regimes in the United Church. Resistance is part of our identity!

Fulkerson's distinction may, however, help us to understand the continual movement between the resisting and ideal reading regimes within the United Church's canonical system. As resisting regimes protest against ideal regimes, they push against the acceptable boundaries of interpretation and practice. If they are eventually incorporated into the ideal regime, they help to establish new boundaries of acceptable belief which in turn are challenged by new resisting regimes. The degree to which they are successfully incorporated depends, in part, upon their ability to remain within the boundaries of the ideal regime even as they are resisting.

For example, feminist biblical criticism in the 1970s and early 1980s was part of the resisting regime within the United Church. However, as it became more popular and better understood, it gradually became incorporated in official documents as a helpful addition to historical-critical studies of the Bible, thus becoming part of the ideal regime. At the same time, feminist criticism needed to be limited by the rest of the United Church's canonical system. To dispense entirely with biblical authority, to dismiss the ultimate authority of the Word of God, to interpret scripture without reference to the gospel of Jesus Christ, or to make ethical decisions without consideration of their social impact on society's marginalized are all violations of United Church traditions. This is not to say that critiques cannot be made that push the boundaries of United Church traditions. To be heard, however, they must be supported by other aspects of the United Church's canonical system.

Herein may lie the greatest problem with the sexuality documents of the 1980s. They were challenging traditional meanings of biblical texts, boundaries of sexual morality and doctrines of anthropology, creation, sin and redemption. At the same time, they virtually ignored aspects of United Church traditions which would support these changes. They did not mention that the method of biblical interpretation used in the 1960 document was very similar to that used in the documents of the 1980s. The documents of the 1980s did not refer to the strong social gospel tradition that has always championed the cause of the other. They downplayed the role of the Holy Spirit and the revelation of God. They gave external scientific analysis and expert opinion more authority than the experiences and faith responses of those within the United Church.

If the sexuality documents of the 1980s had demonstrated the consistency of their conclusions with the liberative aspects of United Church traditions, they may well have received more support. These sexuality documents refer sparingly, if at all, to past interpretations of scripture and United Church traditions. Thus, they ignore their own canonical system and its formative impact on the theological understandings and biblical interpretations of United Church parishioners. In effect, congregations were asked by the documents not to stretch the boundaries of their ideal reading regime, but to dispense with them. This may partially account for the wide gap between the theological conclusions of the writing teams and the responses from pastoral charges. Conservative reform groups then accused the United Church of forsaking its heritage. This is one of the reasons that Tanner has emphasized the importance of tradition. Resistance to the oppressive status quo will be much more effective if it is supported by a faith tradition. Otherwise, groups supporting the status quo can rightly claim that they are the only ones upholding the historic faith.

Another reason to identify United Church traditions is to acknowledge the social construction of the documents. Even though the documents may ignore or resist tradition, they were still produced within the tradition's web of signifiers. Certain words retain meanings and associations unique to United Church contexts, and formed out of its past traditions. If passages of scripture are given new interpretations in the documents, they are usually contrasted with traditional, plain sense meanings assumed by United Church members. The fact that all documents give scriptural support indicates the importance and authority of scripture within the United Church. Acknowledgment of these and other aspects of United Church traditions makes explicit their formative role in the documents.

Thirdly, identifying United Church traditions helps United Church parishioners know who we are. As we hear stories about the roots of our multiple traditions, we will better understand our multiple, sometimes contradictory identities. This will enable us to draw upon the strengths of our traditions as well as to recognize their oppressive aspects. Connecting with our social gospel heritage gives us solid support as we take unpopular stands with society's marginalized. This will challenge the current reputation of the United Church as a weak, liberal and amorphous body, shape shifting with the times. If we acknowledge our own tradition's beliefs and practices that have contributed to oppression, we will be better able to take responsibility for our historical acts of abuse, and to recognize ways in which our beliefs and practices may still be contributing to oppression. This evaluation may lead us to change the selection and organization of particular beliefs and practices that have proven oppressive in our history. Of particular concern are the evangelical doctrines that have been used to espouse Christian superiority and to justify imperialist colonization of the First Nations in Canada, as well as Third World nations who were recipients of United Church missionaries. To use Fulkerson's nuanced terms, Christian traditions must be viewed with the potential for oppression in light of their oppressive use throughout history. For this reason, traditions must be carefully sifted and measured against the concerns of marginalized and colonized peoples.

A fourth reason to identify United Church traditions is to realize the correctives they offer. We are to evaluate our traditions, as mentioned in the previous paragraph, but our traditions can also evaluate us. The meanings of certain traditions and scripture that have been constructed within particular communities have a formative influence on subsequent uses and meanings. Thus, as Fulkerson suggests, they are stabilized and have a certain degree of agency within their social construction. One effect of this agency is to limit the endless possibilities of interpretation according to the community's own canonical system. The system provides its own checks and balances against which new understandings and challenges are measured.

Similarly, Tanner recommends that one responsibility of theologians is to be aware of the historical interpretations of scripture and Christian traditions in order to offer these as checks and balances for contemporary interpretations. According to Tanner, theologians should call to mind certain traditions that have been lost in the overemphasis of their dialectical counterpart. For example, the 1980 document emphasizes the embodied immanence of God, but fails to keep in dialectical tension the transcendent otherness of God that is emphasized in the *Basis of Union*. As a result, it suggests images of God and Jesus that reflect the interests and identity of dominant groups while subsuming the identities of others into these dominant images. If embodied presence is held in tension with transcendent otherness, pronouncements of particular images of God would be viewed as incomplete and partial. The other would not be as easily colonized and subsumed.

For the above reasons, biblical interpretation and ethical deliberation needs to be conducted in reference to the traditions of one's own faith community. Within a Protestant denomination, however, the identification of these traditions is not an easy task. The United Church has multiple traditions which are selected and organized differently by the diverse communities within it. In order to identify its traditions, attention must be given to its constitution. In addition, attention must be given beyond its own bounds to other faith communities. As Protestants our faith community includes the immediate community of one's denomination and the wider community of the universal body of Christ, as both Tanner and Kwok emphasize. Protestants affiliated with the World Council of Churches acknowledge that we are baptized into the one holy catholic Church.[11] I will now examine these aspects of community and diversity.

Community and Diversity

The United Church is formally comprised of four denominational traditions: Methodist, Presbyterian, Congregational and Evangelical United Brethren. Most United Church congregations can still be identified according to their former affiliations with these denominations through their architecture, liturgy, doctrine, and faith practices. In addition to these four traditions, some congregations have been affiliated with yet other denominations before joining the United Church. Many individuals within the United Church also bring multidenominational and multifaith backgrounds. This mix of diverse faith traditions affects the manner in which congregations will select and organize Christian materials. While general observations can be made about common United Church tradition, each congregation will emphasize different aspects, as well as other traditions with which they are familiar. Thus, each congregation will have its own functional canonical system within the formal, overarching canonical system of the United Church.

Included within the United Church's canonical system are resisting regimes of those who offer correctives to the dominant regime. These regimes select and organize Christian materials in a different manner than the dominant regimes. As a result, they will arrive at new meanings of the Christian materials which will inevitably challenge the traditional meanings held by the dominant regime. Within the United Church, the basis of their challenge is usually related to the coherence of Christian traditions, or the oppressive effects of certain beliefs or practices. Renewal groups which tend to favour the patriarchal status quo usually question the coherence of the dominant regime's theology, while groups which are marginalized by the patriarchal status quo usually reveal the oppressive effects of particular beliefs or practices observed by the dominant regime.

These multiple, diverse discourses within the United Church often result in conflict over doctrine and faith practices. In order to resolve this conflict, the United Church has attempted to reach consensus on the issues at hand, such as sexual orientation, with little consideration of the formative impact of its own diverse faith traditions. The 1988 document did give considerable attention to past United Church faith statements and ethical guidelines, as well as noting the diversity of belief within United Church congregations. However, because it was not based upon consensus amongst the liberal, dominant regime and the two opposing resisting regimes, it was not accepted. In all of the sexuality documents, attention was given to the doctrines and faith practices of other denominations in their theological and ethical deliberations, but such ecumenical dialogue is hampered if the United Church is less clear about its own diverse faith traditions. For this reason, it would be helpful for the United Church to begin the identification of its multiple faith traditions within its own diverse communities. Once it is familiar with its own various uses of Christian materials, it can then enter into dialogue with other Christian communities to further examine the coherence and liberative or oppressive effects of these particular uses.

While the United Church has actively engaged in ecumenical dialogue with the contemporary faith communities, it has placed less emphasis on dialogue with historic faith communities, and yet both contemporary and historic communities constitute the wider body of Christ. Tanner and Schüssler Fiorenza can both help with this connection to the historic body of Christ. Tanner can help us connect with dominant Christian traditions, while Schüssler Fiorenza can help us connect with marginalized Christian traditions. Tanner's selection and organization of historic Christian materials can be contrasted with their use in different contemporary Christian communities. These contrasts can provide insight into multiple meanings, coherence, and effects of Christian beliefs on the marginalized. Schüssler Fiorenza's rhetorical reconstruction of the early Christian communities allows those who had no voice in the formation of the dominant Christian traditions to be heard. Her reconstructions of Christian tradition can be contrasted with both Tanner's dominant, historical Christian traditions and the canonical systems of contemporary faith communities. These contrasts can provide further insight into the multiple meanings, coherence, and effects of Christian beliefs on the marginalized.

Dialogue amongst diverse faith traditions within the body of Christ helps to identify formative traditions, and to assess them according to both their coherence with other beliefs and practices, and their impact upon marginalized and colonized people throughout the world. At the same time, disagreement is inevitable with this type of dialogue. Both Tanner and Kwok recognize the vital importance of such dialogue, in spite of its potential volatility, and urge Christian communities to risk conflict and work towards solidarity. Tanner suggests that communities can avoid derisive division by welcoming, not fearing, disagreement as they establish communities of argument. Rather than attempting to agree over the meaning of particular Christian materials, they could simply agree with the choice of materials, and agree to disagree over their meaning. This may be the key for the United Church to remain united amidst diversity. It could agree, together with its different resisting regimes, on the central importance of scripture, the avoidance of literalism in its interpretation, the use of christological norms, support for the marginalized, and recognition of diversity, even though it may disagree over the meanings of these aspects of its faith traditions. One difficulty with this solution is its lack of political impact. In order to avoid absolute relativism and the preservation of the status quo, liberative criteria must also be established. In the following section, we will be examining criteria that arise out of faith communities and help them to respect diversity while attending to the marginalized.

Authority and Revelation

As part of the universal body of Christ, Christian communities must be accountable not only to their own canonical system, but also to the wider Christian communion. According to the social gospel traditions and the World Council of Churches' mandate to seek peace, justice and the integrity of creation, Christian communities must also be accountable for the welfare of the whole of creation, with particular attention given to the marginalized of society. Ultimately they must be accountable to God.

Criteria for the evaluation of this multiple accountability must extend beyond a poststructural focus on the particular. At the same time the criteria must not fall back into a modern universal or metanarrative that collapses diversity and absolutizes the particular. In this section I will identify aspects of each feminist's methodology that contribute towards the development of such criteria and are helpful within the context of a Protestant denomination. I will first consider criteria arising from Christian traditions. Following this I will consider the importance of historical and contextual adequacy. On the basis of these two areas I will then consider pragmatic criteria that are globally conscious.

Common Christian Criteria

Common criteria can be established amongst Christian communities with the help of Tanner's concept of style. Although scripture, historical faith statements, and faith practices contain an endless possibility of meanings, their selection and organization by various communities have produced certain parameters and criteria to limit and guide these meanings. As different communities of faith connect across space and time, their use of Christian materials and derived criteria are contrasted. It is in these interconnections that the United Church can better realize the potential oppression and liberation of its own traditions. It can also find similarities in the use of Christian materials and in criteria by which they can be judged.

It is out of this dialogue or narration of stories from different traditions that Tanner, Fulkerson, and Kwok derive Christian guidelines. Fulkerson names potential universals of sin, grace, and agapic love. Tanner establishes criteria based upon God's transcendence and God's creative agency. Kwok encourages ecumenical dialogues that promote a unity of the body of Christ which respects its own diversity. Thus, through their identification, selection and organization, Christian traditions can produce general guidelines that provide criteria and corrections in the proclamation of the gospel. As these guidelines are continually formed and reformed, they call us to seek not the presentation of a fixed gospel, Kwok reminds us, but the discernment of the living Gospel.

As an example of the general import of these guidelines for the United Church, we will look at Tanner's guideline of relativity. She observes that Christians use common materials in a similar manner: everything is used in reference to God. Even though some will select and organize their materials and practices differently, the style in which they use the material is the same. If all things are referred to God, all things are relativized before God. This has direct implications for a Christian community's concept of authority.

According to Tanner, if a community defers to the transcendence of God, all decisions and authoritative pronouncements will be relativized. We see in a mirror dimly and know only in part. If we declare any decisions to be God's definitive will or claim absolute authority for particular interpretations of scripture and tradition, we transgress into idolatry. Only God is absolute. Our understandings are constructed out of a mesh of interwoven webs of influence. They are particular to our social locations. Therefore, raising the particular to the infinite is demonic, as Paul Tillich reminds us. Indeed, some of the most evil atrocities committed by Christians have been authorized by the absolutizing of our own xenophobic standards. Because of the oppressive aspects of Christian history, western Christians in particular need to be most cautious in our use of authority. If we keep the transcendence of God always before us, Tanner believes that this will prevent the absolutizing of our own positions and give us pause to listen humbly to others. Even those with whom we are radically opposed may have words of truth that need to be heard. However, the operative word here is "may." Marginalized people should not be expected to listen to vitriolic diatribes directed against them. This serves only to further their oppression. As mentioned before, careful consideration needs to be given to issues of power, privilege, and safety, as conditions for dialogue are established.[12]

The writers of the United Church documents would agree that only God is absolute. They would not want to replace divine authority with their own, and they would want to remain open to the ongoing revelation of the Holy Spirit. Likewise, the writers do not give the biblical texts ultimate authority. Although scripture is engaged as a source of God's revelatory authority, it is Jesus the Christ who is given ultimate authority. While scripture provides a functional authority for faith practices and daily living, the basis of its authority lies in its witness of Christ. Where biblical passages appear to contradict the gospel, they are considered non-authoritative. Thus, it is not scripture itself that is sacred but the Word of God that is revealed within and transcends it. Only as it reveals Jesus Christ, the living Word, is it authoritative.[13] As pointed out earlier, there are similarities between this position, Kwok's reference to the living Gospel and Tanner's later emphasis upon the Word of God.

These concepts reinforce the relative authority of scripture in reference to God. Submitting scripture to the authority of God's Word recognizes the human limitations and inconsistencies of scripture's revelation of God. Especially in light of the oppressive uses of scripture against women, gay and lesbian people, and colonized nations, the authority of biblical texts and their interpretations must be tempered. At best, they are rhetorical constructions of God's realm and the gospel, and must be understood and critiqued as such.

The Word of God is related not only to God's transcendence but also to God's immanence through the person of Jesus the Christ. Therefore, scripture is not only tempered in its authority, but is also judged by its own portrayal of the life and ministry of Jesus. Jesus' radical love for social outcasts and his constant striving to break the chains of oppression offer evaluative criteria that have proven particularly important for the social gospel tradition of the United Church.

One of the difficulties with the use of general guidelines, such as a christological norm, is that they can be particularized in a meaning and manner that best suits the interpreter. Norms can be established which benefit the dominant identities of the writing teams under the pretense of divine authority. For example, the ambiguity of Jesus' response to sexual issues in the biblical texts allows the sexuality documents to select christological norms that support their pre-formed beliefs. The 1960 document admits difficulty in knowing the spirit of Christ, because the New Testament presents differing interpretations of Jesus' thought. With this admission in mind, it suggests that the spirit of Christ be based on Jesus' revelation of the underlying purpose and order of the Kingdom of God.[14] On this basis, it restricts sexual expression to marriage in part to maintain societal order. The 1980 document suggests that a Christo-centric reading of scripture will hear God's "yes" uttered in Christ.[15] This yes is to life, to the celebration of sexuality and to the freedom from sexual taboos. On this basis, it opens up the possibilities for pre-marital, extra-marital, and same gender sexual relationships that are mutually supportive and socially responsible. The 1988 document recommends that the Bible be interpreted according to the compassion, faithfulness, and justice of the spirit of Christ.[16] Its corresponding norms call for sexual relationships that are just, loving, health-giving, healing, and sustaining of community.

There is always a danger of equating one's understanding of the spirit of Christ with one's own interests. In fact, this may be inevitable. For this reason, Tanner cautions that all decisions and particularizations of general guidelines must be relativized. However, there are two additional sources of criteria that can prevent a lapse into absolute relativism or a justification of the oppressive status quo: historical and contextual adequacy and globally conscious pragmatism.

Historical and Contextual Adequacy

One of the reasons that Schüssler Fiorenza is reluctant to give up the use of historical criticism is because of its political viability. Even if it is used rhetorically, thereby allowing multiple meanings of the text, it still limits the potential number of historically adequate readings. Historical criticism, combined with archaeology, anthropology, and sociology, suggest that some readings are more credible than others, and thus allow the stories of those who have been marginalized, silenced, and abused throughout history to be heard, and not subsumed into contemporary identities. Likewise, Tanner suggests that the multiple meanings of Christian materials are limited by their coherency with each other. She also emphasizes, along with Kwok and Fulkerson, that Christian materials are borrowed materials from the surrounding culture, thereby making it impossible to separate gospel from culture, Christian materials from secular materials. Intertextual relations with the surrounding context are integral to a Christian community's identity.

These positions all suggest that cross-disciplinary work with the social and physical sciences, anthropology, archaeology, literary theory, and political theory is invaluable in understanding the nature of Christian communities, and their faith practices and beliefs. Critiquing the scientific method does not mean dispensing with scientific findings. It only means that scientific conclusions cannot be absolutized. However, they can still be considered. Placing the different conclusions and theories from the different disciplines together in critical dialogue limits the number of credible conclusions, including those of theology. Thus, theological documents that examine issues of sexuality should be in dialogue with the social sciences. This dialogue can limit the number of credible conclusions, thus adding a criteria of contextual adequacy that prevents the absolute relativization of the document's conclusions.

In order to demonstrate the difference between historical and contextual adequacy, and unquestioned reliance upon scientific conclusions, I will review the sexuality documents' use of the social and medical sciences. Through this review, we will understand how dangerous a modern reliance upon scientific claims is for marginalized people, while still recognizing the value of critical dialogue with the sciences.

The United Church documents seldom questioned scientific and scholarly opinion. When dealing with controversial issues of sexuality, the documents often presented competing views followed by definitive explanations based upon scientific and historical-critical findings. Modern methods of empirical analysis were not questioned, thereby granting them unconditional authority. Their social location and social construction was ignored. One of the documents suggested that scientific findings were the most trustworthy source of truth, and hence of God's revelation.[17]

This concept of truth is based on an elevation of abstract essentialism. Kwok recommends an alternate concept based upon a pragmatic, relational understanding. If this latter concept is used, the focus in the sexuality documents will be less upon empirical findings and more on right relationships. By implication, God will then be sought not in hidden, essentialist truths, but in justice-centred relationships.

The sexuality documents began to move in this direction in the 1980s, although their deference to empirical science retained the elevation of abstract truth. This contributed to the earlier documents' emphasis upon the causes of homosexuality, as well as the emphasis of the 1980s documents upon the fixed nature of sexual orientation. The cause of homosexuality was a particular concern of the 1960 document. If homosexual relations were sinful then God had to provide the possibility of healing and of transformation to heterosexuality. To know the social and psychological causes of this "disease" would enable a more effective transformation.[18] The 1980 and 1984 documents both discussed the causes of homosexuality, but emphasized that scientific findings were showing that sexual orientation was not a choice. However, the 1984 document still called for a study of the nature and origins of homosexuality.[19] The 1988 document stated that one needed to find the cause of homosexuality only if one needed to find a cure. If only heterosexuality is considered natural, there must be causes for the aberrations of homosexuality and bisexuality. However, if they are all considered natural variations of sexual orientation, the cause becomes immaterial.[20] If sexual orientation could be proven to be part of an unchangeable essence of humanity, it could be viewed as part of God's creation, regardless of the type of orientation. Because bisexuality challenges the essentialist assumption that sexual orientation is fixed, it has still not been seriously considered by the United Church. The element of choice is threatening to all sides.

The assumption that sexual orientation is part of a fixed, unchangeable essence also limits God's creation to essential, physiological characteristics. If we can prove that sexual orientation is a genetic trait, it could be argued that, like blue-eyed people, lesbian and gay people are created by God to be lesbian and gay. Conversely, it could also be argued that, like a birth defect, sexual orientation is a disability that may be able to be "corrected" with future technological research.[21] This last possibility dramatizes the danger of unquestioned scientific conclusions and essentialist philosophy.

Fulkerson encourages sexual orientation to be viewed along with race and gender as a social construction. Along with the other three feminists, she warns against the horrific dangers of essentialism. The identification of particular characteristics of sexual orientation, race or gender inevitably excludes those who don't fit, and subjugates those who do into absolutized categories. Medical experiments conducted by the Nazi regime on mentally and physically disabled people, gay men and other expendable undesirables have demonstrated the potential horrific treatment of the essentialized other.

If scientific studies are understood within their own social locations and political interests, the voice of scientific authority is no longer clear, nor unanimous. Identity becomes a site of multiple, sometimes conflicting, discourses. The creativity of God is no longer reduced to a particular essence, but is understood within the complexity and diversity of our world. It is ongoing and unfolding, never static or fixed.

It is within this context of multiple, conflicting discourses that scientific, cultural, and historical claims should be considered. Critical dialogue amongst a variety of disciplines and their findings will enable historical and contextual adequacy without absolutizing any particular claim.

Global, Pragmatic Criteria

The second source of criteria which prevents absolute relativism and the preservation of the oppressive status quo is based upon liberative, pragmatic concerns. All four feminists are aware that pragmatic, emancipatory norms are necessary within their methods. While all are cautious about the establishment of any universal norms that subsume diversity, they also recognize the need for universal guidelines which can be particularized in diverse forms within local communities. Hence, each feminist suggests universal guidelines related to emancipatory, pragmatic concerns. These global, pragmatic guidelines are an important contribution to the development of a more adequate theological method within the United Church context.

Tanner is not all inclusive in her use of Christian materials. She admits that some traditions may well contribute to oppression. Therefore, she selects and organizes material that will best challenge the oppressive status quo. On the basis of two Christian principles she forms pragmatic, emancipatory norms. God's transcendence relativizes the authority of human constructions. God's creative agency honours the diversity and particularity of every creature. Anything claiming absolute authority contravenes these norms. Anything devaluing or otherwise oppressing any of God's creatures is also a contravention. With these two norms in mind, the United Church's dialogue with its own diverse communities can be guided by respect for the diversity and particularity of every person, including lesbian, gay and bisexual people. Any conclusions and judgments made must be understood as partial and relative to God.

On the basis of a community's discursive construction of the Christian principles of sin, grace, and agapic love, Fulkerson identifies internal norms produced by the community to measure its own resistance to patriarchal capitalism. These "feminist stipulations of relevance" are shaped by the community's Christian identity and are pragmatic, asking what effects a particular ordering of discourse have on the marginalized. Within the United Church, those who are marginalized from the benefits of patriarchal capitalism must be considered when conducting theological and ethical analysis within its canonical system.

With the help of postcolonial analysis, Kwok establishes pragmatic norms that honour diversity and allow a global systemic analysis of structures of colonization. Through her ecumenical work, she also calls for the unity of the body of Christ that honours its diversity. In order to achieve this unity, she suggests a solidarity of connections, mutuality and inclusivity amongst faith communities. Within this context Kwok poses ethical criteria for judging biblical interpretations and theological methods. They must contribute to the liberation and humanization of the global community, emphasizing freedom, justice, peace, and reconciliation.

Kwok does not limit this solidarity to Christian communities, but draws on the traditions of other faiths to respect the multiple cultural and faith identities of Asian people. As people have been immersed in multiple faith traditions, their readings of any one will be influenced by the others. This is the case not only of people living in Asian countries. Many United Church congregations, especially those which are of an ethnic minority, include people who have multifaith backgrounds. Many First Nations United Church congregations are beginning to reclaim traditional

Aboriginal teachings. For these congregations a parallel reading process with the traditions of each faith will help identify the multiple webs of signification that are already present. It will also welcome the insights and critiques which each faith brings. In addition, these critiques will give those who do not have a multifaith background additional insights into the oppressive and liberative aspects of various orderings of Christian traditions. Thus, a multifaith hermeneutics will benefit all Christian communities and contribute to a globally conscious dialogical imagination. Out of this dialogue amongst Christian communities and different faith traditions, globally accountable criteria can be developed.

Interfaith dialogue could have had a significant impact in the sexuality documents. Although the writing teams of the sexuality documents consulted with other denominations, they did not consult with other faith and cultural traditions. Learning about the *berdache* and "Two Spirited Peoples" of the First Nations, as well as the "cut sleeve" of the Ming dynasty in China would have disputed the prevailing belief that homosexual activity was a western, Caucasian phenomena.[22] It would also have demonstrated the respect afforded those with non-traditional gender roles and sexual behaviour.This would, of course, be offset by condemnatory positions of other faith traditions.

Schüssler Fiorenza also posits ethical criteria to judge biblical interpretation. Her criteria are developed out of historical and contemporary faith communities of emancipatory wo/men. They are pragmatically based and clearly favour emancipatory over kyriarchal discourse. Although she acknowledges the multiple identities, oppressions and privileges faced by many, she privileges those who are faced with multiplicative oppressions.

The pragmatic, liberation basis for each of these feminists allows the establishment of emancipatory criteria from within the community of faith. Such criteria could well emerge from the United Church's social gospel tradition, and help it to more adequately attend to the other. This was missing from all but the 1988 document. The primary emphasis in the sexuality documents, apart from the 1988 document, was to educate and include into a system, rather than educate and liberate from oppressive structures. They also did not stress the need to connect with other communities of faith in order to develop a global consciousness and globally accountable criteria.

In conclusion, the writers of future United Church documents need to take an intertextual approach in their interpretation of scripture and use of theological methods. To begin, they should connect with the canonical system of the United Church in order to listen to its own faith communities. This includes the resisting regimes of those marginalized from church structures. They also need to listen to those marginalized in our society, especially when dealing with issues affecting them. When addressing their marginalization, they need to address questions of structural oppression, and not simply the inclusion of everyone into the existing structures.

The great diversity of faith communities within the United Church will bring different, sometimes conflicting, biblical interpretations, ethical criteria and theological opinions. These all need to be measured against the United Church's own faith traditions, with particular attention given to the traditions which support the marginalized. In addition, they need to be measured against the beliefs and concerns of other Christian communities, and accountable to the wider body of Christ, to those who are marginalized and colonized around the world, and to the welfare of the earth and its inhabitants. Criteria arising out of the common use of Christian material and out of global, pragmatic concerns that prove adequate to our historical and cultural contexts will allow the development of universal principles that can be particularized by diverse communities.

Throughout this process each community needs to be open to the critiques of other faith communities, as well as marginalized peoples around the world. This will contribute to the unity of the body of Christ and solidarity with other faith traditions as we seek to end oppression and celebrate diversity. Within this faith journey, we must be "faithful to God's call to be just, loving, health-giving, healing, and sustaining of community."[23]

Notes to Chapter 8

1. *Gift, Dilemma and Promise*, 78.

2. Thanks to Karen Ridd for pointing out this middle-class bias.

3. *Together in Faith: Inclusive Resources About Sexual Diversity for Study, Dialogue, Celebration, and Action* (Toronto: The United Church of Canada, 1995), 44–47.

4. Nancy Pinnell, quoting from an anonymous source.

5. For a report on the stories of discrimination and abuse that lesbian, gay and bisexual ministers have faced in the last decade, after the 1988 report was approved, see The Division of Ministry Personnel and Education, and The Division of Mission in Canada of The United Church of Canada, *Lesbian, Gay, and Bisexual Persons in Ministry*, Consultation Report, edited by Ken De Lisle (December, 1999).

6. Rosemary Radford Ruether, *Sexism and God-Talk: Toward a Feminist Theology* (Boston: Beacon Press, 1983).

7. These principles are taken from *The Basis of Union*. See The United Church of Canada, *The Manual* (Toronto: United Church Publishing House, 1995), Section 2.0.

8. I wish to thank Charlotte Caron for noting this liturgical contribution.

9. See "Special Issue: Christianizing the Social Order: A Founding Vision of The United Church of Canada," *Toronto Journal of Theology* 12, no. 2 (Fall); *A Long and Faithful March: 'Towards the Christian Revolution' 1930s/1980s*, ed. Harold Wells and Roger Hutchinson (Toronto: United Church Publishing House, 1989); Ben Smillie, *Beyond the Social Gospel: Church Protest on the Prairies* (Toronto: United Church Publishing House, 1991); Sandra Beardsall, "Methodist Religious Practices in Outport Newfoundland," dissertation (Toronto: Victoria University and University of Toronto, 1996).

10. See Smillie, *Beyond the Social Gospel*.

11. World Council of Churches, *Baptism, Eucharist and Ministry*, Faith and Order Paper, vol. 111 (Geneva: World Council of Churches, 1982), 2–3; The United Church of Canada, *The Manual*, B 2.15.

12. For an excellent discussion of this see Sharon Welch, *A Feminist Ethic of Risk*, revised ed. (Minneapolis: Fortress Press, 2000).

13. The use of various terms in the sexuality documents to refer to the christological norm for biblical interpretation may well indicate a number of different christologies operative within these documents. This would be an interesting exploration for future work. To begin this discussion, see Kathryn E. Tanner, "Jesus Christ," in *The Cambridge Companion to Christian Doctrine*, ed. Colin E. Gunton, Cambridge Companions to Religion (Cambridge: Cambridge University Press, 1997).

14. *Sex, Love, Marriage*, 7.

15. *In God's Image*, 18.

16. *Sexual Orientations, Lifestyles and Ministry*, 36.

17. *In God's Image*, 11.

18. *Sex, Love, Marriage*, 14–16.

19. *In God's Image*, 56–57; *Gift, Dilemma and Promise*, 68–71.

20. *Sexual Orientations, Lifestyles and Ministry*, 48–51.

21. The 1988 document outlines a few of these different views of sexual orientation. See *Sexual Orientations, Lifestyles and Ministry*, 49–51.

22. For further reading see Walter L. Williams, *The Spirit and the Flesh: Sexual Diversity in American Indian Culture* (Boston: Beacon Press, 1992); Bret Hinsch, *Passions of the Cut Sleeve* (Berkeley: University of California, 1990); Viven W. Ng, "Homosexuality and the State in Late Imperial China," in *Hidden From History: Reclaiming the Gay and*

Lesbian Past, ed. Martin et. Duberman, al. (London: Penguin, 1991); Grace M. Jantzen, "Off the Straight and Narrow: Toward a Lesbian Theology," presentation at King's College, London (April, 1995).

23. *Sexual Orientations, Lifestyles and Ministry*, 3.

Chapter 9

Toward a More Adequate Feminist Theological Method

To conclude I will propose both presuppositions and starting points for feminist theologies that will better enable issues of marginalization and diversity to be addressed within Protestant denominations. Although my hope is that this method will be helpful for a variety of Protestant churches, and perhaps some Roman Catholic parishes, it will be of particular benefit to those Protestant churches which have traditionally taken liberal, modern approaches in their theological methods. The presuppositions underlie the critiques of modern, liberal approaches used in theological methods. The starting points will involve a two-step process that Protestant churches can take as they develop theological methods that can better attend to the other. The first step is to identify the canonical system of one's own faith community and its relationship to the wider body of Christ and to other faith traditions. The second step is to evaluate these faith traditions according to their coherence, their historical and contextual adequacy, and their oppressive and liberative potentials. This two-step process of identification and evaluation should occur within certain parameters of accountability that are ultimately accountable to God.

Presuppositions

1. **Theological statements, biblical interpretations, and historical accounts are local creations of meaning.**
This first presupposition stresses that all theological, biblical, and historical interpretations are limited by the social location and interests of the interpreter, and are rhetorical constructions that have political implications. They do not *represent* a reality, but *create* it in the interaction with readers and their communities. In addition, it would be helpful for interpreters to

remember that historical texts themselves are rhetorical constructions, usually written by those who have been in dominant positions. Interpreters need to examine the texts and their own interpretations critically, asking themselves how their interpretations might contribute both to marginalization and colonialization, as well as to liberation and the *basileia* of God.

Because each interpreter brings a different set of interests from different social locations, interpretations are as diverse as the number of interpreters. The infinite number of potential interpretations renders biblical and historical texts unstable. They do not contain one stable, objective, factual meaning, as authorized by academic experts, that is universally valid.

2. Christian traditions and biblical texts are stabilized through communal use.

The selection and organization of particular biblical texts, historical doctrines, creeds, and practices of historical and contemporary Christian communities limit their potential meanings. When one biblical text is read alongside a particular doctrine within the context of a particular practice it will take a different shape than when juxtaposed with other doctrines and practices. The same biblical text will become a very different text as it is used with different combinations of Christian material across different communities. As different communities select and organize Christian material, they shape the material itself and bring temporary stability to it within that setting.

In addition to the selection and organization of Christian materials, societal influences will also shape the material and its meanings. For instance, a Presbyterian church in Canada may read the same biblical text alongside the same historical confessions, doctrines and creeds as a Presbyterian church in Korea, but the contrasting societal influences may shape the biblical text and its meaning differently in each country. As an example, Ephesians 6:1–3 may be understood by the Canadian church to support institutionalized care for aging and disabled parents. The same passage read by the Korean church may be understood to support adult children caring for their aging and disabled parents within their own home, rather than shutting them away in an institution. The contrasting societal views regarding the care and respect of elderly people will shape how this biblical text is heard.

On the basis of this presupposition, it is more difficult to make universal judgements about a text's patriarchal bias. Some communities may read or perform a text that has traditionally been used to suppress women in a more liberative way. As an example, a Southern Baptist church which was committed to social justice ministries, including the provision of a food bank, an AIDS hospice, and refugee housing, read Ephesians 5:21–33 as requiring the husband to be more submissive to the wife than the wife to the husband, because to love with the love of Christ is love with the ultimate act of submission.[1] While patterns of historical use of particular arrangements of Christian material may allow judgements about their liberative or oppressive *potential*, unequivocal judgements rip them from their communally-constructed stability, and impose upon them a false stability removed from communal influence.

3. **Systemic analysis of domination acknowledges the social construction of identity and renders liberal notions of equality and inclusion insufficient.**

Just as Christian material is stabilized within communal use, individual identities are stabilized, however momentarily, within communal circles of influence. We are all socially constructed by our social positions and participation within particular communities. Because we are shaped by multiple, shifting social influences, our identities are multiple and shifting. This renders static definitions of group identities, such as gender, problematic because every woman's experience as a woman is shaped differently.

While historical patterns of gender discrimination suggest the viability of the subject "woman," Fulkerson suggests that this subject needs to remain unstable until particularized within a social location. In other words, while generalizations about women's experiences are important political strategies, they must always remain open to the critique of women whose experiences differ from these generalizations. Otherwise, those defining gender will inevitably choose definitions that most closely match their own socially constructed experiences. These definitions determine whose characteristics are central and whose are peripheral, placing those who created the definitions at the centre.

For example, a statement that women share a common experience of sexist discrimination ignores how this experience is radically changed when associated with experiences of racism. An Aboriginal woman's experience of sexism may be intricately linked to her experience of racism. If women of white-skinned privilege separate the two and deal only with sexism, the experiences of First Nations women would not be adequately represented. Their experiences of racism would become peripheral to their experiences of sexism, thereby placing First Nations women on the periphery of this definition of gender.

Western feminist methods have typically raised experience above critique as an unequivocal source of authority. This elevation has failed to recognize the social construction of experience and has assumed the priority of individual experience. Along with Fulkerson, Kwok shatters these assumptions by refuting the autonomy of the individual and emphasizing the instability of one's identity. For instance, I experience marginalization as a Canadian (in relation to the United States), as a woman, as a lesbian, and having a mixed race family with six Cree and Saulteaux grandchildren. At the same time, these experiences of marginalization are heavily influenced by my experiences of white-skinned, educational and middle-class privilege. At times aspects of my identity that are marginalized become privileged (I may be asked to speak at a gathering because I am a woman and a lesbian) and certain aspects shift over time and place (I may lose my job and middle-class status). My multiple, shifting identity is continually being shaped and reshaped by the multiple circles of influence in which I live.

Without an analysis of the social construction of experience and identity, any discussion of gender, sexual orientation, or other identity remains locked in an essentialism that erases multiple identities and absolutizes differences. That which is assumed to be essential to the experiences of women or of lesbians and gays is actually particular to the experiences of those proposing this essence. As an example, it is usually out of a place of privilege that feminists are able to write. Their description of women's experiences is therefore informed by their places of privilege (usually U.S., middle-class, and formally educated). Any experiences of gender that differ from this privilege become secondary. Thus, the identities of women marginalized by colour, class, nationality, and educational access are subsumed into the identities of privileged women. In addition, when reference is made to non-dominant groups, differences between them and the privileged group tend to be essentialized as "other" and differences within these groups are often flattened.

When non-dominant groups are subsumed into a privileged definition of identity their obliteration is a form of violence. This violence is heightened when theologians give divine sanction to these privileged definitions of identities as attributes of God. These characteristics can then be assumed to be divinely ordained, further obliterating the existence of those who differ from these stable, fixed, and privileged identities.

It is for these reasons that I suggest definitions of identity, such as gender or sexual orientation, must be understood as social constructions within a particular context. While generalized definitions are important for purposes of political strategy and communication amongst different social groups, their own social construction must be acknowledged. The subjects of identity need to be understood as unstable until they are socially constructed by the multiple circles of influence within particular contexts. It should also be recognized that this socially constructed stability of particular definitions of identity is only momentarily stable. Because the social context will include overlapping and contradictory circles of influence arising from multiple associations, the corresponding identities will be continually shifting and changing.

Acknowledging the social construction of identity will also entail a recognition of the method by which the identity was constructed. Which interpretive strategies were used to reach these particular conclusions? If these form part of the authoritative basis for these claims, how are the claims adjudicated against competing claims of communities which have no access to these strategies? For example, how could a community which has no access to tools of historical criticism be taken seriously in its challenge of biblical interpretations that are based upon historical criticism? Kwok would take this critique further by connecting the control of knowledge with the control of colonized peoples. If western modes of analysis form the basis of particular claims, must competing claims use the same western form of logic to be heard? If so, this would further devalue a colonized people's own philosophical methods and communal traditions.

The colonized would once again be subsumed into the identity of the colonizer.

Identity politics also shape liberal political strategies of inclusion. Invitations of inclusion extended by those whose identities are privileged in society invariably set the terms of that inclusion according to their own interests and identities. Seldom are the structures which benefit their dominant identities challenged. Marginalized people are therefore welcomed into the very structures which keep them marginalized. This logic of identity subsumes the identities of marginalized and colonized peoples into identities of dominant groups. In order to address issues of diversity and marginalization, a theological method needs to move beyond a liberal model which welcomes inclusion and assumes the equality of all. It needs to recognize power differentials and systemic structures of multiplicative oppression. It also needs to recognize the social construction of identity and move beyond individualism to communally-based analysis. This leads to the first step in the development of a theological method that will more adequately attend to issues of diversity and marginalization within Christian communities.

Communal Beginnings

Instead of beginning with experience, as feminist theologies usually propose, I join with Schüssler Fiorenza in urging us to begin with an analysis of the social location of experience.[2] This will entail an identification of the multiple circles of influence and communal affiliations that shape the experience. In order to better understand the diverse experiences of oppression and resistance for women, and for lesbian and gay people within a church community, it is helpful to begin this analysis by looking at the church's canonical system. This will engage a community's diverse stories of experiences, beliefs, scriptural interpretations, traditions, ethos, practices, normative assumptions, and goals such as saving souls and/or working against injustice. If stories of experience are engaged without reference to the other components of a community's canonical system, their social construction within this community will not be understood. Experience could then be isolated and raised above critique to support a totalitarian ideology that dismisses contrasting experiences. If traditional doctrine is cited without reference to diverse faith practices or experiences, it could be used to suppress diversity and support a totalitarian ideology that upholds the patriarchal status quo. In order to acknowledge and respect the diversity within the community, the multiple aspects of its canonical system must be considered.

One of the communal norms that will shape biblical interpretation is the assumed sense of scripture. This is the basic, normative sense of the text that seems obvious or direct to the community. It is the exposé that needs no additional warrants for its authority. It is the familiar and therefore authoritative meaning according to a particular community's conventions for reading. This does not mean that a community will necessarily agree with this assumed sense, but will acknowledge that it represents the familiar, traditional reading and that any alternative readings would require additional warrants of support. The assumed sense will vary across communities, as each community with its canonical system will shape the text and its meaning differently, even though the communities themselves may assume that their traditional reading of the text is shared by all other Christian communities.

To attempt to understand one aspect of any community's canonical system apart from the others could potentially distort the community's own meaning of this aspect. For instance, an affirmation of the authority of the Bible may suggest that critical readings of scripture will be ruled out. However, if this affirmation is placed alongside a belief that the Bible is not to be equated with the Word, but is human testimony to the Word, then critical readings of scripture may be required in order to discern the Word.

Included within a community's canonical system are the resisting regimes. Attention to these groups will allow voices marginalized within the church body to be heard. They may offer correctives to the dominant regime in one of two ways. They could reveal incoherencies in the manner in which the dominant regime selects and organizes Christian materials. Resisting regimes could also correct the dominant regime by revealing the oppressive aspects from the community's canonical system.

In order for the resisting regimes to be taken seriously within their own denomination, they need to operate within the bounds of their church's canonical system. While they may be challenging some of their church's dominant conventions, their voice will not be given much authority unless they support their alternative positions with other components of the dominant conventions. Resistance movements that protest too many of the dominant conventions begin to place themselves outside of the community, thereby weakening their effect on the community. As an example, social justice has always been a strong, historical component of the United Church's dominant regime. The resisting regime convinced the United Church in the 1960s that the ordination of married women was an issue of justice rather than personal morality. The same argument was used for the ordination and commissioning of lesbian and gay candidates in the 1980s. Once this link with social justice was made, the leadership of the church began to encourage its membership to include the concerns and commitments of these resisting regimes into the dominant conventions of the church.

If the challenge of resisting regimes is accepted by the dominant regime, they may become part of the dominant regime, although the transition will be lengthy and confusing. For instance, as the United Church began to listen to the voices of the First Nations, women, and lesbian and gay people, policies and colonial beliefs that were racist, sexist, and heterosexist began to be changed. The unwritten assumptions and ethos which accompanied these oppressive policies and beliefs remain in place, however, presenting a confusing mix of contradictory dominant conventions. Although the General Council of the United Church effectively cleared the way for the ordination and commissioning of lesbian and gay candidates over ten years ago, it is still rare that a congregation will call an "out" lesbian or gay minister.

Eventually the implicit rules catch up to the stated beliefs and form an unambiguous dominant convention. This transition can be seen in the Southern Baptist Convention, which was formed in part over its support for slavery.[3] While racist and colonialist beliefs still abound, the dominant regime of the Southern Baptist Convention is now unambiguous in its condemnation of slavery.

One further aspect of a community's canonical system is its relationship with its wider societal context. As a society changes, so do faith communities. This is particularly apparent with the United Church. Political changes in Canada invariably are reflected within the United Church. The social gospel movement was associated with the rise of the CCF (Co-operative Commonwealth Federation) and socialized medicine.

Increasing resistance to centralized power in Ontario is accompanied by increasing resistance to the power of the United Church's head office in Toronto. Fragmentation and threatened splits in the country are reflected in the withdrawal of membership and threatened splits in the United Church.

This impact of society upon the faith communities is due in part to the multiple affiliations of the members of these faith communities with other communities. The identities of its members are multiple and shifting according to their multiple and shifting connections with different circles of influence. Where these circles converge, the dominant regime of the faith community will be strengthened. Where they clash, internal resisting regimes may be strengthened.

This dynamic fluctuation of external and internal influences upon a community shapes the manner in which it will read scripture, select and interpret traditions, and practice its faith. By exploring the intertextual formation of community we are better able to understand the limits of resistance that are possible within the community's canonical system. We are also better able to understand the shifting nature of identity and social location. As Canada becomes increasingly multicultural and multifaith, the social location of Christian churches will include interaction with other faith communities, and churches will recognize an increasing number of their own members who have multifaith identities. In their interaction with society, faith communities will also be more aware of their impact upon marginalized people in the Canadian society and in the world. Their historical relationships with the marginalized and colonized form part of their canonical system and can be challenged or affirmed by resisting regimes.

A recognition of the intertextual formation of communities allows a recognition of the diversity of their own members, and their intricate, conflictual relationship with external circles of influence. It also allows an analysis of the shifting relations of power between resistance regimes and their dominant regime, as well as between privileged and marginalized affiliates of the community.

Accountability and Authoritative Criteria

As we seek to live into grace, our relationship with God entices us to yearn for healing relationships with our earth and all of its creatures. As we yearn, the Spirit moves us to action, and we find ourselves in the middle of a power struggle between dominance and resistance, privilege and marginalization. Questions of authority and revelation will arise. Positions, decisions and actions will need to be evaluated. Conflicting opinions about theology and ethics will require criteria and accountability. I propose four primary areas of accountability for a feminist theological method within a Protestant community, all of which are ultimately accountable to God. The first area is to the marginalized of our own society, who are both within and outside of the faith community. The second is to the denomination's canonical system, and the third to the wider body of Christ within the present and the past. The fourth area of accountability is to the wounded earth and all of its marginalized peoples of the present and past. These are not given in order of priority, but intended to work together as our accountability weaves back and forth, informing each area and being informed by our relationship with God.

One way in which we can be accountable to God within a Protestant context is to hold a belief of God's transcendence in dialectical tension with a belief of God's radical immanence. As Tanner emphasizes, the radical transcendence of God relativizes all human constructions, including the Bible. Nothing can claim absolute authority, but must be viewed in relationship to God as finite and limited.

God's radical immanence as revealed through the person of Jesus challenges followers of Christ to seek agapic ideals in relationships and communities, while opposing all forms of oppression and domination. By reading scripture and evaluating faith practices in light of the Word of Wisdom, God's emancipatory love becomes the authoritative criteria. This criteria of emancipatory love pushes into the future, promising God's presence and guidance through the empowerment of the Spirit of Christ as we strive towards the kin-dom of God.

Accountability to Society's Marginalized

Feminist theologies are accountable to women and therefore to a wide diversity of marginalized groups to which women belong. In acknowledgement of the shifting nature of power and privilege, the identification of these marginalized groups within our own society is an ongoing process. It is made more difficult when different marginalized groups offer competing concerns. I will present two examples of this complexity. First, would it be possible to be accountable both to a First Nations congregation and to its minister who has just been asked to leave because she has been outed as a lesbian? Would it make any difference if the pastor is of dominant, British ethnicity? What would analyses of past and present forms of colonization reveal? Secondly, within a liberal church is one to be accountable to a minority reform group which is demanding an end to the use of inclusive language and opposes the ordination and commissioning of lesbian, gay, and bisexual candidates? This reform group is marginalized from the power and leadership of the church. Does a liberative theology that is accountable to the marginalized therefore include this marginalized group?

These examples highlight the need for a complex analysis of intertextual relations in order to understand the shifting nature of dominance and marginalization, and the type of power which marginalized groups have. As the margins shift amongst communities and circles of influence, so does the centre of power. Even though reform groups may be marginalized within a denomination, they may still enjoy societal and congregational privileges afforded their heterosexual, middle-class and Caucasian identities. Even though an ethnic minority congregation has power in the ousting of their pastor, the balance of power shifts in their relationship with the wider denomination as they struggle to uphold their own cultural identity.

It is for this reason that liberal policies of inclusion are insufficient. We cannot be accountable to every form of marginalization, nor include every marginalized perspective. Those who are marginalized because the centre of power in the church has shifted away from their particular forms of privilege may still enjoy these privileges within society. It is those who are marginalized because of their identities, and not because of a loss of privilege, to whom we are to be accountable.

As relations of power are identified, historical relations of colonization must be realized. Scars of colonization do not disappear, but continue to shape present relations. Although the institution of slavery has been eliminated, its legacy is still visible in systemic structures of racial discrimination. Although the assimilation policies of the residential schools have been changed, their legacy is still visible through the high proportion of abused Aboriginal inmates in the British penal system. Paternalistic imperialism is still operating in Canada as the First Nations struggle to achieve self-government.

Accountability to those who are marginalized in our society includes not only an analysis of the complex and shifting factors of marginalization and colonization, but also a commitment to "hearing them into voice."[4] It is vital that the input of those most affected by certain theological deliberations be consulted. Equally important, it should be recognized that one person from a marginalized group not be assumed to represent that particular marginalized identity. Rather, people marginalized in society should be recognized as subjects with multiple, shifting identities shaped by multiple, complex discourses. This recognition will render insufficient simple policies of inclusion that tend to reify differences between dominant and marginalized identities, obliterate differences within the marginalized group, and establish the terms of inclusion according to the interests of the dominant identities. Instead, analysis of power imbalances and structures of oppression must be made. This will necessitate dialogue with other disciplines, including history, archaeology, anthropology, sociology, psychology, political theory, and economic analysis in order to best understand the complexities of marginalization and colonization. It will also necessitate imaginative dialogue in which marginalized people will be invited to express themselves in as comfortable, familiar, and safe a manner as possible.[5]

Accountability to a Denomination's Canonical System

The second area of accountability concerns a community's use of Christian materials. The organization and selection of Christian materials will be shaped by that community's historical traditions and identity. For a feminist theological method to be operative within a particular community, it must be accountable, in part, to the canonical system of that community. It can do this by demonstrating connections to and logical consequences from the community's historical traditions and faith practices. Without this accountability to a community's canonical system, a feminist theological method could ignore sources of revelation and guidance found within the community's traditions and could be dismissed much more easily by the community.

As particular biblical texts and Christian doctrines have been selected and organized by a community, their multiple meanings are stabilized. As one biblical passage is juxtaposed with another, in light of the assumed sense of the biblical texts, in light of one doctrinal statement juxtaposed with another, in light of one faith practice with another, the potentially limitless meanings of each are restricted. This stabilization of meaning grants the texts agency to limit and adjudicate the community's positions, practices and decisions. In this manner, scriptural passages and doctrinal statements can stand against a community to offer correctives or affirmations and to suggest normative theological principles. For instance, a United Church reading of Luke 4:16–21, with a reading of Isaiah 58 and 60:1–2, with a doctrine of sin, with stories of the social gospel movement, with stories of ecumenical task forces on corporate responsibility supports a materialist reading of scripture and names the liberation of the oppressed as a normative christological principle.[6]

When the assumed sense of a biblical text conflicts with its juxtaposition with other texts, doctrines, beliefs and faith practices, or with readings from its own resisting regimes, criteria will be needed to judge the most appropriate reading, belief or practice for that community. These criteria will be initially derived from the community's canonical system, including their selection and organization of Christian materials. Once a community has identified its traditions and central doctrines, these can be used to determine the coherence of the disputed meaning with the community's dominant conventions. This will enable the correction of an overemphasis upon or neglect of certain beliefs or faith practices within their canonical system.

For instance, the radical immanence and embodiment of God is frequently emphasized within the United Church, often to the exclusion of God's transcendence. Connections could be made with the United Church's historical faith statements and Reformed doctrines, all of which emphasize God's transcendence. These connections could produce a dialectical tension that holds together God's radical immanence as lover, co-sufferer and freedom fighter, while simultaneously acknowledging the human limitations and insufficiencies of these divine referents. The radical immanence of God through Jesus the Christ helps us focus upon God's partnership with humanity to usher in the reign of God, while God's radical transcendence helps us realize the transient, imperfect nature of our contributions and our resultant dependency upon God. This emphasis upon God's transcendence would prevent particular positions from claiming incontestable authority, and instead require them to remain open to critique.

While it is important that a community understand its own canonical system and derive evaluative criteria from it, it is equally important that the community not base its judgements exclusively upon its own canonical system. The two dangers of an exclusive adherence to internal criteria established by the community are isolation and a tendency to preserve the oppressive status quo. The other three areas of accountability help to address these dangers, and make it imperative that each area be considered in light of the others.

Accountability to the Wider Body of Christ

Accountability to the universal body of Christ, as emphasized by Kwok, prevents a myopic cocooning of a community of faith and acknowledges diversity of Christian traditions, beliefs, and faith practices. It also reveals the potential danger of particular beliefs and practices as they have been used to support domination and colonialism. Through dialogue with other Christian communities, the use of Christian materials and the internal criteria established by each community can be contrasted. In their varying selection and organization of Christian materials, they can provide alternative perspectives and understandings of revelation that can offer both insights and correctives to each other. They can demonstrate the oppressive effects of particular uses of Christian materials within their context, and help privileged communities understand their role in the continued domination of marginalized communities. They can also suggest alternative patterns of belief and action.

Dialogue with different Christian communities need not be limited to the present. Rhetorical reconstructions of historical communities allow dialogue with both the dominant and marginalized voices of our Christian heritage. The works of Tanner and Schüssler Fiorenza help us access the doctrines, creeds, beliefs, and faith practices of historical Christian communities from different perspectives. Tanner proposes doctrines which she has found to be fundamental to historical Christian communities within dominant Christian traditions. Schüssler Fiorenza proposes alternative, liberative faith practices of marginalized groups within these historical Christian communities who have been excluded from dominant Christian traditions. As we listen to both of these voices, we will be able to take history seriously without lapsing into historical positivism.

As contemporary Christian communities interconnect with one another and with rhetorical constructions of historical Christian communities, they will find divergences and commonalities in their use of Christian materials. It is on the basis of these commonalities that Christian communities can derive general criteria of coherence and liberation. Because of the divergences, however, these guidelines can only be generalized. They contain a general practical import that can then be particularized in different ways in different communities according to the community's canonical system.

The World Council of Churches has been able to arrive at a few general criteria which might be helpful in this consideration. Their call for peace, justice, and the integrity of creation can provide a general practical import that will be enacted in differently in different communities. Material on sexuality and on the Decade of Churches in Solidarity with Women in Church and Society have contrasted various positions in denominations around the world and arrived at general principles and suggestions.[7]

Accountability to the Earth and its Marginalized Peoples

As Christian communities move into the fourth area of accountability for the wounded earth and its marginalized peoples, Christian dialogue extends into multifaith dialogue with other faith communities that seek the same welfare. This can contribute to mutual critique and solidarity. As Kwok points out, readings of Christian materials from other faith perspectives provide additional insight into their oppressive and liberative potentials. Different faith communities can evaluate the particularization of Christian principles from their own perspectives and contexts. When various faith communities have been colonized by Christians, their critique has the added impact of a marginalized perspective.

The contribution of the church to colonization affected not only human beings, but also the earth. The holistic thought typical of Asian philosophy and Aboriginal teachings connects the welfare of the people with the welfare of the earth. It challenges the church to extend its liberative criteria to the earth and all of its creatures, and to find ways in which the silent and forever silenced ones of the wounded earth can also be heard.

When faith communities enable the voices of marginalized and colonized people to be heard, and sincerely attempt to address the roots of their marginalization and colonization, they may begin to walk in solidarity with the marginalized. This type of solidarity is difficult and exacts a price from those who benefit from the oppressive status quo. As a result, faith communities may face extreme internal opposition as they attempt to be in solidarity.

There may be disagreement over the most appropriate and effective approaches to solidarity. However, strong differences of opinion and belief are to be expected and even welcomed within the multiple, conflicting discourses that comprise Protestant churches. If these faith communities can agree to disagree in communities of argument while holding in common the use of Christian materials and the evaluative criteria of coherence, historical and contextual adequacy, and the liberation of the oppressed, they may be able to remain united amidst diversity. However, the ability of a faith community to retain its political edge in support of the marginalized while encouraging a community of argument is a significant challenge.

In order to prevent their depoliticization, Protestant communities could commit themselves to an ongoing process of assessment in light of the above areas of accountability. They can continually measure the coherence of particular theological positions to their own canonical system and to the faith traditions of other communities. They can also assess their historical and contextual adequacy through updated multidisciplinary study. This will allow a developing understanding of the complexities of multiplicative oppressions and will continuously inform and correct appropriate emancipatory action to be taken for the welfare of the earth and its marginalized peoples. Within this ongoing process, Protestant churches must always remember that they are ultimately accountable to God. God's radical transcendence will remind them of their finite, limited understandings, while God's radical immanence through the Word will call them to an emancipatory love that attends to society's marginalized, challenges sources of marginalization and colonization, and strives towards visions of the *basileia* of God.

Notes to Chapter 9

1. This was suggested in a sermon at Dolores Street Baptist Church in San Francisco in 1985.

2. For further discussion on women's experience, see George Schner, "The Appeal to Experience," *Theological Studies* 53 (March 1992): 40–59; Loraine MacKenzie Shepherd, "The Deceptive Monolith of Women's Experience: Struggling for Common Feminist Visions Amidst Diversity," *Toronto Journal of Theology* 11, no. 2 (1995).

3. Robert G. Torbet. *A History of the Baptists*, third edition (Valley Forge: The Judson Press, 1963): 288; William W. Barnes, "Why the Southern Baptist Convention Was Formed," *The Review and Expositor* 41, no. 1 (January, 1944): 3–17.

4. This familiar phrase within feminist circles has been attributed to Nellie Morton.

5. Sharon Welch has one of the most helpful approaches to hearing and working with those who are marginalized in society. See *A Feminist Ethic of Risk*, revised ed. (Minneapolis: Fortress Press, 2000).

6. This example was taken from a meeting of the United Church's national Church in Society Unit of the Division of Mission in Canada in November, 1997.

7. The World Council of Churches has concluded an Ecumenical Decade of Churches in Solidarity with Women in Church and Society, and has produced a study guide of statements on Sexuality and Human Relations from its member churches. See Robin Smith, *Living in Covenant with God and One Another: A Guide to the Study of Sexuality and Human Relations Using Statements from Member Churches of the World Council of Churches* (Geneva: World Council of Churches, 1990).

Glossary

Aboriginal. The original inhabitants of a land, including First Nations, Inuit, and Métis. See the Canadian Royal Commission on Aboriginal Peoples (1996).

absolutism. The acceptance of unconditional, ultimate, and universally valid principles.

androcentric. Male-centred.

anthropocentric. Human-centred.

attending to the other. To listen, learn and be changed by those who are marginalized in society.

basileia. Kingdom, kin-dom, realm, reign, or commonweal of God.

biblical positivism. See "textual positivism."

colonialism. The social, political, and religious control of a wealthier power over a subjugated people and their land.

critical modern. A methodological approach based upon rational inquiry and a constant analysis of any tendencies towards *absolutism and *totalitarianism.

deconstruction. A method of literary criticism that uncovers the inconsistencies and hidden presuppositions of a text. It assumes that language can only refer to itself rather than to an external reality.

de facto **norms.** Standards for acceptable behaviour or appearance that are based upon the specifics (facts) of a particular situation.

de jure **norms.** Standards for acceptable behaviour or appearance that are based upon universally applicable values (laws) of right and wrong.

destabilize. To challenge singular meanings or definitions of concepts or entities so as to allow for multiple perceptions.

dialectical. Based upon opposing beliefs or values held together in tension.

dialogical. Based upon a contextual, conversational style of communication through various mediums (e.g. verbal, written).

discourse. A text and its context as it interacts with the everyday world.

discursive reality. The creation of an entity, concept or situation by our language and interactions. See "pre-discursive reality."

epistemological privilege of the oppressed. The insight and knowledge of dominated people is given greater weight than the insight and knowledge of the dominant groups.

epistemology. The study of the nature, sources, limits, and validity of knowledge.

essentialism. A philosophical belief that something contains core characteristics that are necessary in making it what it is.

ethnocentrism. Evaluating other racial, cultural, or ethnic groups according to criteria specific to one's own group.

etymology. The study of the origin of words and their evolving meaning.

extra-linguistic reality. See "pre-discursive reality."

extratextual. The reference to something outside and unrelated to a literary text. See "intertextual" and "intratextual."

First Nations. See "Aboriginal."

foundationalism. A philosophy based upon secure and certain premises and beliefs.

hegemony. The predominant authority of one state or culture over others.

hermeneutics. The act of interpreting texts, allowing that text and reader influence each other in the interpretation.

heterogeneous. Diverse in character or content.

historical criticism. A study of biblical texts within their historical settings, using *modern, scientific methods.

historical positivism. An assumption that historical "facts" can be unearthed and understood with absolute certainty if objective, rational scientific methods are used.

homoousia. "Of the same substance," used in reference to the nature of each member of the Trinity.

ideology. A set of beliefs, values, and attitudes which shapes one's world view.

imperialism. The imposition of power, authority, or influence of one group or nation over another.

indeterminate subjects/texts. Subjects and texts whose identity, description, or meaning is always shifting, never stable or fixed.

individualism. A belief that the interests and rights of the individual are of paramount importance and are freed from the constrictions of social relations and norms.

internal critique. Critical analysis that arises from within a group or organization concerning itself.

interstructuring. The overlap and mutual influence of different social systems such as race relations and gendered relations or dominant social structures and marginalized communities.

intertextual. The relationship between literary texts or between literary texts and their contexts. See "extratextual" and "intratextual."

intratextual. A focus solely upon a literary text, with no reference to external influences. See "intertextual" and "extratextual."

kyriarchal. "Master-centred," used by Elisabeth Schüssler Fiorenza to refer to the classic Greek interlocking systems of domination which benefit elite, Western-educated, propertied, Euro-American men.

liberal. Favouring the principles of liberalism; marked by the social, political, and intellectual rights and freedom of the individual.

literal sense. The traditional sense of a text as written, without added layers of allegorical or metaphorical meanings.

literalism. The adherence to a literal interpretation of a text.

logic of identity. A dominant subject swallowing the identity of a subordinate person or group into its own identity.

metanarrative. An overall story or theory which guides the interpretation and limits the meaning of a subset of stories or theories.

metaphysical. Relating to reality that lies beyond that which is perceptible through the senses.

modern. Favouring rational, scientific approaches that produce universally valid, verifiable conclusions.

monolithic. Pertaining to a single, indivisible identity or structure.

mujerista theology. Theology from a Latin American woman's perspective.

multiplicative. As used by Elisabeth Schüssler Fiorenza to describe the effects of multiple oppressions experienced by one person. The impact is not merely multiplied by the number of oppressions (doubled or tripled), but exponentially multiplied (one oppression multiplied by another, multiplied by another).

nihilism. A rejection of moral principles, laws, and institutions, and a belief that existence is senseless and useless.

occlude. To shut out someone or something.

ontological. Relating to the concept of being or existence.

paradigm shift. A significant change in the framework of concepts, results, and procedures.

plain sense. See "literal sense."

politics of identity. See "logic of identity."

positing. To state as a fact.

positivism. A philosophy that follows empirical, scientific, objective methods and rejects *metaphysical speculation. See "historical positivism" and "textual positivism."

postcolonial. Critiquing systems of power that subjugate and colonize a people. This critique is multidisciplinary, often drawing upon *postmodern theory, *social critical theory, and critique of the capitalist system.

postcritical. Moving beyond modern, critical analyses of Christian doctrine and faith practices, with reference to *postliberal positions.

postliberal. Understanding traditional doctrine as "rules" that govern Christian faith communities and their interpretation of scripture. This position is critical of liberal *individualism and of *modern, *historical-critical approaches to scripture.

postmodern. Rejecting *modern claims to objective and universal truth, representations of reality, essential characteristics of identity, and underlying foundations of meaning. This approach understands meaning to be constructed by communities and not unearthed by experts.

poststructural. Often used interchangeably with postmodern, but usually in reference to literary theory and *deconstruction. This philosophy states that language constructs, rather than describes, reality. Language cannot refer to anything outside of itself. It is based upon contrasting differences, describing what something is and, by extension, is not.

pre-discursive reality. Reference to a reality that precedes or transcends our language and interactions.

problematize. To reveal the complex dynamics of a supposedly simple term or concept.

queer theory. Analysis of issues related to lesbian, gay, bisexual, transgendered, and transsexual identities. Postmodern theories are often utilized in this analysis.

reconstruction. As used by Elisabeth Schüssler Fiorenza to indicate a piecing together of historical evidence to create a more plausible historical account or text.

referents. An object or idea to which a word refers.

regula fidae. Rules of faith, which are determined by general agreement in the church and evolve over time.

reification. The reduction of a person into a commodity (Marxist theory); the conversion of an idea into something solid and rigid.

relativize. To consider something in relation or proportion to something else.

representational fallacy. The false assumption that one can accurately represent something or someone else. One's descriptions of others may be more descriptive of one's self.

rhetorical criticism. A study of the literary devices employed by an author to persuade the reader to accept the author's point of view.

semiotics. The study of *signs within systems of communication.

sensus literalis. See "literal sense."

sign. A set of sounds or marks on a page (signifier) together with their meaning (signified) within a particular language and social system. See "semiotics."

signified. See "sign."

signifier. See "sign."

sitz im leben. "Setting in life;" the context of a text.

social critical theory. A critique of capitalist societies and the modern emphasis on objective, scientific methods, offered by the Frankfurt School in the mid-1900s.

sola scriptura. "By scripture alone," recognizing scripture as the primary, if not only, source of authority.

soteriology. The doctrine of salvation, especially as effected by Jesus Christ.

stabilize. To limit the potential meanings of a concept or the potential identities of a subject.

standpoint theory. The belief that someone marginalized on the basis of their identity (gender, race, sexuality, class, ethnicity, etc.) has additional insight and knowledge that those of privileged identities lack.

teleological. Concerned about the goals or end result.

textual positivism. An assumption that the "true" meaning of a text can be found if objective, rational scientific methods are used. According to Elisabeth Schüssler Fiorenza, isolation of the text from historical reality also constitutes textual positivism.

third world. The term "two-thirds world,"while indicating the proportion of the world's population, does not seem to be used as widely by theologians in these countries. Most of them prefer the term "third world," in part to emphasize their economic situation in relation to the rest of the world.

totalitarian. Dictating control and demanding absolute obedience.

totalizing. Subsuming diverse elements into a whole and thereby eliminating any features that do not fit.

universality. Having universal applicability.

universals. A concept or term that can apply globally.

unstable. A fluid definition of an identity or concept that contains endless possibilities of meaning. See "stabilize."

womanist. An African Canadian or African American woman who challenges racism and sexism, along with other interlocking systems of oppression.

Chronological Bibliography

Works by Mary McClintock Fulkerson

Review of *Womanguides*. *Journal of the American Academy of Religion* 54, no. 3 (Fall 1986): 607–08.

"Women, Men, and Liberation: Old Issues, New Conversations." *Quarterly Review* 8, no. 4 (Winter 1988): 76–89.

Review of *Inheriting Our Mother's Gardens*. *Theology Today* 46, no. 4 (January 1990): 430–32.

"Contesting Feminist Canons: Discourse and the Problem of Sexist Texts." *Journal of Feminist Studies in Religion* 7, no. 2 (Fall 1991): 52–73.

"Sexism as Original Sin: Developing a Theacentric Discourse." *Journal of the American Academy of Religion* 59, no. 4 (Winter 1991): 653–75.

"Theological Education and the Problem of Identity." *Modern Theology* 7, no. 5 (October, 1991): 465–482.

"Gender—Being It or Doing It? The Church, Homosexuality, and the Politics of Identity." *Union Seminary Quarterly Review* 47, no. 1–2 (1993): 29–46.

Changing the Subject: Women's Discourses and Feminist Theology. Minneapolis: Fortress Press, 1994.

"Documents on Human Sexuality and the Authority of Scripture." *Interpretation* 49, no. 1 (January 1995): 46–58.

Review of *She Who Is*. *Religious Studies Review* 21, no. 1 (January 1995): 21–25.

"*Theologia* as a Liberation *Habitus*: Thoughts Toward Christian Formation for Resistance." In *Theology and the Interhuman: Essays in Honor of Edward Farley*, edited by Robert R. Williams, 160–180. Valley Forge, Pennsylvania: Trinity Press International, 1995.

"Changing the Subject: Feminist Theology and Discourse." *Literature & Theology* 10, no. 2 (June, 1996): 131-147.

"Toward a Materialist Christian Social Criticism: Accommodation and Culture Reconsidered." In *Changing Conversations: Religious Reflection & Cultural Analysis*, edited by Dwight N. Hopkins and Sheila Greeve Davaney, 43–57. New York: Routledge, 1996.

"Contesting the Gendered Subject: A Feminist Account of the *Imago Dei*." In *Horizons in Feminist Theology: Identity, Tradition, and Norms*, edited by Rebecca S. Chopp and Sheila Greeve Davaney, 99–115. Minneapolis: Fortress Press, 1997.

"Feminist Exploration: A Theological Proposal." *International Journal of Practical Theology* 2, no. 2 (1998): 208–221.

" 'Is There a (Non-Sexist) Bible in this Church?' A Feminist Case for the Priority of Interpretive Communities." *Modern Theology* 14, no. 2 (April, 1998): 225–42.

"Grace, Christian Controversy, and Tolerable Falsehoods." *Grace Upon Grace: Essays in Honor of Thomas A. Langford*, edited by Robert K. Johnston, L. Gregory Jones, and Jonathan R. Wilson. Nashville: Abingdon Press, 1999.

Works by Kwok Pui-lan

"Image of Birth." *East Asia Journal of Theology* 1, no. 1 (1983): 128–29.

"God Weeps with Our Pain." *East Asia Journal of Theology* 2, no. 2 (October 1984): 228–32.

"The Feminist Hermeneutics of Elizabeth Schüssler Fiorenza: An Asian Response." *East Asia Journal of Theology* 3, no. 2 (October 1985).

"God Weeps with Our Pain." Revised from 1984 article with same title. In *New Eyes for Reading: Biblical and Theological Reflections by Women from the Third World*, edited by John S. Pobee and Bärbel Von Wartenberg-Potter. Geneva: World Council of Churches, 1986.

"Claiming a Boundary Existence: A Parable from Hong Kong." *Journal of Feminist Studies in Religion* 3, no. 2 (Fall 1987): 121–24.

"Worshipping with Asian Women: A Homily." *Asia Journal of Theology* 1, no. 1 (April 1987): 90–95.

"Mothers and Daughters, Writers and Fighters." In *Inheriting Our Mothers' Gardens: Feminist Theology in Third World Perspective*, edited by Letty Russell, Kwok Pui-lan, Ada María Isasi-Díaz and Katie Geneva Cannon, 21–34. Louisville: The Westminster Press, 1988.

"Discovering the Bible in the Non-Biblical World." *Semeia* 47 (1989): 25–42.

"The Emergence of Asian Feminist Consciousness of Culture and Theology." In *We Dare to Dream: Doing Theology as Asian Women*, edited by Virginia Fabella and Sun Ai Lee Park. Hong Kong: Asian Women's Resource Centre for Culture and Theology, 1989.

"Meditation." *One World*, no. 155 (May 1990): 15.

"The Mission of God in Asia and Theological Education." *Ministerial Formation*, no. 48 (January 1990): 20–23.

"Gospel and Culture." *Christianity and Crisis* 51, no. 10/11 (July 15 1991): 223–24.

"The Image of the 'White Lady': Gender and Race in Christian Mission." In *The Special Nature of Women?* edited by Anne Carr and Elisabeth Schüssler Fiorenza. Concilium Series. London: SCM Press, 1991.

Chinese Women and Christianity: 1860–1927. Edited by Susan Thistlethwaite. American Academy of Religion Academy Series, No. 75. Atlanta: Scholars Press, 1992.

"Claiming Our Heritage: Chinese Women and Christianity." *International Bulletin* 16, no. 4 (October 1992): 150–52, 154.

"Speaking from the Margins." *Journal of Feminist Studies in Religion* 8, no. 2 (Fall 1992): 102–05.

"Chinese Non-Christian Perceptions of Christ." In *Any Room for Christ in Asia?* edited by Leonardo Boff and Virgil Elizondo. Concilium Series. London: SCM Press, 1993.

"Racism and Ethnocentrism in Feminist Biblical Interpretation." In *Searching the Scriptures: Volume I: A Feminist Introduction*, 101–16. New York: Crossroad, 1993.

"Ecology and the Recycling of Christianity." In *Ecotheology: Voices from South and North*, edited by David G. Hallman, 107–11. Geneva: World Council of Churches, 1994.

"The Future of Feminist Theology: An Asian Perspective." In *Feminist Theology from the Third World*, edited by Ursula King. London: Society for Promoting Christian Knowledge, 1994.

"Business Ethics in the Economic Development of Asia: A Feminist Analysis." *Asia Journal of Theology* 9, no. 1 (April 1995): 133–45.

Discovering the Bible in the Non-Biblical World. The Bible and Liberation Series. Maryknoll: Orbis Books, 1995.

"The Global Challenge." In *Christianity and Civil Society: Theological Education for Public Life*, edited by Rodney L. Petersen. Maryknoll: Orbis Books, 1995.

"Chinese Christians and Their Bible." *Biblical Interpretation* 4 (January, 1996):127–129.

"Women and Protestant Christianity at the Turn of the Twentieth Century." In *Christianity in China: From the Eighteenth Century to the Present*. Edited by Daniel H. Bays, 194–206, 405–406. Stanford: Stanford University Press, 1996.

"Response to the *Semeia* Volume on Postcolonial Criticism," *Semeia* 75 (1996): 211–217.

"Discovering the Bible in the Non-Biblical World: The Journey Continues." *The Journal of Asian and Asian American Theology* 2, no. 1 (Summer 1997): 64–77.

"Ecology and Christology." *Feminist Theology* 15 (May, 1997): 113–125.

"The Sources and Resources of Feminist Theologies: A Post-Colonial Perspective." In *Yearbook of the European Society of Women in Theological Research*. Vol 5, *Sources and Resources of Feminist Theologies*, edited by Elisabeth Hartlieb and Charlotte Methuen, 5–23. Kampen, Deutschland: Kok Pharos Publishing House, 1997.

"Jesus/The Native: Biblical Studies from a Postcolonial Perspective." In *Teaching the Bible: The Discourses and Politics of Biblical Pedagogy*. Edited by Fernando F. Segovia and Mary Ann Tolbert. Maryknoll: Orbis Books, 1998.

"Reflection on Women's Sacred Scriptures," *Women's Sacred Scriptures*, edited by Kwok Pui-lan and Elisabeth Schüssler Fiorenza, Concilium Series (London: SCM Press, 1998).

"Mending of Creation: Women, Nature, and Eschatological Hope." In *Liberating Eschatology: Essays in Honor of Letty M. Russell*. Edited by Margaret A. Farley and Serene Jones, 144–155. Louisville: Westminster John Knox Press, 1999.

"Response to Archie Lee's Paper on 'Biblical Interpretation in Postcolonial Hong Kong.'" *Biblical Interpretation* 7 (April, 1999): 182–186.

Introducing Asian Feminist Theology. Introductions in Feminist Theology Series. Cleveland: Pilgrim Press, 2000.

Works by Elisabeth Schüssler Fiorenza

" 'For the Sake of Our Salvation.' Biblical Interpretation as Theological Task." In *Sin, Salvation, and the Spirit*, edited by Daniel Durken. Collegeville, Minnesota: The Liturgical Press, 1979.

In Memory of Her: A Feminist Theological Reconstruction of Christian Origins. New York: Crossroad, 1983.

"Response to 'from Study to Proclamation' by Walter J. Burghardt." In *A New Look at Preaching*, edited by John Burke. Good News Studies, vol. 7. Wilmington, Delaware: Michael Glazier Inc., 1983.

Bread not Stone: The Challenge of Feminist Biblical Interpretation. Boston: Beacon Press, 1984.

"Emerging Issues in Feminist Biblical Interpretation." In *Christian Feminism: Visions of a New Humanity*, edited by Judith Weidman, 33–54. San Francisco: Harper & Row, 1984.

Schüssler Fiorenza, Elisabeth and David Tracy. "The Holocaust as Interruption and the Christian Return Into History." In *The Holocaust as Interruption*, edited by Elisabeth Schüssler Fiorenza and David Tracy. Concilium Series. Edinburgh: T. & T. Clark Ltd., 1984.

The Book of Revelation: Justice and Judgment. Philadelphia: Fortress Press, 1985.

"Claiming Our Authority and Power." In *The Teaching Authority of Believers*, edited by Johann Baptist Metz and Edward Schillebeeckx. Edinburgh: T & T Clark Ltd., 1985.

"The Will to Choose or to Reject: Continuing Our Critical Work." In *Feminist Interpretation of the Bible*, edited by Letty M. Russell. Philadelphia: The Westminster Press, 1985.

The Inside Stories: Thirteen Valiant Women Challenging the Church. Interview. Edited by Annie Lally Milhaven. Mystic, Ct.: Twenty-Third Publishers, 1987.

"The 'Quilting' of Women's History: Phoebe of Cenchreae." In *Embodied Love: Sensuality and Relationship as Feminist Values*, edited by Paula M. Cooey, Sharon A. Farmer and Mary Ellen Ross. San Francisco: Harper & Row, Pub., 1987.

"Rhetorical Situation and Historical Reconstruction in I Corinthians." *New Testament Studies* 33, no. 3 (1987): 386–403.

"The Ethics of Biblical Interpretation: Decentering Biblical Scholarship." *Journal of Biblical Literature* 107, no. 1 (March 1988): 3–17.

"Biblical Interpretation and Critical Commitment." *Studia Theologica* 43, no. 1 (1989): 5–18.

"The Politics of Otherness: Biblical Interpretation as a Critical Praxis for Liberation." In *The Future of Liberation Theology: Essays in Honor of Gustavo Gutiérrez*, edited by Marc Ellis and Otto Maduro. New York: Orbis Books, 1989.

"Text and Reality—Reality as Text: The Problem of a Feminist Historical and Social Reconstruction Based on Texts." *Studia Theologica* 43 (1989): 19–34.

"Biblical Interpretation in the Context of Church and Ministry." *Word & World* 10, no. 4 (Fall 1990): 317–23.

"Changing the Paradigms." "How My Mind Has Changed" Series. *The Christian Century* 107, no. 25 (September 5–12 1990): 796–800.

Revelation: Vision of a Just World. Edited by Gerhard Krodel. Proclamation Commentaries. Minneapolis: Fortress Press, 1991.

But She Said: Feminist Practices of Biblical Interpretation. Boston: Beacon Press, 1992.

Discipleship of Equals: A Critical Feminist Ekklesia-Logy of Liberation. New York: Crossroad, 1993.

"Introduction: Transforming the Legacy of *The Woman's Bible*." In *Searching the Scriptures: Volume I: A Feminist Introduction*, edited by Elisabeth Schüssler Fiorenza. New York: Crossroad, 1993.

"The Bible, the Global Context, and the Discipleship of Equals." In *Reconstructing Christian Theology*, edited by Rebecca S. Chopp and Mark Lewis Taylor. Minneapolis: Fortress Press, 1994.

"Introduction to the Tenth Anniversary Edition: Remember the Struggle." In *In Memory of Her: A Feminist Theological Reconstruction of Christian Origins*, 10th Anniversary Edition. New York: Crossroad, 1994.

"Introduction: Transgressing Canonical Boundaries." In *Searching the Scriptures: Volume II: A Feminist Commentary*, edited by Elisabeth Schüssler Fiorenza. New York: Crossroad, 1994.

Jesus: Miriam's Child, Sophia's Prophet: Critical Issues in Feminist Christology. New York: Continuum, 1994.

"Breaking Silence—Becoming Visible." In *The Power of Naming: A Concilium Reader in Feminist Liberation Theology*, edited by Elisabeth Schüssler Fiorenza. Concilium Series. Maryknoll: Orbis, 1996.

"The *Ekklesia* of Women: Revisioning the Past in Creating a Democratic Future." In *The Call to Serve: Biblical and Theological Perspectives on Ministry in Honour of Bishop Penny Jamieson*, edited by Douglas A. Campbell. Sheffield: Sheffield Academic Press, 1996.

"The Ethos of Interpretation: Biblical Studies in a Postmodern and Postcolonial Context." Presentation. The Association of Korean Theologians. Usong, The Republic of Korea, October 26, 1996.

"For Women in Men's World: A Critical Feminist Theology of Liberation." In *The Power of Naming: A Concilium Reader in Feminist Liberation Theology*, edited by Elisabeth Schüssler Fiorenza. Concilium Series. Maryknoll: Orbis, 1996.

"G*d at Work in Our Midst: From a Politics of Identity to a Politics of Struggle." *Feminist Theology* 13 (S 1996): 47–72.

"Introduction: Feminist Liberation Theology as Critical Sophialogy." In *The Power of Naming: A Concilium Reader in Feminist Liberation Theology*, edited by Elisabeth Schüssler Fiorenza. Concilium Series. Maryknoll: Orbis, 1996.

"Ties that Bind: Domestic Violence Against Women." In *Women Resisting Violence: Spirituality for Life*, edited by Mary John Mananzan et. al. Maryknoll: Orbis Books, 1996.

"Jesus and the Politics of Interpretation." *Harvard Theological Review* 90, no. 4 (October, 1997): 343–58.

"Justified By All Her Children: Struggle, Memory, and Vision." In *The Power of Naming: A Concilium Reader in Feminist Liberation Theology*, edited by Elisabeth Schüssler Fiorenza. Concilium Series. Maryknoll: Orbis, 1996.

"Discipleship of Equals: Reality and Vision." In *In Search of a Round Table: Gender, Theology & Church Leadership*, edited by Musimbi R. A. Kanyoro. Published for the Lutheran World Federation. Geneva: WCC Publications, 1997.

"Reading the Bible as Equals." In *In Search of a Round Table: Gender, Theology & Church Leadership*, edited by Musimbi R. A. Kanyoro. Published for the Lutheran World Federation. Geneva: WCC Publications, 1997.

"Struggle is a Name for Hope: A Critical Feminist Interpretation for Liberation." *Pacifica* 10 (June 1997): 224–48.

"Celebrating the Struggles, Realizing the Visions." Keynote address at "Soul to Soul: Women, Religion & the 21st Century," Graduate Theological Union, Berkeley, Feb. 26 – March 1, 1998. *Journal of Women and Religion* 16 (1998): 16–27.

Sharing Her Word: Feminist Biblical Interpretation in Context. Boston: Beacon Press, 1998.

"Ecclesia Semper Reformanda: Theology as Ideology Critique," *Concilium* 1 (1999): 70–76.

"The Emperor Has No Clothes: Democratic Ekklesial Self-Understanding and Kyriocratic Roman Authority." *The Non-Ordination of Women and the Politics of Power*, edited by Elisabeth Schüssler Fiorenza. London: SCM Press, 1999.

Rhetoric and Ethic: The Politics of Biblical Studies. Minneapolis: Fortress Press, 1999.

"To Follow the Vision: The Jesus Movement as *Basileia* Movement." In *Liberating Eschatology: Essays in Honor of Letty M. Russell*, edited by Margaret A. Farley and Serene Jones. Louisville: Westminster John Knox Press, 1999.

Works by Kathryn E. Tanner

"Theology and the Plain Sense." In *Scriptural Authority and Narrative Interpretation*, edited by Garrett Green, 59–78. Philadelphia: Fortress Press, 1987.

God and Creation in Christian Theology: Tyranny or Empowerment? Oxford: Blackwell, 1988.

Review of *Eternal God: A Study of God Without Time*. *Theology Today* 47, no. 1 (April 1990).

Review of *Intimations of Divinity*. *Theology Today* 46, no. 4 (January 1990): 449–50.

Review of *Faith After Foundationalism*. *Journal of the American Academy of Religion* 59, no. 4 (1991): 855–58.

The Politics of God: Christian Theologies and Social Justice. Minneapolis: Fortress Press, 1992.

"Respect for Other Religions: A Christian Antidote to Colonialist Discourse." *Modern Theology* 9 (January 1993): 1–18.

Review of *Mimetic Reflections: A Study in Hermeneutics, Theology, and Ethics*. *The Journal of Religion* 73, no. 1 (January 1993): 117–18.

"A Theological Case for Human Responsibility in Moral Choice." *Journal of Religion* 73 (October 1993): 592–612.

"Creation, Environmental Crisis, and Ecological Justice." In *Reconstructing Christian Theology*, edited by Rebecca Chopp et. al. Minneapolis: Fortress Press, 1994.

"The Difference Theological Anthropology Makes." *Theology Today* 50 (January 1994): 567–79.

"Human Freedom, Human Sin, and God the Creator." In *The God Who Acts: Philosophical and Theological Explorations*, edited by Thomas F. Tracy, 111–35. University Park, Pennsylvania: The Pennsylvania State University Press, 1994.

Review of *Religion, Theology, and American Public Life*. *Religious Studies Review* 20, no. 3 (July 1994): 212.

Review of *The Body of God*. *Modern Theology* 10, no. 4 (October 1994): 417–19.

Review of *Communication and Cultural Analysis*. *Church History* 64, no. 4 (December 1995): 747–48.

"The Care That Does Justice: Recent Writings in Feminist Ethics and Theology." *Journal of Religious Ethics* 24, no. 1 (Spring 1996): 171–91.

"Public Theology and the Character of Public Debate." *The Annual of the Society of Christian Ethics* (1996): 79–101.

"Theology and Popular Culture." *Changing Conversations: Religious Reflection & Cultural Analysis*. Edited by Dwight N. Hopkins & Sheila Greeve Davaney, 101–120. New York: Routledge, 1996.

"Jesus Christ." In *The Cambridge Companion to Christian Doctrine*, edited by Colin E. Gunton. Cambridge Companions to Religion. Cambridge: Cambridge University Press, 1997.

"Social Theory Concerning the 'New Social Movements' and the Practice of Feminist Theology." In *Horizons in Feminist Theology: Identity, Tradition, and Norms*, edited by Rebecca S. Chopp and Sheila Greeve Davaney, 179–97. Minneapolis: Fortress Press, 1997.

Theories of Culture: A New Agenda for Theology. Guides to Theological Inquiry. Minneapolis: Fortress Press, 1997.

"Response to Max Stackhouse and Eugene Rogers." *Sexual Orientation & Human Rights in American Religious Discourse*. Edited by Saul M. Olyan & Martha C. Nussbaum, 161–68. New York: Oxford University Press, 1998.

"Scripture as Popular Text." *Modern Theology* 14, no. 2 (April 1998): 278–97.

"Why Are We Here?" *Why Are We Here? Everyday Questions and the Christian Life*. Edited by Ronald F. Thiemann & William C. Placher, 5–16. Harrisburg, Pennsylvania: Trinity Press International, 1998.

"Justification and Justice in a Theology of Grace." *Theology Today* 55, no. 4 (January, 1999): 510–23.

Author Index

Subject Index

absolutism, 17

accountability, 8, 26, 37, 39, 154, 155, 225; to academy, 24; to body of Christ, 93, 204, 212–13, 229–30; to canonical system, 204–07, 227–29; to Christ, 206–07; to community of faith, 24; to earth & its marginalized, 93, 101, 158, 204, 212–13, 230–32; to God, 204, 216, 225; to the past, 52, 143; to society's marginalized, 204, 225–27; to women's movement, 20, 151, 212

agapic care, 58, 64, 71, 144, 155, 157, 205, 211, 225

androgynous, 170, 178, 196

anthropology, 108, 198, 207, 208, 227

Aristotelian philosophy, 18

Aryan Race, 81–82

Asian: Christians, 77, 79, 85, 86, 97, 141, 143, 192; contexts, 78, 79, 85, 86, 87, 92, 97, 101, 211; hermeneutical traditions, 77, 80, 84, 98, 99; identities, 77, 83–84, 85, 150, 211; philosophies, 82, 86, 231; religions, 77, 78, 79, 85, 86, 87, 88, 90, 97, 100, 143, 147; women theologians, 15, 23, 28, 78, 82, 99. *See* also solidarity: definition

assumed sense of scripture, 147, 154, 197, 222, 228. *See* also literal sense; plain sense

attending: to diversity, 11, 48, 58, 83, 156, 157, 196, 221; to marginalized, 11, 157, 193, 196, 221; to the other, 8, 10, 57–58, 71, 212, 216; to tradition, 120, 141, 172

authoritative criteria, 7, 25–27, 36, 87; agapic care, 64, 144, 157; Bible,

30–32, 45, 63, 68–69, 89, 120–22, 146–48, 169, 174, 175, 177–79, 206, 222, 225; body of Christ, 144, 229–30; canonical criticism, 128; canonical system, 65–70, 153–54, 227–29; Christ, 25, 123, 206–07, 225; Christian materials, 118–20, 124–28, 153–54, 204–07; doctrinal rules, 114–18, 126–29, 146–48, 152–53, 210–11; ekklēsia of wo/men, 25, 26, 39, 157; experience, 51, 169, 219; faith communities, 92–93, 99–101, 148–52, 181; feminist stipulations of relevance, 62; God's *basileia*, 25, 157, 144, 232; historical adequacy, 26, 141–46, 207–10; historical criticism, 189–96, 208–10; liberation, 11, 64, 94, 130, 154–55, 156–57, 210–12, 225–27, 230–32; living Gospel, 87, 157; plain sense, 120–24, 154; scientific experts, 179–81; Spirit, 172; tradition, 124, 169, 175, 180

basileia of God, 21, 24, 25, 26, 35, 42, 157, 144, 217, 232

Beijing Massacre, 91

birth control. *See* contraception

bisexuality, 7, 164, 167, 176, 181, 182, 187, 191, 193, 214, 196, 209, 211, 226. *See* also homosexuality; lesbian and gay issues; sexual orientation; transgendered

Buddhism, 77, 86, 90, 92

canon: of Asian religions, 90; biblical, 28, 30–32, 39, 45, 87, 90, 92, 100–01, 107, 120, 158, 180; as criticism,